D0072608

MESSIAEN'S LANGUAGE
OF MYSTICAL LOVE

STUDIES IN CONTEMPORARY MUSIC AND CULTURE
VOLUME 1
GARLAND REFERENCE LIBRARY OF THE HUMANITIES
VOLUME 2050

MESSIAEN'S LANGUAGE OF MYSTICAL LOVE

EDITED BY
SIGLIND BRUHN

GARLAND PUBLISHING, INC.
A MEMBER OF THE TAYLOR & FRANCIS GROUP
NEW YORK AND LONDON
1998

Library of Congress Cataloging-in-Publication Data

Messiaen's language of mystical love / edited by Siglind Bruhn.
      p.   cm. — (Studies in contemporary music and culture ; v. 1)
(Garland reference library of the humanities ; vol. 2050)
   ISBN 0-8153-2747-1 (hardcover : alk. paper)
    1. Messiaen, Olivier, 1908–1992—Criticism and interpretation.
2. Music—Philosophy and aesthetics. I. Bruhn, Siglind. II. Series.
III. Series: Studies in contemporary music and culture (Garland Publishing,
Inc.) ; v. 1.
  ML410.M595M49   1998
  780'.92—dc21   98-12602
                                            CIP
                                            MN

Cover photograph of the nave of the Cathedral of Notre-Dame, Amiens, built
between 1220 and 1264. Photograph courtesy of the French
Government Tourist Office.

Printed on acid-free, 250-year-life paper
Manufactured in the United States of America

CONTENTS

Part Three:
Praising God with Saint Francis and the Song of Birds

Part Four:
Poetry, Angelic Language, and Contemplations

Introduction

Since the beginning of sacred music in the Christian tradition, composers have created musical symbols to express transcendental ideas. These included the use of certain keys and modes, the choice of specific intervals perceived as connected to religious concepts (from the chromaticism in laments over human sinfulness to the representation of God's perfection in the octave), the shaping of pitch lines for special images of visual symbols (see e.g. the manifold melodic outlines tracing the shape of the Cross), as well as the translation of Christian terms into their numerological equivalents and their embodiment in the form of rhythmic, metric, or otherwise countable units. This development reached its peak in the sixteenth and early seventeenth centuries when an already very elaborate musical rhetoric coincided with a heightened desire for mystical expression.

Olivier Messiaen (Avignon 1908 – Paris 1992), while undoubtedly an heir to this tradition, has created a musical language that is highly idiosyncratic. Influenced by mystics like Saint John of the Cross and Sainte Thérèse de Lisieux, his spirituality permeates all his works, from the explicitly sacred to the allegedly secular. As he never tired of telling his interviewers, his music can be subsumed under three themes: God's Love as it is extended to the world through the birth of His Son (the Incarnation), the human emulation of God's Love (the myth of Tristan and Isolde as the epitome of idealized love which, even in its most exemplary form, is only a poor and blurred reflection of divine love), and the glorification of God in his non-human creatures (bird song, both as a manifestation of God's love as expressed in nature and of the praise that God's creation offers its creator).

This volume of essays aims to explore the various aspects of Messiaen's spiritually committed musical language, drawing on his own remarks in subheadings and prefaces, his biblical and theological citations, his allusions to works of visual art, and on the language spoken more indirectly by the musical tropes themselves.

The two essays in the first part introduce the person behind the music: Messiaen the teacher who never formed a 'school', the humanist who coached widely different creative talents, encouraging each to become more fully him- or herself, and the theologian who drew on complex mathematics to transform his rhetorical message into music. Part II follows with three investigations into the principal aspects of his compositional technique and their relationship to his religiously based concept of restraint. The three essays in Part III focus specifically on the celebratory angle of the subject matter Messiaen's music explored: the combination of humility and glorious praise of God in Franciscan spirituality and the song of birds. The volume concludes with three inquiries into language and structure in the broader sense, and into the spiritual motivation that underlies a spectrum that spans from a musical alphabet through the complex symmetrical design of a cyclic composition to the composer's own poetry.

Soliciting essays for a volume dedicated to a composer whose music, thought, and spiritual attitude have for many years been a major inspiration for me has been challenging and richly rewarding. Working with an international team of authors and editing their thought-provoking articles for publication has been a wonderful experience and a great pleasure. I wish to extend my sincere gratitude to all contributors for making this volume possible. My particular thanks go to Joseph Auner, general editor of the series on "Studies in Twentieth-Century Music" of which this book forms a part, for his very prompt, always enlightening, and invariably kindly advice and support.

As can be expected when several scholars discuss a single composer, the essays collected here contain some points of overlap. Where observations made in one article were repeated in another, such repetitions have been eliminated. Thus Ian Darbyshire, e.g., has kindly agreed to cut out substantial documentation for points made in his essay since the examples are discussed in extensive detail elsewhere, and Roberto Fabbi has consented to limit himself to merely touching upon the issue of synaesthesia, since this is central in Jean Marie Wu's contribution. In other cases, however, both the series editor and I felt that the various treatments of the same material can be a strength rather than a weakness, since recapitulations of a topic in different contexts often create a cumulative effect.

Much thought has been given to Messiaen's specific terminology and its rendering by various authors. While several contributors grant the composer the right to idiosyncrasies of language, others feel strongly that traditions of the English language should have priority; thus you will find Ian Darbyshire arguing against the use of the word "interversion" while other authors saw no reason to deviate from Messiaen's choice of term. However, spelling and capitalization in the titles of

Messiaen's works have been standardized throughout this collection in accordance with the article on Messiaen in *The New Grove Dictionary of Music and Musicians,* ed. Stanley Sadie (London: Macmillan, 1980). Transliterations of Indian rhythms follow the "Table of 120 *deçi-tâlas* according to Sharngadeva" in Appendix II of Robert Sherlaw Johnson's *Messiaen* (London: J.M. Dent and Berkeley, CA: University of California Press, 1974 and 1989; now Oxford: Oxford University Press).

Ann Arbor, July 1997
Siglind Bruhn

Messiaen's Language
of Mystical Love

PART ONE

The Composer as Humanist, Mathematician, and Theologian

Messiaen's Teaching at the Paris Conservatoire: A Humanist's Legacy

Jean Boivin

In his foreword to the first volume of Messiaen's long-awaited *Traité de rythme, de couleur et d'ornithologie*, French composer Alain Louvier recognizes his teacher's contribution to contemporary music thinking:

> To read this treatise is to marvel at the genius of Olivier Messiaen, at his universal spirit, curious about everything, which brings to the waning days of our century a great gust of divine inspiration. The work is that of a Renaissance Man, of a Leonardo da Vinci, free of the chore of pleasing princes, whose rhythmic invention disdains passing fashions in order to partake exclusively of the glories of God, Nature, Time and Space.[1]

The three volumes of Messiaen's posthumous treatise available by March 1997 already reached a total of over 1,300 pages. The complete seven-volume set will be immense, nourished by Messiaen's thirty-seven years of teaching at the Paris Conservatoire (1941–78) and a lifetime of research in the fields of music analysis, composition, rhythms both ancient and modern, bird songs, and theology. The thorough reader will share Alain Louvier's admiration for Messiaen's cultural openness and his vast knowledge of the musical repertoire, from the Middle Ages to the avant-garde. The introduction to the treatise (the first two chapters of the first volume) is devoted to definitions of rhythm and time. It brings together, strikingly, a variety of approaches as shown by the broad and far-reaching list of references proposed to the reader, which includes: Confucius, Pythagoras, Dürer, Victor Hugo, Saint Paul, Teilhard de Chardin, Shakespeare, Einstein, Virgil, Shri Aurobindo, Edith Piaf, and H.G. Wells. One should think that Leonardo da Vinci might not have been offended by Louvier's audacious pairing.

Messiaen's treatise confirms what has long been said about him as a pedagogue. Former students of amazingly diverse aesthetic allegiances have pointed out the French composer's rare ability to reach beyond technique or theory to the universal questions of creativity and inspiration. Among those who have celebrated Messiaen's uncommon teaching qualities are Pierre Henry, pioneer of musique concrete; Pierre Boulez and Karlheinz Stockhausen, post-Webernian serialists; Iannis Xenakis, strongly opposed to serialism and inventor of stochastics; François-Bernard Mâche, who joined forces with Pierre Schaeffer to explore the "objet sonore"; Tristan Murail and Gérard Grisey, two younger members of the so-called Parisian "spectral" school. The list could go on and on. In one extraordinary statement, Iannis Xenakis regards his meeting with Messiaen (in the early fifties) as a most challenging spiritual encounter.

> At last I had found the man I had been searching for by the feeble glow of my dark lantern. And more than a man; this was a sort of sunshine which lit up music, of the past as well as the future, with the same generous beatific light as in those stained-glass rainbows he so cherished. The most dazzling truth he revealed in his teaching and in his works was that everything is possible in music (as, of course, in all the arts and sciences) on one condition: that creation proceed from a rich, full inner necessity, untouched by aesthetic dogmas and ideologies, guided by a talent in which reason and intuition commingle.[2]

In an earlier publication,[3] drawing on exclusive interviews with nearly a hundred of Messiaen's former students, I have described his approach to teaching and its historical impact on contemporary music (European and non-European alike). In the following pages, I will further argue that Messiaen's rare human profile can help explain his undeniable influence as a teacher and thus illuminate his major contribution to twentieth-century musical life.

PORTRAIT OF THE TEACHER AS A HUMANIST

Messiaen was officially designated head of a harmony class at the Paris Conservatoire in 1942. He had started in this function in the late spring of the previous year, only a few months after being freed from a prisoner's camp in Silesia, where he had suffered severe physical and spiritual privations. War-time Paris was occupied by the German army with Nazi-approved entertainment dominating the cultural scene. Many male students of the Conservatoire were held prisoner in work camps; some Jewish teachers had lost their jobs. Despite the demanding task of teaching harmonic progressions and voice-leading in such difficult conditions, Messiaen felt the inner need to reunite, in private, a small group of disciples he had regularly seen before the war. Those were now joined by some of Messiaen's better students at the Conservatoire (e.g., Pierre Boulez and pianist Yvonne Loriod[4]). With them Messiaen could discuss musical questions closer to his own creative preoccupations, such as ancient Greek meter and new symmetric scales, which he called "modes of limited transposition." United in the same breath were reflections on plainchant and bird songs, harmony and colors, series of durations, and the splendors of God's creation.

Other Conservatory teachers chose music examples from academic treatises by revered fellow members of their institution. Messiaen, barely into his mid-thirties, preferred to extract the rules of perfect harmonization directly from scores by great masters, such as Debussy's *Prélude à l'après-midi d'un faune*. He would sit at the piano and analyze the successive and distinct appearances of the famous flute theme. He pointed out the formal links of the music with Mallarmé's symbolic verses and gave ample comments on the refined orchestration. In order to isolate characteristic traits in the melodic, harmonic, or rhythmic writing, Messiaen referred liberally to Debussy's later scores as well as to a large pool of works, ranging from Rameau's opéra-ballet *Castor et Pollux* to Ravel's *Gaspard de la Nuit*. Each exercise in harmonization was to be written in the style of a given composer whose works had been discussed in class. Above all, it was to be truly composed and mentally heard.[5] Students coming from more traditional classes were amazed to suddenly "talk Music"; as the musical language of one famous composer after another was deciphered and discussed, Messiaen seemed to engage, across the time barrier, in a stimulating debate with each one of them, recomposing as it were the work at hand.

Even at this early stage of his career as a pedagogue, Messiaen's inquiries into the repertoire ranged widely, including Claude le Jeune's *Le Printemps* (a Renaissance choral work based on Greek principles of poetic declamation), Machaut's *Notre-Dame Mass*, François Couperin's harpsichord pieces, Mozart's instrumental works and operas, Chopin's *Études*, Wagner's *Ring*, Albeniz's *Iberia*, and Stravinsky's *The Rite of Spring*, among others. The young teacher ventured as far as Bartok's violin sonatas, Schoenberg's *Pierrot lunaire*, Webern's early works, and Berg's *Violin Concerto* at a time when these composers were almost absent from the French music scene.

Messiaen's apparently eclectic choice of models set him apart instantly. Most of his colleagues at the Conservatoire prudently stayed close to the *esprit français* and warned their easily impressed pupils not to go beyond Fauré's or, at the most, the young Ravel's modal harmonic conceptions. In the thirties, Messiaen already stood head and shoulders above that "horrible neo-classical music" so favored at the time.[6] From the start, an unbridgeable gap separated Messiaen, fundamentally a harmonist and a rhythmician, from that other influential French pedagogue, Nadia Boulanger, who deeply revered Renaissance polyphonists, Monteverdi's madrigals, and J.S. Bach's *Well-Tempered Clavier*. Messiaen's constructive approach also stood miles apart from the pessimistic vision of modern music expressed by Arthur Honegger, once associated with the Groupe des Six, who taught for some years at the École Normale.

By then, Messiaen had already written imposing works such as two organ frescoes (*La Nativité du Seigneur*, 1935, and *Les Corps glorieux*, 1939), two extraordinary song cycles (*Poèmes pour Mi*, 1936-37, *Chant de Terre et de Ciel*, 1938), and some orchestral works (*Les Offrandes oubliées*, 1930, and *L'Ascension*, 1934). His instrumental music was noted for its often ecstatic slow pace, the strange modal melodic contours, the sensuous harmonies, unheard-of timbres and registrations, and exotic rhythmic formulae. In the vocal works, all of these elements supported the composer's own curiously personal yet effective poetry.

Interestingly enough, and unlike many other composers of the period, Messiaen was more than willing to answer any serious questions that his personal style might raise. The treatise *Technique de mon langage musical*, written in 1942,[7] served as a textbook for some of his most eager students, famished by years of Nazi propaganda and general condemnation of the subversive avant-garde, French or foreign. Even if one disregards the fact that Messiaen was barely thirty-three years old at the time and only starting to be recognized, this detailed summing up of his musical idiom was—and remains—an astonishing statement of confidence. Every aspect of the music had been given much thought. Numerous recent works were lavishly quoted to illustrate each theoretical point. Though the comforting names of Mussorgsky, Grieg, and Debussy were invoked in the text, and plainchant offered as a melodic model, the whole process seemed unbelievably, *eccentrically*, modern. Any daredevil who would follow this path could never claim the Prix de Rome, the supreme goal to which all the teaching efforts of the author's colleagues at the Conservatoire were directed. Yet Messiaen's open mind and far-reaching investigations of Greek meters, modality, and palindromic rhythmic motifs, sowed precious seeds in the minds of such fast-emerging musicians as Jean-Louis Martinet, Pierre Henry, Maurice Le Roux, and Pierre Boulez. One can say, together with Serge Nigg, that the post-war European musical revolution had already started:

> [...] it was during the darkest and most sinister years of the war, when hope of any kind seemed chimerical, that was most deeply felt the obscure sensation of an artistic Renaissance: this intellectual freshness experienced by those who take active part in a RENEWAL.[8]

The Parisian premiere in April 1945 of the *Trois petites Liturgies de la Présence Divine*, written on the eve of the Liberation, brought Messiaen instant fame. As is often the case, public success came with the critics' wrath. Both reactions added a new attractiveness to Messiaen's class at the Conservatoire, already smacking of heresy and "sulphur," to quote Boulez.[9] Controversy has its price, however. In 1946, a vacant position as head of a composition class was not granted to Messiaen, despite the wish of a delegation of students led by the untamed Boulez. Official recognition was offered instead to the older, more "artistically correct" Darius Milhaud. The conservative members of the Institut de France, responsible for the nomination, had feared Messiaen's harmful influence on young musicians. But thanks to the visionary advice of Conservatoire director Claude Delvincourt, the unorthodox organist was instead offered a tailored-to-measure analysis class that rapidly became the *rendez-vous* for non-conformist composers-to-be. Many of these young lions could not adjust to the Conservatoire's strict curriculum and Messiaen's class was the only one they freely attended. This explains why the names of Stockhausen and Xenakis, two famous composers deeply marked by Messiaen's unique approach, do not appear on any official lists.

AN INTERNATIONAL FIGURE

From the end of the forties, "Messiaen's class" (the name has become a reference in itself) attracted a large number of composers: Marius Constant, Gilbert Amy, Betsy Jolas, Alexander Goehr, Michaël Lévinas, and George Benjamin, to name but a few of those who reached international stature. Messiaen also occasionally taught abroad during summer months: in Budapest (1947), Tanglewood (1947 and 1949), Darmstadt (in 1949, 1952, 1953, and 1961), Saarbrücken (1953), and Buenos Aires (1963).[10] These teaching sessions were often coupled with important performances of his major works. As a consequence, young composers of many nationalities, including some Americans,[11] were attracted to Messiaen's class at the Paris Conservatoire. While some only paid visits ranging from a few weeks to a few months in length (as in the case of Peter Maxwell-Davies, Mikis Theodorakis, György Kurtag, and William Bolcolm), others took a complete three-year commitment. Slowly but surely, Messiaen became a world-wide celebrity through both his music and his teaching. Those two dimensions of his musical career had become inseparable.

To limit the list of Messiaen's students to composers would be misleading. A complex net of organists, pianists, and conductors has assured for many years to come a living tradition of performing Messiaen's music throughout the world. His thought-provoking ideas on music and creation have been transmitted to younger generations through both the teaching of his earlier students and the writings of commentators who sat in his class, including Odile Vivier (author of the first French monograph on Edgar Varèse), Serge Gut (a renowned Liszt specialist), and Daniel Charles (exegete of John Cage). At least four authors of significant books on Messiaen are former students: Harry Halbreich, Alain Périer, Pierrette Mari, and Michèle Reverdy. More popular sectors of "functional" music creation, such as music for film and theater, are represented as well. This makes for fascinating study.[12]

In 1966, long after he had gained international celebrity, Messiaen was deservedly nominated head of a true composition class. Interestingly enough, the nearly sixty-year-old composer was then still perceived by many talented young musicians as a free-thinking artist and a true master of his craft. He had managed to evolve constantly while remaining true to himself. As such, he stood almost alone among composers of his generation, having survived radical transformations in taste and conceptions of what modern music is or should be about. His works were regularly played in such progressive events as the *Domaine musical* concerts (created in Paris by Boulez), as well as by more conservative ensembles dispersed around the world. A few titles (e.g., the *Quartet for the End of Time* and the *Turangalîla-Symphonie*) had even become real "classics" of the concert repertoire—a rarity in nontonal twentieth-century music. Still, the mature composer now and again created commotions (a famous instance being the uproar of the Donaueschingen premiere of *Chronochromie* in 1960, followed by a similar scandal in Paris a year later). This man could definitely not be ignored.

In the mid-seventies, a few years before his retirement, a group of Messiaen's composition students formed a Parisian performance collective baptized L'Itinéraire. The founders (among others Michaël Lévinas,

Tristan Murail, Gérard Grisey, François Bousch, and Michel Zbar) were devoted to exploring the realm of harmonic resonance and electronic transformations of timbre, often resulting in a slow-moving static sound continuum. They viewed the author of *La Transfiguration de notre Seigneur Jésus-Christ*, together with György Ligeti and the recently-discovered Italian composer Giacinto Scelsi, as their spiritual guides. Till the end of his career, Messiaen's discourse still stirred creative minds. Through years of teaching, he had won the respect of a large public and of almost three generations of younger composers. No other composer-teacher in the century could claim the same, not even Schoenberg or Boulanger, strongly associated as they were with exclusive trends (serialism for the former, Stravinskian neoclassicism for the latter).

"LE VENT DE L'ESPRIT"[13]

So what was it, one can aptly ask, that was so striking about Messiaen's class? What did he have to say about music that was to attract as it did such a broad spectrum of musicians? How did he engage and inspire composers of such varying and even opposing aesthetics? The answer is not a simple one since Messiaen possessed many remarkable and complementary talents that all seemed to resonate when he addressed a group of students as one complex and vibrating colored chord.

First, Messiaen, whose reputation as an organist was deservedly well-established, also proved to be a remarkable pianist, as attested notably by his recordings of the *Quartet for the End of Time* and of the *Visions de l'Amen* (in duet with Yvonne Loriod).[14] His class renditions of Mozart's concertos or of Debussy's *Préludes* have been highly praised; for many students they remain unforgettable. His sight-reading talents were equally extraordinary. In his childhood and adolescence he enjoyed running through operatic scores like Berlioz's *La Damnation de Faust*, Mussorgsky's *Boris Godunov*, Wagner's *Tristan*, and Debussy's *Pelléas et Mélisande*. Such fine works were to define both his lifelong musical taste and his approach to the keyboard. So colorful and orchestral was his pianistic touch that former student Alain Louvier swears he could actually hear the horns, even the crossed or uncrossed flute and clarinet parts, as Messiaen worked through the highly complex orchestral scores of Stravinsky's *The Rite of Spring*, Debussy's *La Mer*, Ravel's *Daphnis et Chloé*, or Berg's *Wozzeck*.

This rare instrumental ability was incessantly called upon to serve a remarkable memory. One might truly assume that Messiaen's acclaimed teaching talents were in large part due to this immediate, tactile and mental virtuosity. Unusual parallels and associations were drawn between works written in distant periods and styles. The melodic contours of a Mozartian theme thus resembled a plainchant neume also located in the first bar of one of Debussy's *Images* for piano. The description of an unstable harmonic progression sustaining a "terrifying" scene from *Siegfried* could easily lead the analyst to a reminiscence of the first movement in Beethoven's Ninth Symphony when a chord appears as if "lit from underneath...."[15] Similarly, demanding passage-works in a Mozart piano concerto evoked in turn Couperin, Chopin, and Ravel, while a leap between registers was to become, in Varèse's language, a "son projeté" (a projected sound), itself a precursor of a modern electroacoustically-treated effect. And so on.... The analyst would cover in a few minutes the entire span of Western music and would play instantly all the passages referred to. More exotic music was not overlooked. Messiaen brought his first post-war students to hear early recordings of Andean folklore, Japanese Nô theater, and Balinese gamelan at the Musée de l'homme in Paris. The sumptuous orchestration of the *Trois petites Liturgies de la Présence Divine* (1944) and the *Turangalîla-Symphonie* (1946–48) testifies to his attentive listening.

Messiaen was very well-read. At a time when a much more rational and abstract discourse was proposed by Leibowitz, Boulez, Xenakis, Stockhausen, Babbitt, and others, Messiaen's deeply emotional and literary response to music was unreservedly shared with his students. This analyst could summon at will, without any sign of pedantry, impressive cultural treasures accumulated through a life-long companionship with the written word. Books on nature, birds, Gothic stained-glass windows, precious stones, astronomy, Renaissance frescoes, or modern painting, were brought in side by side with major scores. Poetic verses ranging from the *Song of Songs* to Paul Éluard's *Capitale de la douleur* were occasionally read aloud and commented upon. Messiaen charmed not only through his commentary on musical techniques but also through his chosen vocabulary and his colorful use of metaphor. The evocative images he suggested remained vivid in the memory of his students decades after they left the class.

Another important feature that made Messiaen's teaching particularly attractive to young composers was his direct response to their often unexpressed needs as contemporary creative artists. He focused on the elements of a score that were modern for a period, be they rapidly shifting modal recitatives in Monteverdi's *Orfeo*, a way of crossing the hands in a harpsichord piece by Rameau, the disintegration of a theme in a Beethoven piano sonata, the special color of an inverted-seventh chord in a Chopin prelude, superimposed metric divisions in Albeniz's *Iberia,* or an irrational rhythmic accelerando by Jolivet. Messiaen wished to show his students that one could be a visionary at any time and in any place; any class he taught soon turned into a composition workshop.

Though he often had to be prompted by his students, Messiaen regularly analyzed his recent works in class. As clearly shown in *Technique de mon langage musical* and in the recent *Traité de rythme*, Messiaen saw his own development as a single phase in the overall evolution of musical language. To explain the complex rhythmic writing found in his *Vingt Regards sur l'Enfant-Jésus* or the *Turangalîla-Symphonie,* the composer had to go through lengthy exposés on ancient Greek meter or thirteenth-century Hindu rhythmic theory. Thus was revealed a continuous line of thought undisturbed by national borders, language barriers, or cultural differences, circulating through Machaut's *Notre-Dame Mass,* Beethoven's mature works, Wagner's Leitmotiv transformations, Bartok's Fifth String Quartet, and the *Sacrificial Dance* at the end of Stravinsky's *The Rite of Spring.* While new developments of this single thread appear in Messiaen's own compositions, it is the sacred task of the younger generation to keep the stream flowing. Composer Gilbert Amy, a student of Messiaen in the early 1950s, confesses he was fascinated by his teacher's telescopic view of music history:

> The most original aspect of his teaching was that all music
> — ... no matter what its origin—was examined at the same
> work-bench, by a kind of syncretism that was unbelievably
> new at the time. [...] Messiaen would willingly take his
> own works—especially the most recent—and submit them
> to the same X-ray exam. [...] No traces of false modesty.
> We were told of his latest discoveries, his newest obses-
> sions as a composer. Was it not the least hypocritical way
> to unite, in an indivisible whole, both the creator and the
> transmitter of knowledge? I was bedazzled, definitively.[16]

WHERE MUSIC BORDERS ON SILENCE

I have dealt so far with a remarkable music analysis teacher, blessed with a rich, vivid, and pragmatic knowledge of the history of Western musical language, whose commentaries on a score radiated out as a web of illuminating digressions. This expertise alone would have ensured Messiaen a secure place—if somewhat difficult to classify—in the history of music teaching. But every encounter with a former pupil brought more indications that his enviable reputation as a pedagogue had more deep-reaching roots.

Even before the War, when a small group of disciples showed keen interest in Messiaen's first compositions and organ improvisations, the thirty-year-old composer was seen both as an original creator and as a rare human being. Informal meetings were held in Messiaen's garden or in the organ loft at La Trinité church. Yvette Grimaud, who was to premiere all of Pierre Boulez's early piano works, said it was like the ancient practice of disciples gathering around a beloved and revered master. Even though music remained at the center of discussions, she first speaks of an "enseignement de vie": "Messiaen tried to transmit to us his inner silence." The greatest force of his teaching, insists Yvette Grimaud, could not be grasped in an instant. "It created a development in the life of those among us who remained true to it."

Practically everyone who was questioned on the subject of Messiaen's teaching methods, even when critical of some aspect or other of his theories and musical ideas, expressed a profound feeling of thankful affection for the man himself. Many praised his kindness and generosity. His tranquil countenance hid a solid strength of will. A "believer" in the musical as well as in the spiritual sense, Messiaen felt sure of his own path and rarely cared to criticize that chosen by others. Stockhausen, who attended his class for a few months during the academic year 1951–52, gave testimony that he never heard Messiaen speak ill of anyone, even though his private and professional life was difficult at the time.[17] When confronted with a work or a style in which he felt little interest, Messiaen generally kept resolutely and calmly silent, a restrained—unequivocal—gesture which his students learned to respect and appreciate. French composer Gérard Grisey, a regular student of Messiaen in the seventies, admits he was disappointed at first when this most admired pedagogue made only sparse and sibylline commentaries on the scores that were brought to him in class. Grisey later realized that by so doing, Messiaen sent him back to himself, to his music, and to the kind of criticism the composer alone can formulate on his own work. "Zen masters act like this with disciples who expect the truth of them."[18]

Let us discuss now some of the recurring themes found in Messiaen's discourse, be it in class, in various interviews and conferences, or in his posthumous treatise. This might help us draw a clearer picture of both the artist and the pedagogue, and better define the long-sustaining nourishment he provided for his students.

COMPOSER OF TIME AND OF THE END OF TIME

Messiaen's fascination with the general concept of Time (and with rhythm, its corollary) has been expressed on various occasions, such as when he was awarded the Prix Érasme in 1971:

> Time is my great love, because it is the point of departure for all Creation. Time presupposes change (thus, matter) and movement (thus, space and life). Time makes us understand Eternity by contrast. Time should be the friend of all musicians.[19]

The *Traité de rythme* opens with a quote from Thomas Aquinas that eloquently demonstrates a real communion of mind between two theoreticians equally captivated by the mystery of the Eternity of God: "Time measures not only what is effectively changing, but what is changeable: hence it measures not just motion, but also rest; the state of a being born to move yet not presently moving."[20] In class, Messiaen explained in minute detail, for weeks on end, Greek metrics or the ancient Hindu rhythmic formulas called *deçi-tâlas*. Seemingly insouciant of Conservatoire schedules, he undertook to open the minds of his often bewildered (and sometimes annoyed) students to the numerous layers of Time: time of the universe, of the stars, of the mountains, of the trees, of microphysics; human time, animal time, insect time, mineral time. The heart and brain of the whole of Western civilization was called upon for assistance and advice, as the composer of *Soixante-quatre durées* discussed diverse definitions of time and rhythm given throughout history. Fortunately enough, Messiaen's later treatise bears precious witness to these unusual discussions. Greek philosophers such as Aristoxenes, Plato, and Heraclites were quoted side by side with the Holy Scriptures, scientists, novelists, poets, composers, and music theorists.

One should not, however, be given the impression that Messiaen is merely playing a learned game of casual name-dropping. His commentaries are generally full of insight. Musical correspondences or applications are never far from his preoccupations. Paraphrasing a comment of Roger Vitrac's on the transparency of Jacques Lipchitz's sculptures, Messiaen affirms in his treatise that such prominent musicians as Edgar Varèse, André Jolivet, Anton Webern, Pierre Boulez, and John Cage— perhaps even Pierre Schaeffer and Karlheinz Stockhausen—have adopted the only two possible attitudes toward silence: either to submit to it or to let it pass.[21] Boulez's interesting approach to silence in his Second Piano Sonata (1948) is linked with Jean Thibault's research on atoms[22]: "[those silences] are so totally opposed to sounds that they belong neither to the sound that precedes them nor to the one that follows. In this conception, silence is a cessation, an absence, a negation. It is the opposite of sound, as night is the opposite of day. It is simply Silence, with a capital S. "[23]

A complete musician, however deeply immersed in theological meditations, can always learn from the observation of simple human life. Messiaen's students were regularly reminded that one dimension should never shun the other, that an acute awareness of everyday reality, counterbalanced by the gift to transfigure it into the universal, reveals the true artist.[24] In his last theoretical opus, Messiaen points out that there are certain moments in life when a great psychological stress alters one's perception of duration, a fact well known by traditional oriental musicians.

> If we examine the present moment, it is clear that waiting and inactivity create an emptiness which slows down the passage of time. By contrast, joy, work, anything that keeps us busy and captures our attention, speeds up the pace. If we consider the past, memory, like a mirror, has the reverse effect on our sense of speed. A slow period leaves us with a general memory lacking special details, lacking images to focus thoughts, lacking interest; even if it was very long by clock time, it now seems short. By contrast, a busy period filled with all sorts of events (hard work both physical and mental, emotional blows, aesthetic shocks, actions both achieved and avoided) will be remembered as long, in fact very long if it was especially action-packed, and its speed seems to stretch or shrink in proportion to the number of memories it has left us.[25]

Composers organize time just as sculptors shape matter. Jean-Pierre Leguay, both a composer and a renowned organist, remembers that if Messiaen undeniably talked a lot about rhythmic cells, he also wisely considered the question from a much broader perspective, urging his students to ponder the overall rhythm of a work, to relate rhythm to the larger form. Such challenging reflections, supported by specific examples (chosen, for instance, from Wagner's three- or four-hour-long operas), have stimulated the progress of numerous composers-in-the-making who attended his analysis or composition class. Guy Reibel, for one, testifies that Messiaen was the first musician he encountered who knew how to describe music as a force, a dynamic element, as an energy in movement.

A POET OF LOVE AND RESURRECTION

It should be obvious by now that words and language were the essential tools of Messiaen's never-ending inquiry into musical creation. His was a truly *oral* teaching, a discourse made of interwoven strings of verb and sound that defies transcription. The rich sonorities he produced at the piano with his astonishingly soft hands were translated on the spot into poetic images. One can only regret that the posthumous treatise, the sum of a lifetime experience in direct communication, must be *read*—and not *heard*—as it was in his class.[26]

This fervent lover of opera, the son of the poetess Cécile Sauvage and of an acknowledged translator of Shakespeare, explored daily the delicate correspondence between *la parola* and *la musica*, an old preoccupation indeed in musical aesthetics.[27] When Yvonne Loriod was asked to play all of the Mozart piano concertos in a series of concerts in the late fall of 1964, in Paris, Messiaen made a special point of analyzing these works, which he greatly admired, for his students. More than twenty years later, the program notes he had written for his wife's performances were published.[28] This precious document stands as one of the first windows opened on Messiaen's class, and although it presupposes from the reader some knowledge of musical terminology, it is still the most largely accessible source for a general public. Startling parallels are suggested between the works in hand and other pillars of Western musical literature. For instance, the *Concerto in E flat*, K. 271 (nicknamed the "Jeunehomme") is linked with the *Funeral March* of Beethoven's *"Eroica" Symphony* and with Bach's passions. The deeply moving cadenza of the slow movement of K. 271 inspired this beautiful meditation:

> Such a passage should be heard in the fading glow of twilight. It is at this symbolic hour that it takes on all its grandeur and recalls the poetry of Death in Ecclesiastes: "...and those that look out of the windows be darkened, And the Doors shall be shut in the streets... the wheel broken at the cistern... and the spirit shall return unto God who gave it. Vanity of vanities, saith the preacher: all is vanity."[29]

Messiaen shows again his sensitivity to human experience, as well as his ability to use metaphor in order to convey the music's deeper meaning. In the first movement from the same concerto, the broadening intervals are compared to a smile becoming warmer and warmer. The larghetto of Mozart's last piano concerto, written in the last year of his life, is "totally bathed in a dying light. The light of the setting sun, beyond which one glimpses the birth of another light, the inner glow of Grace, and the almost affectionate waiting of the greatest of invitations, that of Death." Leading further into this path, the analyst associates another grave moment in the same concerto with a sentence pronounced by one of the characters in *Pelléas et Mélisande*: "Yours is the face most grave and friendly of those who will not live long."[30]

The analogies with Debussy's opera are not fortuitous. Messiaen was given the score at the age of ten, less than twenty years after the controversial premiere of the opera, and he always considered this unexpected and sensitive present as one of the most significant events of his entire musical education. He had played through Debussy's idiomatic score so often, singing every role in a soft tenor voice, he practically knew the whole opera by heart. The complete analysis of the work, interspersed with numerous extra-musical detours, could well demand many months. Every page gave Messiaen ample ground for discussing the subtle correspondence, so characteristic of Debussy's mature vocal style, between words and music. Furthermore, the complex psychological and philosophical implications of Maeterlinck's diffused symbolist play, magnified by the music, were the source of countless admiring comments. Messiaen's complete analysis of the work, interspersed with countless extra-musical detours, could well demand many months. As could be guessed, students expecting a more conventional approach were sometimes irritated by this interdisciplinary marathon. Others were truly fascinated, even deeply moved.[31]

From Vincent d'Indy's composition treatise onward, the French school of music analysis—if such a thing exists—has shown strong links with the romantic literary tradition. Similarly, music criticism in this country of letters has often resembled what is known to French high-school students as lyrical "description de texte." In this respect, Messiaen's process is far from extraordinary.[32] Here, originality lies in the composer's rare choice of extra-musical sources: medieval dawn-songs, fairy-tales, French playwrights and poets, foreign authors (e.g., Shakespeare, Poe, Rilke, Tennyson, the Chinese book of *I Ching*, all in translation), philosophical essays, popularized accounts of scientific theories, and, of course, the Holy Scriptures. Which leads us to the most important dimension of Messiaen's intimate world, his Christian spirituality.

"I WAS BORN A CHRISTIAN"

Much has been said and written regarding Messiaen's life-long endeavor to "highlight the theological truths of the Catholic faith" through his musical compositions.[33] Admirers might be surprised to learn that Messiaen rarely directly discussed his spiritual beliefs in class, except when he agreed to analyze one of his own works bearing a religious title (this he did more readily toward the end of his teaching career than in the fifties). In such cases, he willingly enumerated the sources of his inspiration, often a quotation from either the Bible or the writings of great theologians such as Thomas Aquinas, Dom Columba Marmion, Romano Guardini, Hans Urs von Balthazar, or Thomas Merton.[34] Messiaen once explained to French musicologist Brigitte Massin that the theological research prior to the composition of a new work was for him almost as important as the actual writing of the score.[35] Since he also wanted every listener to know precisely what inspired the music in the first place, he wrote extensive program notes for each of his works. These explanatory commentaries invariably appear on the published score and accompany every recording he supervised. When asked by a journalist to comment on a recent composition, Messiaen would most probably go back to his own text, even to the extent of reading it meticulously.[36]

From the start, Messiaen's faith has been a very public affair. It was he who brought modern religious music out of the church and into the concert hall. Messiaen's candid self-affirmation as a resolutely religion-motivated composer, as early as in the late twenties, clearly isolated him from his fellow students at the Conservatoire. Even Paul Dukas, his composition teacher, was somewhat taken aback by his pupil's choice to take the Eucharistical Banquet as the subject of his first orchestral piece.[37] The more his reputation as a composer spread in Europe and America, the more it was known that his strong religious convictions were inseparable from his artistic creation. This fact made many early listeners rather uncomfortable. What was often perceived as unreserved religiosity inspired numerous contemptuous critical comments in the press. France has been a secular state since the beginning of the century, and anti-clericalism was always strong among the intelligentsia. Avowed Catholic writers like Paul Claudel, François Mauriac, and Georges Bernanos remained exceptional figures. The distaste for outward religious demonstrations seemed even stronger after the Second World War, since genuine Christian faith had proved unable to prevent the horrible events, when they did not reinforce anti-Semitism in the right-thinking bourgeoisie. Leftist political opinions, quite popular at the time, were considered antithetical to religious beliefs. The most apolitical avant-garde world was no exception. The feeling of social marginalization, of reluctant acceptance by his colleagues and peers, persisted throughout Messiaen's life, even when he acquired an international stature.

This label of "Catholic composer" may have put off some young musicians from trying to study with Messiaen in Paris, especially in the sixties and early seventies, when the American "Peace and Love" anti-war movement inspired students globally to reject the social conventions, the morals, and the religious values of their elders. On the other hand, Messiaen's perceptible spiritual aura, his awareness of oriental philosophies and mythologies, appealed to many younger musicians, who did not necessary share his beliefs. Japanese composer Makoto Shinohara was surely one of them.

> This is a man who, with infinite patience and curiosity, continually explores music where abstract and concrete elements are in tune with each other; music which touches him. He flees the noisy dusty city for the broad calm countryside, to observe—while others sleep—nature and life around. Hoping to understand all that is comprehensible, he reflects on what has always united man and nature. He meditates profoundly on the mysteries which human thinking can penetrate. It is in showing me how to feel and to recognize this incomparable territory that his teaching has revealed unsuspected horizons to me. My respect for my master grows stronger every day, and his sensitive, inspired words, his humble solitary face, will live forever in my heart.[38]

Another telling testimony is that of French composer Jacques Charpentier, who discovered Messiaen's music during a pivotal trip to Asia and India. The fascinating non-European musical universe had in a certain sense thrown him across Messiaen's path.

> I must say that in the wake of my exposure to Indian music, I was filled with profound amazement at THIS MAN, who, throughout my years of study with him [in the mid-Fifties], taught us not just musical knowledge but something far more precious: musical *conscience*. Messiaen once wrote: "Only a great artist, a great artisan as a Christian believer can be, can bring to this age the living water for which it so thirsts!" After several years spent close to such a wise and loving master, this "great artist," this "great artisan," this

"Christian believer" in the sense that Messiaen meant, became for me none other than Messiaen himself... He alone has the means and the will to awaken in us a sense of the absolute, a sense which confers, on the faculties of the heart and soul, their highest meaning.[39]

"WHAT IS WRITTEN IN THE STARS... "[40]

According to pianist and ethnomusicologist Yvette Grimaud, Messiaen always had a great reverence for realms beyond his expertise. Astronomy, for instance, exerted a strong fascination on him. The imagery and symbolic meaning of the stars, planets, and constellations were evoked in many of his works (e.g., the piece called *Amen des étoiles, de la planète à l'anneau* in *Les Visions de l'Amen* for two pianos). This remained a constant inspiration throughout his career. Since the composer's eyes were too weak to permit him to observe for himself Saturn's moons, he read many illustrated essays on astrophysics and followed the highly publicized conquest of space. Speaking of the amazing discoveries of this century in this field, like that of the quasars in 1960, Messiaen reaffirms his unshakable faith:

> This dizzying expansion of our concept of the universe, incommensurate in time and space, opens a new path by which to approach the mystery of Eternity. To think that divinity has no beginning, that it existed before all these phenomena of which we speak, long before; and that there is really no "before" imaginable, that the word itself is inexact, because eternity transcends both "before" and "after." And to think that divinity wished to be near us in the Incarnation of Christ... I think that far from being terrified by astronomical discoveries, the believer should be strengthened in the faith.[41]

One is bound to think of Renaissance philosophers (notably Descartes) who saw no difficulty whatsoever in the parallel existence of rational thinking and theology. Messiaen showed again and again the ability to merge various dimensions of life and thought into one coherent creative system. In this respect, one particular student impressed him more than any other: the Greek Iannis Xenakis. When the young man came to him in the early fifties, his musical baggage was very light. His studies of mathematics, engineering, and architecture had been interrupted by the German invasion of Greece; severely injured in the resistance movement, he was forced to flee to France where he finally found employment in the workshop of the architect Le Corbusier. In his search for advice about his ever-stronger needs for musical expression, the disfigured and emotionally shaken refugee finally sought out Messiaen. Though obviously lacking in basic technical training, the young man heard nothing but encouragement. He had in the Conservatoire teacher's eyes many qualities to build upon: he was Greek, had a heroic past, had read the classics, and possessed extensive knowledge of mathematics and physics. He should thus forget about harmony lessons and seek his own personal place in twentieth-century music. Messiaen's good counsel proved to be one of the most inspired and far-reaching intuitions of his whole career as a pedagogue, since Xenakis rapidly became a prominent composer using laws of physics and computer technology to construct complex worlds of sound totally unheard of before.[42]

REAPING THE HARVEST

As seen within the evolution of the European avant-garde, Messiaen's class reveals itself to be a fascinating microcosm of various modern musical tendencies. The emergence of a strong post-Webernian serial current in the early fifties is historically tightly bound to the French composer's research on rhythm and to his serial approach to durations, dynamics, and modes of attack. The fact is that Messiaen, though severely critical of Schoenberg's achievement as a dodecaphonic composer, was the first teacher in France to acknowledge the surprising rebirth and development of the movement in this country.[43] He also took quite seriously the highly structural compositions to emerge among his first students, namely Pierre Boulez, Jean Barraqué, Karel Goeyvaerts, Karlheinz Stockhausen, and Michel Fano. All felt strongly indebted to Messiaen's famous *Mode de valeurs et d'intensités* (part of the *Quatre études de rythme* for piano), composed in Darmstadt in 1949—and one of his rare unreligious scores to date.[44] Even Boulez, seldom inclined to acknowledge any gratitude toward the French educational system, recognized Messiaen as a spiritual father, though his praises were at that time characteristically mixed with some venom.[45] As for Michel Fano, another member of the group of free-thinkers who gathered around Messiaen in the late forties,[46] he more then once paid tribute to his teacher in enthusiastic terms:

> Passion, generosity, an endless fount of knowledge of musical art, suddenly flooded our barren fields. Week after week, [there was] fervent exploration of unknown territory,

guided subtly by a Master more eager to suggest than to impose. If Truth existed, as surely it did for Messiaen, he never felt it gave him the right to turn it into a catechism. Showing, revealing, leading each one to become himself, while profoundly respecting others, such was the enriching activity of this veritable Master—he who brought us to know and love *all* musics, even those from which he felt himself most distanced... His extremely cultivated nature brought into any discussion of music a whole network of enquiries and new questions. That he knew how to meet the needs of a pivotal generation, deeply troubled by the musical turmoil of their times, is an ineffable, unforgettable gift.[47]

In the fifties, "integral serialism" was proclaimed by Boulez and his followers to be the only road a composer could decently follow. This precipitated a terrible stylistic crisis and unfortunately began to silence a number of talented composers, forced to take sides. After a period of intense reflection (and a few completed scores), a group of works based on bird songs and nature appeared as Messiaen's personal response. This apparent turn toward less abstract grounds (compared to the influential *Études de rythme, Messe de la Pentecôte,* or *Livre d'orgue*) proved again to be inspirational for a new generation of students who felt nowhere at home, neither in the severe pointillism of Darmstadt nor in the closed studios of tape-music devotees. Messiaen stood as a persuasive example for anyone eager to construct a personal imaginary world. Composer François-Bernard Mâche, one of the few to participate simultaneously in Messiaen's class and in Pierre Schaeffer's *Groupe de recherche* on "concrete music," believes that the composer of *Oiseaux exotiques* stood for freedom of choice and independence, against the changing fashion of the day.

Messiaen incarnated the necessity of the waking dream— that liberty which he offered his students he demonstrated by allying, in a manner as strange as it was convincing, the spirit of systematic method, and that of no method at all. Whether exploring the limits of numerology or naturalism, he always imposed on his compositional experiments a higher law: Intuition. It seems to me that this was the most valuable part of his teaching: beyond the numerous processes of creation he invented, and the remarkable products that came from them, there is the global intuition of the work, which is not a sum of the parts but a primal vision which works itself out as one writes.[48]

From a general point of view, one could say that the composer-teacher stressed by his every action the importance of giving much thought to every parameter of sound (pitch, dynamics, duration, timbre), considered, if necessary, in isolation from the others. The *Traité de rythme* bears witness to his revolutionary conception of rhythm, but also to his life-long admiration for plain-song's eternal principles of elevation and deposition of the linear phrase (*arsis* and *thesis*), of its joyous and ever-renewed inventiveness. Similarly, Mozart and Debussy provided countless treasures of melodic genius. Furthermore, Messiaen's "vision" of harmony as essentially colored and non-directional, although certainly very French, was found by many altogether stimulating. In the vast *Catalogue d'oiseaux* (1956–58), every chord was conceived—and should be perceived—as a resonant and telling "objet sonore," almost in the Schaefferien sense of the word. It sometimes took the composer days to find the right combination of tones to represent most vividly dusk on the Atlantic shore or sunset in the Dauphiné mountains. To quote Quebec composer Serge Garant, Messiaen showed through his music and general discourse that there should be no schism between research and music, that the creative imagination can be structured without impairing spontaneous expressivity.

> He taught me that one can think music as an architect thinks the construction of a building, that is, in a manner both rational and sensitive. I learned from him that what we call "inspiration" should never get the upper hand of the intelligence that organizes the materials. The curious thing is that Messiaen never said this sort of thing explicitly. But thanks to the way he taught, one became permeated with a certain necessity to construct music, to compose music at once sensitive and intelligent. I would even go so far as to say "intelligible," that is legible at the level of the structural plan.[49]

Still, once the score laid on his piano had been patiently and objectively broken down into pieces, Messiaen would confess that real artistic beauty and truth lie beyond any technical considerations. Many would agree, and leave the class in a state of dynamic wonder.

RISING ABOVE THE TURMOIL

In the face of harsh criticism, which in the first half of his career shaded over into private insults more than once, Messiaen displayed impressive courage and tenacity. Novices in the craft, frightened by the relentless race of the avant-garde, gained confidence at his side.[50] Did he not keep writing, in a strikingly individual yet constantly evolving language, musical frescoes of unrestrained expansiveness and (for some) uncomfortable length? In class, he who once prayed for the End of Time never gave the impression of measuring his own. Unmindful of Conservatoire time-tables, he appeared totally absorbed in the manifold beauties of a score; as if, one student remembers, talking in his sleep. Quebec composer Gilles Tremblay recounts that while ecstatically commenting on Debussy's *Pelléas et Mélisande*, the analyst was every so often constrained to silence, able only to confess: "I can not talk any more, it is just too beautiful."

In the late sixties and through the seventies, the aging Messiaen still was graced with sensitive antennas. He immediately recognized as valid the new paths opened by students some forty years younger than he. Discreet as always, he helped them clear the way to unexplored ground. He presented in class, side by side with reliable masterpieces, recent scores and recordings that proposed a direct approach to sound, for instance that of the new Polish school led by Penderecki. György Ligeti he thanked promptly for the rich and beautiful harmonic realm his music brought to the rather dry cerebral style prevailing in the early sixties. Pierre Schaeffer's *Traité des objets musicaux,* published in 1966, was likewise discussed and the recordings that came with it played on the gramophone, provoking animated debates amongst the supporters and the detractors of electroacoustic music. Devoted as he was to instrumental composition, Messiaen repeatedly stated that the electronic medium was one of the most important revolutions ever to occur in music-making; had he been younger when it appeared, he might well have been induced to change course.[51] Talented performers were also regularly invited to his class. Guests, teacher, and students explored together the untapped resources still offered by conventional instruments. Even such an accomplished orchestrator as Messiaen acknowledgedly learned from these visits, as the striking horn solos in *Des Canyons aux étoiles...* (1974) bear proof.

Over the thirty-seven-year span of Messiaen's pedagogical activity at the Conservatoire, contemporary music went through numerous, sometimes violent, upheavals. It is a highly significant fact that his class remained, continually, a real center of creativity. This teacher's curiosity about the latest developments was seen, first, in his reliable presence at numerous concerts and second, in his constant interest for his students' compositional essays (whatever the official title given to his class, be it harmony, analysis, music aesthetics, or composition). The most celebrated composers came to see him in the old building of the

Rue de Madrid; they brought along their latest scores—and sometimes recordings—which they analyzed for the benefit of his students, deeply impressed by such informal encounters. Through decades, the class of Messiaen served as a "salon" where one discussed what was happening or was going to happen on the musical scene. Young apprentices in search of their identities undeniably profited from such a warm creative atmosphere. Messiaen's ability to make the connections between the past and future constitutes, according to Japanese composer Makoto Shinohara, "the work of all great men."[52]

AN ENDURING LEGACY

An exact appraisal of Messiaen's impact on each of his students remains difficult to assess, perhaps even impossible, as the creative process can never be easily summed up. One could dislike Messiaen's music but still benefit from his teaching. On the other hand, beside being one of the foremost European composers of this century, Messiaen was also an exceptionally cultured man equally at ease discussing theological problems, Yeats' poetry, ornithology, oriental philosophy, or the paintings of Jerome Bosch. Multiple influences were at work in his discourse, and his hundreds of students were certain to latch on to at least one or more.

From the composer came rich new ideas about matters of rhythm, orchestration, modal harmony, melodic writing, and form. Here was a creator of remarkable works who freely invited others into his private garden while never imposing his own solutions. As we have seen, this attitude was reflected in his role as a teacher. Generosity, respect, passion, erudition, humanity, those are the key-words that recur under the pen of his former students. Messiaen the pedagogue was indistinguishable from Messiaen the man, self-assured yet curious, open to discussion, understanding of the ardor of youth, patiently canalizing the vehemence of the artist struggling to grow. A brief yet concentrated glance at an unfinished score was sometimes all he needed to help a timid creator in discovering his own path in the jungle of modern music. This complete musician spoke of masterpieces without obsequiousness, keeping his hands on the keyboard, exhorting his students to develop their inner ears and to compose bearing in mind that music, even though it must be thoughtfully conceived, is above all meant to be *heard*. Such a rare conjunction of diverse human qualities made Olivier Messiaen, for several generations of students, a "Master" in the full oriental sense of the term.

Without any doubt, many music teachers around the world show a real and sincere passion for the art of sound. But probably few of us succeed as well as did Messiaen in transmitting this passion to others. He knew, to quote Stockhausen, the art of "bringing back the dead to life,"[53] of showing how composers of the past may still nourish today's creative minds. Daniel-Lesur, one of the three organists to premiere Messiaen's long organ cycle *La Nativité du Seigneur* in 1935, believes that the musician's message "is spreading more impressively than ever. For he was filled with grace, shining with radiance, drawing on both his faith and his love of music."[54] His versatility, his liberalism in sharing both knowledge and experience, are what made Messiaen one of the most eminent music teachers of our time.

NOTES

[1] In Olivier Messiaen, *Traité de rythme, de couleur et d'ornithologie*, vol. I (Paris: Leduc, 1994), p. viii. We heartily thank Dr. Christine Beckett of Sherbrooke and McGill universities for her precious help in translating from the French most of the testimonies and quotations included in this chapter, as well as for her numerous suggestions on how to improve our English prose. We are also deeply indebted to Pierre Chénier for his many helpful comments.

[2] In Harry Halbreich, *Olivier Messiaen* (Paris: Fayard/Fondation SACEM, 1980) p. 520.

[3] Jean Boivin, *La classe de Messiaen* (Paris, Christian Bourgeois, 1995), 483 pp. The book is a shortened and revised version of our Ph. D. thesis entitled *La classe de Messiaen: historique, reconstitution, impact*, 3 vol. (Université de Montréal, Faculté de musique, 1992), 755 pp.

[4] A life-long devotee of Messiaen's music, Yvonne Loriod became the composer's second wife in 1961. She is to be warmly thanked for the immense task of preparing for edition, with the help of composer and former student Alain Louvier, Messiaen's unfinished *Traité de rythme*. She followed her husband's detailed instructions, given to her before his death (which occurred in April 1992).

[5] An early theoretical work written by Messiaen in 1939, *Vingt leçons d'harmonies*, encourages the student to imitate the style of various composers ranging from Monteverdi to Ravel. It was published by Leduc in 1944 and translated into English in 1957 (Paris: Leduc).

[6] In Brigitte Massin, *Olivier Messiaen: une poétique du merveilleux* (Aix-en-Provence: Alinéa, 1989), p. 179.

[7] Published in French (Paris: Leduc, 1944), and in an English translation (Paris: Leduc, 1956).

[8] In an unpublished Conservatoire document prepared for Messiaen's 80th birthday, April 1988.

[9] Boulez often used this image when questioned about Messiaen's class, for example in his foreword to the latter's *Traité de rythme* (1994), p. V.

[10]In July 1987, ten years after his retirement from the Conservatoire, Messiaen was invited by director Claude Samuel to lecture at the Centre Acanthes, near Avignon. This was his last official teaching engagement. A documentary film has been made on the occasion by Olivier Mille, *Les leçons d'Olivier Messiaen* (Paris: ARTLINE/FR 3/LA SEPT/SNC, 1988, 59 min).

[11]Other Americans' names found on the list of Messiaen's pupils are Philip Corner, William Albright, Roland Jackson, Alvin King, Robert Newell, Edward Weinmann, Janice Giteck, Gerald Levinson, and Brian Schober (the last two attended his composition class in the seventies). Messiaen's impact on American music remains an interesting subject of research.

[12]In Canada, the province of Quebec was a very fertile ground for Messiaen's theories and ideas. In the fifties, the rapid formation of a young avant-garde movement was directly linked with various travels of young French Canadian composers to Paris, where many attended Messiaen's class. This group was lead by Serge Garant (1929-1986), who soon after his return assumed in Montreal a role equivalent to that of Boulez in Paris with the *Domaine musical* concerts. I summarized Messiaen's prominent influence on Quebec's composers in an article entitled "Olivier Messiaen et le Québec: une présence et une influence déterminante sur la création musicale de l'après-guerre," *Canadian University Music Review*, 17/1 (1996), pp. 73-97. Another recent article, focused on Garant's studies in Paris, is to be published in the *Cahiers de la Société québécoise de recherche en musique*, 1/1-2 (1997).

[13]"The wind of the spirit." The title refers to the last part of Messiaen's *Messe de la Pentecôte* (1950), a stunning "sortie."

[14]In fact, Messiaen mastered the piano long before he got acquainted with the organ, which he came to relatively late in his youth, when one of his teachers at the Paris Conservatoire, Jean Gallon, noticed his gift for improvisation. Thereafter, Messiaen became well versed in a huge repertory of organ works, from Bach and Daquin to Widor, Tournemire, and Dupré.

[15]Recollection of a former student, the French musicologist Françoise Gervais.

[16]In Harry Halbreich, *Olivier Messiaen*, pp. 518-519.

[17]In *Melos*, December, xxv/12 (1958), p. 392, reproduced in *Texte Band II* (Cologne: DuMont Schauberg, 1964), pp. 144-145. Messiaen's first wife, violinist Claire Delbos, became seriously ill and had to be hospitalized after the birth of their first and only son. She died in 1959.

[18]In an unpublished document prepared by the Conservatoire de Paris for Messiaen's 80th birthday, April 1988.

[19]Quoted by Brigitte Massin in *Olivier Messiaen: une poétique du merveilleux*, pp. 113-114.

[20]Messiaen, *Traité*, vol. I, p. 7.

[21]*Ibid.*, p. 48.

[22]*Vie et transmutation des atomes* (Paris: Albin Michel, 1942).

[23]Messiaen, *Traité*, p. 28. Boulez, though rather a *persona non grata* in the Conservatoire from which he had fled in disgust, was invited to come and present his Second Piano Sonata to Messiaen's students as soon as it was published (1950). The initiative was to have a strong impact on many young composers attending (e.g., Michel Fano and Jean Barraqué). The first volume of the *Traité* includes an analysis of the rhythmic structure of an excerpt from the sonata (p. 50).

[24]This absence of duality in Messiaen's mind between worldly and spiritual matters explains why critics were shocked more than once to discover that in his first post-war works, sensual love is just as important a motivation as is the adoration of Christ. Robert Sherlaw Johnson once aptly remarked that the composer speaks of both human love and love of nature not as being opposed to his faith but as being "complementary to it and implied in it." Sherlaw Johnson, *Messiaen* [Berkeley and Los Angeles: University of California Press, 1989], p. 40.

[25]Olivier Messiaen, *Traité*, vol. I, p. 10.

[26]Even though Messiaen's treatise is filled with countless excerpts from important scores, including his own, reading it still falls short of the almost metaphysical experience related by his students. The highly acclaimed—and long awaited—analysis of Stravinsky's *The Rite of Spring,* posthumously published in volume two (1993, pp. 93-147) is certainly worth attentive reading and studying, but it also emphasizes in my opinion the limitation of any written transcription of an exposé intended to be listened to. In a short scene from Denise Tual's and Michel Fano's film *Olivier Messiaen et les oiseaux* (SOFRACIMA, Denise Tual, Fondation Royaumont, 1973, 80 min.), we are shown Messiaen commenting in class on the prelude of Act One from Debussy's opera *Pelléas et Mélisande.* The valuable sequence reveals, if only in a glimpse, the strong physical and aural dimension of his approach. A true suspense grasps the students' attention throughout, as well as ours. I propose a transcription of the scene in my book on Messiaen's class (*op. cit.,* pp. 211-224).

[27]Let us not forget that following the mature Berlioz and Wagner, and to many critics' dismay, Messiaen always set his own texts to music (with the sole exception of a melody on one of his mother's poems, composed in his youth). He explained more than once that the poems of the *Trois petites Liturgies de la Présence Divine,* for instance, were expressly meant to be *sung,* not read aloud.

[28]Olivier Messiaen, *Les 22 concertos pour piano de Mozart* (Paris: Séguier-Archimbault-Birr, 1987), p. 121.

[29]*Ibid.,* p. 33. Translation of the Bible (Ecc. 11: 3-8) was taken from King James version.

[30]*Ibid.,* pp. 116-117.

[31]Fragments of this fascinating analysis, which we discovered through the notes taken by Messiaen's former students, are to be included in a yet to be published volume of the *Traité de rythme* (vol. VI). Other works by Debussy should also be included in this volume, such as the *Prélude à l'après-midi d'un faune, La Mer,* and the piano works, *Preludes* and *Images.* All were favorites of Messiaen, often discussed in his class.

[32]Messiaen's models in the field of music analysis were primarily Vincent d'Indy's composition treatise (*Cours de composition musicale,* 2 vol., [Paris: Durand, 1912]) and the teaching of both Paul Dukas and Maurice Emmanuel. The former was Messiaen's composition teacher and a renowned critic, while the latter's study on Greek metrics deeply influenced the composer of *Cinq rechants.* We must remember that Messiaen, though he was the son of an English teacher, could not read any other language than French. The Anglo-Saxon's tradition of music analysis was thus remote from him. Translations were still fairly rare when he started his pedagogical career, and there was no sign that he ever came to know Schenkerian theories, for instance.

[33]Olivier Messiaen, *Musique et couleurs, nouveaux entretiens avec Claude Samuel* (Paris: Belfond, 1986), p. 21. The composer proclaimed more than once that he saw the Holy Scriptures as a "true" fairy-tale.

[34] From the Bible, Messiaen chose more regularly the Psalms, *Song of Songs*, the Epistles of Paul, and the *Book of Revelation*. Among other religious sources he readily made use of are an anonymous work entitled *L'Imitation de Jésus-Christ*, St. Francis's *Fioretti*, Ernest Hello's *Paroles de Dieu*, and the writings of various saints such as Bonaventure, Bernard, St. John of the Cross, and Theresa of Avila. For an interesting study of the composer's religious inspiration, see Brigitte Massin, *op. cit.* Prior to the present publication, some illuminating papers were also written in English on the subject, such as those by Wilfrid Mellers and Ian Matheson in *The Messiaen Companion*, Peter Hill editor, (London and Boston: Faber and Faber, 1995), pp. 220-233, 234-248.

[35] B. Massin, *op. cit.*, pp. 145-150.

[36] I met Messiaen in his Paris apartment in the spring of 1987 to discuss his teaching career at the Conservatoire. Before leaving, I could not resist the temptation to ask him a few questions about *Le livre du Saint-Sacrement* (1984), an important and lengthy organ composition that had been recently premiered in the city. Though obviously tired, the aged composer very kindly obliged for the benefit of the French-speaking audience of the Radio-Canada Broadcasting Corporation programs. Before the interview started, Messiaen briefly left the room to fetch his program notes, which he patiently read in their entirety in a soft tone. Uncertain whether those extensive prefatory texts could be included in a standard radio broadcast of the work, I prudently inquired if an unknowing hearer could nevertheless enjoy the music. Messiaen appeared somewhat annoyed by the prospect and assured me that the preparatory description was "very important." Unfortunately, the interview was never broadcasted as intended.

[37] As told by Messiaen to Brigitte Massin in *Messiaen et la poétique du merveilleux*, pp. 45-46. *Le Banquet Eucharistique* (1928) remained unpublished. An early organ piece from the same year, *Le Banquet céleste*, was also inspired by this rather unconventional theme. Messiaen's first acknowledged orchestral piece, *Les Offrandes oubliées* (1930), subtitled "Symphonic Meditations for Orchestra," is based on yet another singular program, the too often forgotten love of Christ sacrificed on the Cross, as noted by Malcolm Hayes in *The Messiaen Companion* (Boston: Faber and Faber, 1995), pp. 159-160.

[38] Translation of Shinohara's testimonies, part of an extensive homage to Messiaen, in *Melos*, xxv/12, December (1958), pp. 391-392.

[39] In *Melos*, xxv/12, December (1958): 387.

[40] *Ce qui est écrit sur les étoiles...* , title of the second piece of *Des Canyons aux étoiles* (1971-74).

[41] In B. Massin, *op. cit.*, pp. 99-100. "Science only confirms the truths found in the Holy Scriptures," also declares Messiaen to B. Massin (*op. cit.*, p. 98).

[42] Before the publication of the *Traité de rythme*, in which the ideas of renowned scientists and scientific popularizes are discussed (e.g., Einstein's relativity theory, Paul Couderc's writings on the expansion of the universe), further evidence of Messiaen's rather naive awe of science was given when he was asked to attend Xenakis' thesis defense at the University of Paris (Sorbonne) in 1976. Xenakis' presentation and the discussion that followed has been published under the title *Arts/sciences*. *Alliages* (Tournais: Casterman, 1979). The exchange of ideas between these two most famous contemporary artists on various topics is certainly worth reading. Among the topics touched on are: a sentence from Parmenides; musical material that can inspire hate or love on the composer's part; laws of atmospheric pressure applied to musical sound; what can and cannot be said about music techniques or aesthetics; the structure of a Bach fugue compared to determinist scientific systems. Other participants in the discussion were Michel Ragon, Olivier Revaut d'Allonnes, Michel Serres, and Bernard Teyssèdre.

[43]In Paris, René Leibowitz's and Max Deutsch's approaches to dodecaphony were much more orthodox and closer to the Second Viennese School in spirit.

[44]Messiaen's essay of serialization of durations, dynamics, and modes of attack, though certainly influential as far as Stockhausen and Boulez are concerned, was in fact a quick and efficient response to a structural problem that preoccupied more than one composer at that time. See Maurice Le Roux's testimony in J. Boivin, *La classe de Messiaen*, p.109. See also Nattiez (ed.), *The Cage-Boulez Correspondence* (Cambridge: Cambridge University Press: 1992).

[45]See Boulez early articles "Propositions" (1948) and "Éventuellement" (1952), collected by Paule Thévenin under the title *Relevés d'apprenti* (Paris: Seuil, 1966), Eng. trans., 1968. Interestingly enough, it is the reconciled Boulez who was asked by Yvonne Loriod to write the foreword to the *Traité de rythme* (vol. I, 1994, pp. iii-iv).

[46]Fano's unpublished *Sonate pour deux pianos*, heard in Darmstadt in 1951, is thought to have inspired, together with Messiaen's *Étude*, Stockhausen's first post-Webernian scores. See Richard Toop's article, "Messiaen, Goeyvaerts, Fano, Stockhausen, Boulez," in *Perspectives of New Music*, vol. 13/1, fall-winter (1974), pp. 141-169. See also Jean Boivin, *op. cit.*, pp. 105-112 and pp.120-125.

[47]In *Olivier Messiaen, homme de foi: regards sur son œuvre d'orgue* (Paris: Trinité Média Communication, 1995), p. 87.

[48]In the unpublished document prepared by the Conservatoire de Paris for Messiaen's 80th birthday, April 1988.

[49]In a Montreal published tribute to Messiaen on the occasion of his 70th birthday, *Variations*, vol. 2, November (1978), p. 8. A series of concerts were given that fall, both in Montreal and Quebec City, in the presence of the composer.

[50]This most precious gift of inner strength is well expressed in George Benjamin's enlightening testimony on Messiaen's teaching, published in *The Messiaen Companion*, pp. 268-273. Benjamin also insists on Messiaen's fabulous sense for harmonic color.

[51]Messiaen tried his hand at electronic music (*Timbres-Durées*, composed with Pierre Henry's help in 1952) but was not really prepared to abandon the written score. The work remained in the composer's desk.

[52]In a Montreal published tribute to Messiaen on the occasion of his 70th birthday, *Variations*, vol. 2, November (1978), p. 19.

[53]In *Melos*, xxv/12, December (1958): 392; reproduced in *Texte* Band II (Cologne: DuMont Schauberg, 1964), pp. 144-145.

[54]In *Olivier Messiaen, homme de foi: regards sur son œuvre d'orgue* (Paris: Trinité Média Communication, 1995), p. 89. Also a composer, Daniel-Lesur was Messiaen's fellow-member in the "Jeune-France" association in the mid-thirties. This group tried to convey a spiritual meaning in modern music, as opposed to the light "divertissement" influence of the Groupe des Six and objectivity of Stravinsky's first neoclassical works.

Messiaen and the Representation of the Theological Illusion of Time

Ian Darbyshire

> Messiaen himself has always claimed to write theological music, as opposed to "mystical" music, which he insists is not his affair.[1]

For Messiaen to describe his music as theological already implies a scientific conception of the nature of music, since theology is the "science of things divine" and hence implies a precision which is not suggested by the word "religious." This scientific capability is exploited by Messiaen through a formalization of the basic materials of his musical language. His appeal to ancient rhythmic principles and the general truths which he believed they contained establishes a link in his music between science and primordiality. The scientific character of music is not limited to a systematic organization of material, which thus bestows on it a type of structure but also asserts that music can be a means for ascertaining knowledge about the world in a manner at least cognate with the modern notion of scientific knowledge. At a deeper level it could be argued that the recognition of "a material" already implies a significant internal structural organization, although a composer may not understand the intellectual history contained within his given materials. Messiaen saw a parallel between some advanced ideas of modern physics concerning the nature and behavior of time and the arguments of theology, both of which could present us with ideas shocking to common sense.[2] The quality of musical material, primarily rhythmic material, is such that it comprehends the intellectual qualities which link the two.[3]

This is literally a radical conception of the nature of music in that Messiaen's philosophy is based on the notions that are etymologically concealed in the word 'music'. 'Music' derives from the Indo-European root MEN, which denotes the 'movements of the mind'; and two of the principal ideas that characterize the derivatives of this root are the realm of the abstract and of the intellect, and the realm of divination and the marvelous, or time and the supernatural:

> All of this makes clear our conception of music: it is there-
> fore an art of thought, intellectual, abstract, unmaterial; an
> art of time (this speaks of the importance of rhythm in
> music), a supernatural art (this speaks of religious aptitudes
> and the psychic power of music).[4]

We could point out that the word "mathematics" is also derived
from the same root; so at the most general level the structure of musical
material and thinking is cognate with, amongst other things, the root of
scientific understanding. Musical representation can be understood as
more or less precise by virtue of this intellectual character. This at once
subverts the criticism which, broadly speaking, holds that there is a
shortfall of connection between Messiaen's musical language and the
ideas more naturally verbally articulated, which that language has pur-
portedly been created to express. This view has recently been succinctly
stated thus:

> We might agree that the music [the second movement of
> Les corps glorieux] could just as appropriately have been
> attended by a different title and prefatory text, or that title
> and text might have engendered completely different
> music. Relatively easy as it is to define and describe the
> technique of Messiaen's "musical language", the extent to
> which it genuinely operates as a musical "language",
> expressive both of the concrete and the spiritual, and
> independent of the verbal exegeses that Messiaen provided,
> remains a moot point.[5]

If the materials of music are imbued with an intellectual character
that is associated with the origins of our basic mental construction of
the world, then a formalization of certain basic musical structures implies representation of a general character. This qualifies how in relation to this general level of representation we should assess Messiaen's
verbal explanations accompanying particular pieces.

Notions of time and of space are of first importance in the formation of the human mind and its mental construction of the world.[6] If we
are so inclined, they are also notions with a theological aspect, as can
be seen from the fact that many divine attributes are described in their
terms, even if in some cases negatively, such as with "timeless" or
"boundless." There is not, in this respect, a radical dichotomy between
fundamental terms in science and theology broadly considered, and the
etymology above is a historical demonstration of this confluence. From
this perspective it is not so much a reconciliation between science and
theology that is the issue, as the similarity of imaginative appeal. Mes-

siaen's familiarity with most of Thomas Aquinas' *Summa Theologiae* is a sign of his familiarity with a world where scientific ideas are involved in theological argument and definition. In our own day, the terms of speculation about whether space and time can be finite without boundaries, where at the origin and "end" of the universe time disappears in quantum uncertainty, are not incomparable to the classical descriptions of divine attributes: "The universe would be completely self-contained and not affected by anything outside itself. It would neither be created nor destroyed. It would just BE."[7] Messiaen himself notes—in a discussion with the composer Iannis Xenakis—that a text of Parmenides describing attributes of the universe ("it IS," "being simultaneously one, continuous," and so on) for him describes God "since only divine attributes are expressed."[8]

It is the representation of time in particular which Messiaen considers to be the business of the musician, although this representation cannot quite be dissociated from notions of space. The deep connection between these two notions, which in modern physics is a precise mathematical and physical one, manifests itself in language metaphorically. The representation of time by sequential cuts on a line, which is a physical and spatial representation, is similar to the idea suggested by the Sanskrit word *tāla* (meaning rhythmic pattern), whose root contains the idea of a physical cutting or arrangement. By virtue of this deep connection, a notion of space will be contained at some level of intellectual sense in rhythmic division.

> Time has always been at the center of my preoccupations.
> As a rhythmist, I've endeavored to divide this time up and
> to understand it better by dividing it. Without musicians,
> time would be much less understood. Philosophers are less
> advanced in this field. But as composers, we have the great
> power to chop up and «retrograde» time.[9]

Messiaen saw what he described as his three principal technical innovations as expressions of the same basic phenomenon. These technical structures are the modes of limited transposition, non-retrogradable rhythms, and symmetrical permutations. Briefly, the modes are symmetrical divisions of the octave which consequently can only be transposed a certain number of times before returning to the original notes; non-retrogradable rhythms are symmetrical rhythms which when written backwards are identical to their forward statement; symmetrical permutations are permutations of a series of musical durations which, because each successive permutation is read in the same reading order, limit the number of permutations from what may be an astronomical number of possible permutations of the original series.[10]

The phenomenon that links these technical structures together is their mathematical limitation, the impossibility of proceeding beyond a certain point of development. Although this represents a formalized conception of music, which extends across the parameters of pitch and rhythm, or sound and time, the mathematical substrate to which they are reduced is not a formally precise one. None of these structures are isomorphic in a precise mathematical sense since each structure has a different degree of symmetry and type of symmetrical structure. Nonetheless, we may suspend our disbelief and suppose that Messiaen's description is satisfactory for his level of mathematical reference, since he is working with a general and elementary idea of number and numeration that he considers to be the key to the secret power contained within these structures, rather than with a mathematically developed notion of symmetry. "This is the charm of impossibilities—they possess an occult power, a calculated ascendancy, in time and sound."[11] ("Calculated ascendancy" is a weak translation of the original French "une emprise chiffrée," the meaning of which is difficult to encapsulate in one phrase but suggests a capture of potentiality by means of numeration.)

A kind of numerical encapsulation is a feature of the ancient Hindu rhythms that Messiaen intensively studied and began to use in his music from the 1930s.[12] Hidden within some of these rhythms were numbers considered to be symbolic of certain ideas. The "charm of impossibilities" is not, however, number symbolism as such, but based on instances of limitation in numeration. This elementary notion of symmetry, which Messiaen detected or built into his basic techniques, made them a kind of musical-mathematical formula, descriptive of a law that holds the secret of the ultimate nature of things. This is the paradox lying at the heart of Messiaen's musical technique: the point where intellectual operations become ineffective is the means to discovery.

With the development of symmetrical permutations the process of numeration allowed Messiaen, so he believed, to make deductions from a theological aspect about our relation to the structure of time and its directionality. The limiting character of the permutational process is not the means of arriving at a more general conclusion about the nature of temporality, but it is the mechanism by which the most interesting rhythms—and by extension a control over the behavior of time—from the original set of durations can be discovered. The nature of temporality is reached from the notion of possible movements of time, which must apply to permutations generally considered.[13] The direction of time is firstly an issue in Messiaen's music in the structure and nature of non-retrogradable rhythms, and these can be seen as a preliminary to the more developed exploration of time through the permutation of an ordered series of durations.

THE REPRESENTATION OF ETERNITY:
TRANSCENDING THE BOUNDARIES OF TIME AND SPACE

A non-retrogradable rhythm possesses mirror, or bilateral, symmetry. However, Messiaen's coining of the term "non-retrogradable" allows for some confusion between the notions of irreversibility and symmetry, with what may seem to be paradoxical consequences for Messiaen's interpretation of the rhythms' intellectual significance. Irreversibility in this context is not referring to the fact that time always flows for us in only one direction, namely forward; rather, it is the intellectual sense of the rhythm which concerns us. Clearly, in this sense a rhythm—or a musical representation of time, which is how a rhythm can be construed—can be reversed: "the mind recognizes in the retrogradation the primitive text redirected towards the past."[14] With a non-retrogradable rhythm no such change in sense can be identified, and so no distinction can be made between the forward or backward direction of time.

The relevance of bilateral symmetry to the physical nature of space is that there is no intrinsic difference of left and right, which means that "position, direction, left and right are relative concepts."[15] The application of this notion to time would suggest that there is no intrinsic difference in the flow of time from past to future or from future to past: physical laws would be symmetrical in relation to backward or forward motion, so that a reversal of time would return one to the original state of a given system. And, in this kind of time symmetry "we reverse the order of events making up the development of the system in such a way that the time intervals between successive events retain their magnitudes."[16]

The conclusion that laws are symmetrical under an inversion of time depends on the idea, if not the actual fact, of the reversibility of the direction of time. Nevertheless, this symmetry can be tested experimentally by the reversal of the physical processes concerned in a given case, even though the actual flow of time cannot be reversed. However, just as time can be inverted mathematically in a set of equations, so the composer can invert time by the manipulation of the sense of his musical material. Mirror symmetry, of which non-retrogradable rhythms are an example, is usually referred to by physicists as time-reversal symmetry. Messiaen's use of the term "non-retrogradable" obscures the issue here somewhat. Compare, for example, these two statements of a non-retrogradable rhythm:

i) ♪♪♩   ii) ♪♪♩

The operation of reversal in either of these two cases is redundant because there is no way of distinguishing which of these two statements is written forward and which is written backward. The reason for this, as of course Messiaen himself explained, lies in the structure of the rhythm, which already contains within itself a retrograde movement. Indeed, explicit retrograde movement is used by Messiaen as a representation of an important theological idea in *Méditations sur le mystère de la Sainte Trinité* (for organ, 1969). Discussing the Theme of God in this piece he comments that

> in order to express that God is boundless just as he is eternal [*immense autant qu'éternel*], without beginning or end in space as in time, I have given two forms to my theme: one forward, one retrograde, as two extremities which face each other and which can fall back on each other [*reculer*: to move backwards, to fall back] indefinitely...[17]

If the two forms of the Theme of God were conjoined, then we would have a non-retrogradable rhythm. Indeed, the notion Messiaen is conveying here is that of circularity, the circle being from ancient times considered the most perfect of geometrical figures because of its complete rotational symmetry. In his first book, *The Technique of My Musical Language*, Messiaen pointed out the effect of "a certain unity of movement (where beginning and end are confused because identical) in the non-retrogradation."[18] It is interesting that in the example quoted from the *Méditations* Messiaen is also representing a spatial idea of boundlessness through rhythmic circularity. From the point of view of duration, though, circular motion would not theologically represent eternity if the absence of boundaries was the sole point of the metaphor: "Conceivably both time and movement could be endless, since any point you choose in time or in circular movement is a beginning as well as an end."[19] It is conceivable, as Aristotle believed, that time had no beginning and has always existed, so the lack of a beginning or end is not the defining characteristic of eternity. Rather, following Aquinas, eternity is characterized by the absence of consecutiveness (of "a before and an after").[20] It is not merely the absence or presence of a boundary but the nature of duration which distinguishes time from eternity. On the other hand, Messiaen's explanation in the *Technique of My Musical Language* concerning unity of motion is probably intended to suggest the absence of motion,[21] since in this rhythmic case there is no meaningful distinction between forward or backward direction. "Non-retrogradable," therefore, has the appearance of an asymmetric term—a term that appears not to express the symmetry of the phenomenon it describes.

There are, then, two levels of interpretation to such a rhythm as we can see if we substitute "non-retrogradable" with "palindromic," the Greek word meaning "running back again": a non-retrogradable rhythm actually affirms the principle of retrogradation, but by doing so closes the movement into a unified whole. At one level of meaning, directionality is important to the rhythm, and considered as a whole unit a non-retrogradable rhythm cannot be called a truly primordial text. At another level, the symmetry involved removes the idea of any inherent directionality, so that a distinction between moving towards the past or the future becomes impossible to sustain. Hence, we may conclude, there is no real motion; thus viewed as a complete unit the non-retrogradable rhythm is an image of the effective simultaneity of the whole of time. And since space is inextricably connected with time—movement is a division of space—this is an image of the whole of space-time: the whole universe.[22]

In fact, Messiaen has already conflated time and space in the quotation above from the preface to the *Méditations*: God has neither beginning nor end in space in the same manner as he has not in time. "*Immense*" is the same word Messiaen uses in movement V of the same piece to denote ubiquity, though in the *Summa Theologiae* these notions are denoted by different Latin words, *infinitus* and *ubique* respectively. For Aquinas, in the *Summa Theologiae*, limitlessness (*infinitus*) applied to God is a formal limitlessness concerned with self-subsistent existence, and that "limitlessness of extension is the kind of limitlessness associated with matter, and such limitlessness, as we have said, is not to be ascribed to God."[23] There is a paradox here, in that a non-retrogradable rhythm is classified on the basis of an inherent limitation, yet the deconstruction of the form of such a rhythm in the case of the Theme of God is a representation of the idea of limitlessness. The paradox may only be a linguistic one; in fact, this example of recursion (*reculer*) is a representation of self-subsistence.

Another way of explaining the principle of non-retrogradability, other than through the analysis of retrogradation within the rhythm itself, is through the principle of identity. In volume I of the *Traité de rythme, de couleur, et d'ornithologie*,[24] Messiaen demonstrates how a group of identical note values can be read backwards but will be indistinguishable as such to the listener:

    i) 1 2 3 4 ♩♩♩♩   ii) 4 3 2 1 ♩♩♩♩

Messiaen then goes on to explain that "this is why there exist rhythms impossible to retrograde or *non-retrogradables*,"[25] such as in the case of the ancient Hindu rhythm *dhenkî*:

    i) 1 2 3 ♩♪♩   ii) 3 2 1 ♩♪♩

Messiaen draws an analogy between this musical feature and the impossibility in wave mechanics of effecting a permanent numeration of particles that have the same physical nature. In the case of four sixteenth-notes, it is impossible to discern any change of position, and hence direction of time, because of the identical nature of each of the notes or, following Messiaen's analogy, each "particle." To explain non-retrogradable rhythms thus is to employ an analogy based on the identity of events rather than on the reversal of temporal direction. On this line of reasoning it is impossible to detect an inversion of time because of the impossibility of numbering, and therefore distinguishing, each "particle." This is an instance of permutational symmetry, as we can see if we examine the scientific analogy Messiaen has drawn:

> The symmetry prevailing is twofold.... Secondly, all electrons are alike: the distinction by their labels 1, 2, ... , n is one not by essence, but by name only: two constellations of electrons that arise from each other by an arbitrary permutation of the electrons are indiscernible.[26]

Identity of elements in the Hindu non-retrogradable rhythm is obvious, but Messiaen's development of more complicated non-retrogradable rhythms weakens this principle of identity, where there may be a large number of clearly different "particles" present.

Messiaen's identification of a link between certain musical principles and mathematical qualities of the world as they are revealed by scientific analysis is illustrated in this analogy. Assertions of such substantive parallels between mathematics and music are not, of course, peculiar to Messiaen (see, for example, the parallels Xenakis has drawn between the development of music and mathematics, and where, it is argued, music has sometimes anticipated advances in mathematics).[27] However, the mix of conclusions at which Messiaen arrives is distinctive. The aim to "shed light on the Truths of the Catholic Faith"[28] is rather more of a claim than mere ornamental illustration of those truths.

The symmetry by which we humans can see time and space existing as a whole is an achievement of intellectual perception; God, who is not bounded by space or time, can see everything at once by the virtue of his very nature. This is the viewpoint of eternity, in which everything exists as an instantaneous whole and where there is no distinction between past, present, or future. Modern physics has reached a similar position when it asserts the relative nature of simultaneity. Again, this reflects an intellectual understanding that sees space and time in physical terms as a single whole.[29] For Messiaen this intellectual victory over space and time, deduced from musical principles, is an indication and foretaste of the sharing of eternal life in God: "regular time moves towards the future—it never goes backwards. Psychological time, or time of thought, goes in all senses: forward, backwards, cut in pieces, at will... [In the life of the Resurrection] we will live in a duration malleable and transformable. The power of the musician, who retrogrades and permutes his durations, prepares us, in a small way, for that state..."[30] It is, for example, entirely appropriate that permutations of durations are used in movement X of *La Transfiguration de Notre-Seigneur Jésus-Christ* (for choir and orchestra, 1963–1969), whose text asks that we may be co-inheritors with Christ of the Kingdom of God. The theological idea of transfiguration has a general, but well-defined, significance relating to the quality of materiality in the Resurrection. The quality of materiality in this "new kingdom" is intimated in the notions of movement to be found in Messiaen's scheme of permutations. The same set of permutations used in this piece is also used in several other pieces, with very similar connotations. The correspondence is with a set of general theological ideas about time, matter, and eschatology that are involved in the definition of transfiguration.

THE DEFINITION AND SUBVERSION OF TIME

Messiaen explored the implications of numbering more extensively in his permutations of an ordered series of durations. These series are scalar arrangements, for example extending from a sixteenth note up to a dotted half note with each successive duration increasing by one sixteenth note (♪ ♪ ♩ ♩ ♩♪ ♩ ♩. ♩ ♩♪ ♩♪ ♩♪ ♩.). Number relates to this line in several ways, and it is through Messiaen's manipulation of these relations that he represents the structure of time. Judging from his pronouncements he believed these representations to be discoveries which the rhythmician/composer by the nature of his materials was privileged to make.

The fundamental point is that it is from numbering itself that we derive the notion of time. The definition of time given by Aquinas, which derives from Aristotle[31] and which Messiaen often quoted, that in "time there is a before and after" whereas in eternity there is no such successiveness, depends on the idea of numeration. Time arises from the measurement—hence numeration—of change. The relevant passage from the *Summa Theologiae* needs to be quoted at some length:

> For in any change there is successiveness, one part coming after another, and by numbering the antecedent and consequent parts of change there arises the notion of time, which is simply this numberedness of before and after in change.

So just as numbering antecedent and consequent in change produces the notion of time, so awareness of invariability in something altogether free from change produces the notion of eternity. A further point: time is said to measure things which begin and end in time, as Aristotle points out, and this is because one can assign a beginning and end to any changing thing. But things altogether unchangeable cannot have a beginning any more than they can display successiveness.[32]

It is instructive to compare the above quotation from Aquinas, which Messiaen had undoubtedly studied, with his own often-quoted mythical explanation of the birth of time and rhythm given in 1958:

Let us not forget that the first, essential element in music is Rhythm, and that Rhythm is first and foremost the change of number and duration. Suppose that there were a single beat in all the universe. One beat; with eternity before it and after it. A before and an after. That is the birth of time. Imagine then, almost immediately, a second beat. Since any beat is prolonged by the silence which follows it, the second beat will be longer than the first. Another number, another duration. That is the birth of Rhythm.[33]

There is a confusion of ideas here caused by the distinction Messiaen makes between Time and Rhythm. The definition of rhythm is actually identical to the definition of time, since it is rhythm which is "first and foremost the change of number and duration." The thing which comes before and after in relation to Messiaen's single beat is eternity, but eternity by definition exists outside of time and so cannot be numbered as an antecedent or consequent of change in relation to that single beat. Relation between time and eternity, and relation between points in time, are not equivalent relations. We can compare this with a modern scientific definition that time is "a dimension that allows two otherwise identical events that occur at the same point in space to be distinguished. The interval between two such events forms the basis of time measurement."[34] The creation of time implies a relation between things—there is otherwise no measurement and no numbers—and so there cannot be a first moment of time any more than there can be a smallest number.

The problem in Messiaen's explanation is, oddly, explicit in his own comments on the first in the list of 120 Indian *deçi-tâlas. Deçi-tâla* number one is called *aditâla,* which means "root of the *tâlas.*" It consists of a single eighth-note (or *laghu,* which is the Indian notational equivalent). In volume I of the *Traité*, where Messiaen discusses this *tâla*, he rehearses an abbreviated form of his description of the birth of time and rhythm, but then proceeds to remark that

> ... in the *aditâla*, the unique root of all of the *tâlas*, we can
> see a magnificent symbol of the causality of the First Cause
> [*Premier Principe*; the scholastic term is *primum
> principium* meaning causal origin], by God the Creator of
> all things, including Time (we have seen that a single beat
> gave rise to Time).[35]

"First" in "First Cause" does not refer to an initiating point on the line of time, but to a logically "first" sustaining cause of the universe, and cannot then double up as a first causal point in time, which would be of the same kind as any other point in time. If there cannot be a first moment, then this single note can only be a symbol of God.

Nevertheless, Messiaen detected a symbolic property in the most basic aspects of musical notation. It is pertinent to remember that Messiaen tended to see in his analysis of the rhythmic principles of the 120 Indian *deçi-tâlas* the sufficient root of all rhythmic development. Not surprisingly, he detected in embryo the principle of "chromaticism of durations," another, if inaccurate, name for a scalar arrangement of durations. The validity of these principles is no doubt connected with their primordiality: "they reascend, perhaps, to the beginnings of humanity."[36] This suggests that Messiaen (so the line of reasoning seems to run) is uncovering what has always been latent in the basic structure of music itself, but also that this is a pathway to the most fundamental aspects of the human mind. It is impossible to perform, or discover, certain operations on music without them having a wider significance.[37] There is, properly speaking, no purely technical aspect of music; experiments in musical techniques are therefore experiments about the several different levels on which music exists, and to which verbal metaphor can provide us with access.[38]

The significance Messiaen draws from his line of durations and their permutation is connected with the point about relation and succession. If time is a before and an after, and time is the measurement between events, then we have the basic ideas for a geometry, since "a system is a geometry provided it can be used to organize points in terms of 'betweenness' along one or more dimensions."[39] The systematic arrangement and investigation of musical durations constitutes for Messiaen a kind of musically represented geometry of time. Just as the geometer uses numbers to divide space and by doing so can make deductions about the structure of space, so the composer uses numbers to divide time and the parts of time.[40]

The operation of division, and hence the creation of parts, constitutes our perception of the physical world: "the 'splitting' of the world into space and time carried out at every moment of my consciousness."[41] The link between this and rhythm can be seen in the metaphor that rhythm, by a beat, "cuts" into duration. By this cut, a unit of measurement, and so the possibility of perception, becomes established. A scale of durations in this context can then appear to be the division of duration, which is a converse way of viewing the successive extension of the line of time.

Ancient Hindu rhythmic notation takes its point of departure from a short note, whereas European notation proceeds from the division of a long note, which Messiaen seemed mainly to take as the whole-note (although the English, and historically correct term, for this note is a semibreve, indicating the much larger single notes which formerly were in use). Messiaen probably saw something symbolic in this. Important scales of durations which he experimented inverting were of 64 durations (used in *Livre d'orgue*, for organ, 1951), 32 durations (used in *Chronochromie*, for orchestra, 1959,[42] and other pieces afterwards) and, so we can see from previously unpublished theoretical notes, 16 durations.[43] Scales of 16 and 32 are divisions of the whole-note into sixteenth-notes and thirty-second notes respectively, and 64 is a transposition of this on to the double whole-note divided into thirty-second notes. Important use, as will be seen below, is made of a twelve-note scale, but the roots of this number are more obviously connected with the influence of serialism.

Messiaen argued that a whole-note could not be appreciated by a listener apart from a smaller unit which could serve as a basis of measurement for that whole-note.[44] For duration to be perceived it must be mentally "cut." Consequently, just as the Indian *laghu* is symbolic, so, within this geometrical conception, the whole-note is symbolic of the duration of eternity; the resulting scale-line of durations is representative of duration in space-time. When Messiaen described the numbers which define the unit length of a duration in his scale he used the term *monnayage possible*—"potential minting." The possible variety of units of division implied by this term, be they large or small, is related to the idea of the continuum of time and space. The idea here refers back even to Aristotle who defined the continuum—the usual model of which is a line segment—as being infinitely divisible. Modern physicists can divide time into extremely small units of measurement but these are not fundamental discrete units of time; in other words, time is continuous. Messiaen's use of a scale of 64 durations, for example, is intended to point towards this variety of measurements of time:

"we're halfway between the microcosm and the macrocosm. So we perceive very long durations with difficulty, and the very tiny durations, which can contrast the long durations, with still greater difficulty."[45]

In the above quotation from Aquinas successiveness clearly means a uniform linear direction, and this, as well as its relation to the linear representation of the sequence of natural numbers 1, 2, 3, ..., is what Messiaen's series of durations is a musical representation of. The parallel is not quite exact because a line segment numbered 1–12 would be twelve units long, whereas on Messiaen's scale each succeeding number (duration) along the line contains within itself its preceding number, so the line is 78 units long. Nevertheless, what is important is the parallel between the sequential numbering along a segment of a directional time-line and Messiaen's scale. Any collection of durations could be permuted, but the permutation of a continuous scale of durations derives its significance from its similarity to the measurement and linear direction of time.

A line in itself has no inherent directionality, and possesses direction only insofar as we may read direction into it by seeing movement from one point to another. Messiaen's series of durations, it could be argued, does have a direction even apart from a sequential numbering because there is a change of duration, an ordered successive change across the line, and it is change which gives a directional arrow of movement and hence the notion of time. In fact, numbering of change in this sense is precisely involved in this rhythmic series: in a numbered scale of twelve sixteenth-notes extending from 1 to 12, each number marks the sequential order of durations and that same number is a property of the duration. 7, for example, marks the duration seventh in sequence in the series, and that same number also defines the duration, which is seven sixteenth-notes long.

However, in order to discover within time a structural weakness and so expose its secondary or derivative quality of existence, Messiaen then applies to this series possible rearrangements of order and various impositions of direction by separating the connection between number as definition of order and number as definition of duration. This is meant to demonstrate that our ordinary understanding of temporal relation is only one possible relation contained in the nature of existence. That point, of course, reveals the significance of the term "symmetrical permutations" because the direction of time, where there is a series consisting of antecedent and consequent or one term being earlier than another, is asymmetrical. The introduction of symmetry at whatever level undermines this. Hence the non-retrogradable rhythms are the starting point for Messiaen's exploration of permutations because the retrograde reading of a series is itself a permutation. At the outset, though, the more familiar serial ordering based on order of magnitude must be understood as an established point of departure for this discovery to be comprehensible.

The first explorations into permutations are concerned with experimentation with different types of movement other than simple forward and retrograde movement. For example, in parts of *Mode de valeurs et d'intensités* (for piano, 1949) we find, among other variants, the following two permutations of a twelve-note group:[46]

```
       1   2   3   4   5   6   7   8   9   10  11  12
i)     1   12  2   11  3   10  4   9   5   8   6   7
ii)    9   4   5   10  3   6   11  2   7   12  1   8
```

The movement of the first example aims to represent a folding-in of the original series from the extremes to the center. The second example follows a "triple line," where the divisions move stepwise but do not all follow the same direction. If the first example, which is a "double line," was pictured by Messiaen as folding inwards like closing a fan or a pair of scissors, then a triple line could by extension be a more complicated spatial metaphor. Thus the second example above could be construed as a stepwise ascending line (9, 10, 11, 12) alternating with an outward-folding movement (4-5, 3-6, 2-7, 1-8).

This may seem a bizarre picture, but it is the result of a further complication in the movements identified in the inversion.[47] Messiaen considered a series that was inverted and partitioned as if three fans were being closed:[48]

```
 1   2   3   4   5   6   7   8   9   10   11   12   13   14   15
 1   5   2   4   3   6   10   7   9   8   11   15   12   14   13   i.e.:
       3                   8                        13
    2     4             7     9                12      14
 1           5       6          10         11             15
```

Whatever the status of Messiaen's spatial metaphors, these permutations are patterned in a manner more interesting than those readily discovered by a systematic exposition of the set of permutations.

Messiaen discovered that by turning the permutational process in on itself, permutations that were patterned in a manner interesting to him were automatically revealed. This procedure he called "symmetrical permutation," a composite manipulation that turns out to be an important symmetry operation because of the resultant significant limited set of permutations. For example, in the set from *Île de feu II* (for piano, 1950), Inversion VII can be interpreted as a multi-directional triple line, while Inversion VIII alternates a retrograde and forward motion up and down the scale 4 by 4, where each change of direction is prepared by a stepwise increasing movement. The sense is of a volupt-uous pattern of movements across the original line.

The primitive directions of forward and retrograde underlie all of these movements but they are no longer simple movements. Messiaen likens the movement of the reading order to the unfolding of a fan, or more prosaically describes it as a double line. The sense is of a simul-taneous forward and retrograde movement, and so we have a movement which is no longer simply "a direction." Turning that movement back in on itself reveals even more extraordinary movements. The complication is then increased by the superposition of inversions in the composition, which gives a "thickness" to the experience of time in a victory over mere succession.

The key to this discovery has been the principle of numeration, because the re-numeration of each permutation allows the same reading order to be re-applied. The composite procedure turns out to be an important symmetry operation because of the significant reduction that results, a reduction from a huge number of possible permutations—479,001,600 for twelve objects—to a limited set of permutations. The permutation of durations—"chopping-up" time—is a mutilation of time's reasonable order; but symmetrical permutations may be a trans-cended reassertion of order because the procedure can reveal particular types of movement. The procedure is symbolic of the mind's eternal dominion over created time. The complicated movements revealed are indicative of a transcendence beyond the limitations of matter, of time or space.

The action of division is the origin of our perception of space and time. As such, the necessity for quantitative determinations to constitute knowledge of those parameters is a sign of our limitation by the bound-aries of matter. Yet, from within this numberedness, and by that means itself, Messiaen finds the roots of eternity. This eschatological per-spective on the physical world is not an unfamiliar expression of the religious instinct: "What you sow is not the body that shall be, but a naked grain ... It is sown in weakness; it is raised in power: It is sown a natural body; it is raised a spiritual body."[49] This explores another aspect of the human mind besides its capacity for scientific analysis. Whatever criticisms—or good-natured amusement—may fall on the strict cogency of Messiaen's eclectic idea of musical discovery, Messiaen was an agent of the curious and primordial weaving of the rational and the fantastic. This is why Messiaen's intellectual achieve-ment remains valuably elusive:

> "I'm partial to the fantastic side of surrealism, to the sort of science fiction that goes beyond reality and science itself."[50]

NOTES

[1] Antoine Goléa, *Rencontres avec Olivier Messiaen* (Paris: Julliard, 1960), p. 47; quoted in Robert Sherlaw Johnson, *Messiaen* (London: Faber and Faber, 1989), p.45, footnote 2.

[2] See, for example, Olivier Messiaen, *Traité de rythme, de couleur, et d'ornithologie*, vol. I (Paris: Leduc, 1994), p. 27: "Holy Scripture always has reason, and science rejoins it once more..." All translations from this treatise are my own.

[3] Messiaen here revives a view similar to that of the mediaeval university's classification of subjects into the Quadrivium. These were the four mathematical sciences, viz., astronomy, geometry, arithmetic, and music.

[4] Messiaen, *Traité*, vol. I, p. 39.

[5] John Milsom, "Organ Music I," *The Messiaen Companion*, ed. Peter Hill (London: Faber and Faber, 1995), p. 62.

[6] Messiaen also points this out in the *Traité*, vol. I, p. 9.

[7] S. W. Hawking, *A Brief History of Time* (London: Bantam, 1995), p.151.

[8] Iannis Xenakis, *Arts/Sciences: Alloys. The Thesis Defence of Iannis Xenakis* (New York: Pendragon Press, 1985), p. 34.

[9] Claude Samuel, *Olivier Messiaen: Musique et couleur: nouveaux entretiens* (Paris: Belfond, 1986), trans. by E. Thomas Glasow as *Music and Color* (Portland, Oregon: Amadeus Press, 1994), p.34. I have changed one word of Glasow's translation (indicated by « »). He translates "*rétrograder*" (p. 36 in the French edition) as "alter."

[10] For more detailed explanations and examples regarding these three techniques see the articles by Roberto Fabbi and Jean Marie Wu.

[11] Samuel, *Music and Color*, p. 48 (p. 51 in the French edition).

[12] The list of 120 *deçi-tâlas* (regional rhythms), as they are called, is given in Sherlaw Johnson, Messiaen, Appendix I, pp. 206-210.

[13] "And what is true of numbers is equally true of points on a line or of the moments of time: one order is more familiar, but others are equally valid." Bertrand Russell, *Introduction to Mathematical Philosophy* (London: Allen and Unwin, 1967), p. 30.

[14] Messiaen, *Traité*, vol. I, p. 43.

[15] Hermann Weyl, *Symmetry* (Princeton: Princeton University Press, 1952), p.20.

[16] Joe Rosen, *Symmetry Discovered*, (Cambridge: Cambridge University Press, 1975), p.67.

[17] Olivier Messiaen, *Méditations sur le mystère de la Sainte Trinité*, (Paris: Leduc, 1969), author's preface on "le langage communicable" (my translation).

[18] *Technique de mon langage musical* (Paris: Leduc, 1944), translated by John Satterfield as *Technique of My Musical Language* (Paris: Leduc, 1956, two volumes), vol. 1, p. 21.

[19] Aquinas, *Summa Theologiae*, trans. by Timothy McDermott (London: Eyre and Spottiswoode, 1964), vol. 2, p. 101 (Question 7, "God's Limitlessness," article 4).

[20]"There always has been motion [so Aristotle argues], and there always will be; for there cannot be time without motion, and all are agreed that time is uncreated, except Plato. On this point, Christian followers of Aristotle were obliged to dissent from him, since the Bible tells us that the universe had a beginning." Bertrand Russell, *History of Western Philosophy* (London: Allen and Unwin, 1979), p. 216. Aquinas writes: "Certain people make the difference consist in time having a beginning and an end whilst eternity has neither. Now this is an accidental and not an intrinsic difference. For even if time had always existed and will always exist, as those hold who think the heavens will rotate for ever, there will remain the difference Boethius points out between time and eternity: that eternity is an instantaneous whole whilst time is not, eternity measuring abiding existence and time measuring change." Aquinas, *Summa Theologiae*, vol. 2, p. 145 (Question 10, "The Eternity of God," article 4).

[21]"If we are right in finding the distinction between eternity and time in the fact that without motion and change there is no time, while in eternity there is no change, who can fail to see that there would have been no time, if there had been no creation to bring in movement and change, and that time depends on this motion and change, and is measured by the longer or shorter intervals by which things that cannot happen simultaneously succeed one another?" Augustine, *City of God,* tr. Henry Bettenson (London: Penguin, 1984), Bk. XI, Chapter 6, p. 435.

[22]"The objective world simply is, it does not happen. Only to the gaze of my consciousness, crawling upward along the life line of my body, does a section of this world come to life as a fleeting image in space which continuously changes in time." Hermann Weyl, *Philosophy of Mathematics and Natural Science*, revised and augmented (by the author), English edition based on a translation by Olaf Helmer (Princeton: Princeton University Press, 1959), p.116. Need I point out that "universe" literally means everything "turned into one"?

[23] Aquinas, *Summa Theologiae,* vol. II, p. 97 (Question 7, article 1).

[24] Messiaen, *Traité,* vol. I, p.26.

[25] *Ibid.,* p.26.

[26] H. Weyl, *Symmetry*, p. 134.

[27] Iannis Xenakis, *Arts/Sciences: Alloys.* Appendix I. "Correspondences Between Certain Developments in Music and Mathematics," p. 99. Also, for example, p.74: "If I want to write, design, or especially, visually represent time, I would have to put it on an axis, as physicists do, as musicians do (first musicians, and later, physicists). It must be pointed out that musicians with the musical staff were the first to invent a Cartesian representation of this principle."

[28] Samuel, *Music and Color*, p. 20.

[29]"To accommodate everybody's nows, events and moments have to exist 'all at once' across a span of time. We agree that you can't actually witness those differing there-and-now events 'as they happen,' because instantaneous communication is impossible. Instead, you have to wait for light to convey them to you at its lumbering three hundred thousand kilometers per second. But to make sense of the notions of space and time, it is necessary to imagine that those there-and-now events are somehow really 'out there,' spanning days, months, years and, by extension (you can magnify the mischief by increasing your changes in speed and the distance to 'there'), all of time." Paul Davies, *About Time* (London: Penguin, 1995), p. 71.

[30]Messiaen, *Traité*, vol. III, p. 352, 353.

[31]See Aristotle's *Physics*, especially Book IV (Δ) and Book VI (Z). For recent discussion see *Aristotle's Physics: A Collection of Essays*, ed. Lindsay Judson (Oxford: Oxford University Press, 1995), especially chapters 7 ("Aristotle on the Reality of Time" by Michael Inwood) and 8 ("Aristotle on Continuity in Physics VI" by David Bostock).

[32]Thomas Aquinas, *Summa Theologiae*, vol. II, p. 137 (Question 10, "The Eternity of God," article 1).

[33]Messiaen, *Conférence de Bruxelles* (Paris: Leduc, 1958) (published in English, French, and German), quoted in Sherlaw Johnson, Messiaen p. 32.

[34]Alan Isaacs (ed.), *Oxford Dictionary of Physics* (Oxford: Oxford University Press, 1996), p. 433.

[35]Messiaen, *Traité*, vol. I, p. 273.

[36]Messiaen, *Traité*, vol. I, p. 259.

[37]"It is just those meanings which attempt to be most exclusively material, which are also the most generalised and abstract—i.e. remote from reality. Let us take the English word cut. Its reference is perfectly material; yet its meaning is at the same time more general and less particular, more abstract and less concrete, than some single word which should comprise in itself—let us say—all that we have to express today by the sentence: 'I cut this flesh with joy in order to sacrifice'. If it is impossible to cut a pound of flesh without spilling blood, it is even more impossible 'to cut'." Owen Barfield, *Poetic Diction: A Study in Meaning* (London: Faber and Faber, 1952, second edition), p. 79.

[38]Messiaen's attempt to find a type of "communicable language" in music in the *Méditations sur le mystère de la Sainte Trinité*—consisting of musical notes which stand for letters or cases—is a paradoxical enterprise, which Messiaen perhaps resolved by describing it as "a game." The paradox manifests itself in a pair of quotation marks in Messiaen's own preface to the score when he says that "music cannot strictly 'say' [*dire*], cannot inform with precision" (composer's preface to the score, my translation). The quotation marks are needed because of the metaphorical nature of the comment. Music's proper character owes more to its mathematical connections. For example, the word "unbegotten" is rendered in the communicable language: its musical effect is striking, but the meaning of the term is clearly represented in the recursive rhythm of the Theme of God.

[39]Roger Scruton, *Modern Philosophy* (London: Mandarin, 1996), p. 358.

[40]Messiaen, *Traité*, vol. III, p. 347.

[41]H. Weyl, *Philosophy*, p. 116.

[42]In the 1-12 series each duration is fixed to a particular pitch. This defines a musical system of fixed points called *sons-durées*. The influence of serialism is apparent here with the fixed points relating to sound in terms of the 12 chromatic notes. When Messiaen used a series of 32 durations for the first time in Chronochromie the connection between duration and sound was correspondingly more complicated; it was also more satisfactory for Messiaen because it allowed greater exploration into the "color" of sounds and their connection with duration. Incidentally, the fact that Messiaen's "coloring" obscures the inversions is not an oversight or a perversity on the part of the composer, but is a philosophically considered thing: the root of the word color means to hide or cover.

[43] See Messiaen, *Traité*, vol. III, pp. 319-343. A scale of 16 durations is used in *Vingt Regards sur L'Enfant-Jésus* (for piano, 1944), but is used in only a retrograde inversion.

[44] See Messiaen, *Traité*, vol. I, p. 32.

[45] Samuel, *Music and Color*, p. 118.

[46] Robert Sherlaw Johnson gives a table of all the permutations in this piece and explains the construction of the three groups in Messiaen, pp. 105-106. The three groups are divisions of single mode consisting of 36 pitches, a durational scale of 1–24 thirty-second notes, 12 attacks and 7 intensities. For movements of inversions generally, see also chapter three of Messiaen's *Traité*, vol. III, p. 319-343.

[47] Messiaen's term "interversion" describing each permutation has customarily, if sometimes diffidently, been retained in English-speaking scholarship. The English noun "interversion" and verb "intervert" are, however, obsolete, and Messiaen's term could be translated with the familiar "inversion," though this may have been thought to result in confusion given the limited musical sense which normally applies to that word. In any case, it is unlikely that "interversion" has been preferred because of subtleties between the prefixes "inter" and "in." In the context of the present article I have used "inversion" and "invert" to avoid the impression that something different from their general non-musical sense is intended.

[48] See Messiaen, *Traité*, vol. III, p. 322.

[49] 1 Corinthians 15, verses 37, 43, and 44.

[50] Samuel, *Music and Color*, p. 14.

PART TWO

Self-Restriction and Symbolism

Theological Implications of Restrictions in Messiaen's Compositional Processes

Roberto Fabbi

In his numerous writings, interviews, and conversations, Messiaen rarely dwells upon that particular characteristic which he himself attributed to some of his theoretical-compositional inventions and which he called *le charme des impossibilités* [the charm of impossibilities]; nevertheless, when the subject does come up, it is treated with importance and some emphasis. In 1944, the author of *Technique de mon langage musical* states that a "charme, à la fois voluptueux et contemplatif, réside particulièrement dans certaines impossibilités mathématiques des domaines modal et rythmique"[1] [charm, at once voluptuous and contemplative, resides particularly in certain mathematical impossibilities of the modal and rhythmic domains]. More than forty years later, he confirms that "un phénomène [...] a dominé, si l'on peut dire, toute ma vie de musicien [...]: 'le charme des impossibilités'"[2] [a phenomenon has, as it were, dominated my whole life as a musician: 'the charm of impossibilities'].

It must be admitted that there is something odd about this 'phenomenon.' Although the expression describing it appears at the beginning of an essay on compositional technique, it is utterly foreign to specialist jargon, conceptually opaque, paradoxical, and attempts to classify precise technical elements with words of almost poetical resonance. It calls into play types of experience that one normally considers to be of an opposing nature: the sensual and emotional experience of 'charm' and the intellectual, rational experience of 'impossibilities.' The image would seem more appropriate in a literary text than in a systematic treatment of musical analysis. The deliberately ambiguous choice of these words in relation to precise sound elements, far from being the unlikely product of some bizarre literary whim, invites us to project merely technical information onto a wider plain embracing the composer's musical, worldly and spiritual ideas. And yet, the same composer who is usually generous when it comes to explaining his ideas in general, is rather concise when it comes to the special implications of the 'charm of impossibilities'; he relegates this happily ambiguous phrase to the description of the mathematical properties of three, albeit highly significant, technical inventions. In a few words, the *charme des impossibilités* as a key to interpret Messiaen is as rich, promising, and fascinating as it is incomplete. The *phénomène* in question is something more general, concealing a deeper motive which transcends and comprehends the mathematics of impossibility and permeates the entire works and poetics of Messiaen. I call this 'something' a way of thinking based on an idea of restriction.

Messiaen's musical language appears to be impregnated with this way of thinking even in its most hidden creases, and it turns up in extremely subtle and sophisticated forms. Restrictions are imposed on the sound material in a large variety of ways, a variety regulated by the intensity of the restrictive device, the manner and level upon which it operates, the parameters to which it refers, and other features. In this context, the impossibilities become an especial case of restriction, by no means the sole example, deriving from geometric-arithmetical symmetries. It is true that music of any period and place is, in some way, subject to restrictions, inasmuch as it obeys rules, however lax they may be. The case of Messiaen is clearly not to be understood in this rather obvious and tautological sense. Here, the idea of restriction is at work on a vast scale and affects every aspect; yet, it is also a clearly defined agent that, despite having many modes of application, is univocal in the sound behavior patterns that it generates: spatialization of time, color fixity of harmony, 'additive' (non-evolutionistic, non-organic) musical flux, etc. Here originatethe unifying qualities, which are able to render homogeneous a diversity of musical ingredients, from the European tradition to non-Western rhythms and complex sounds found in nature.

The natural place to search for the roots of this restrictive idea and its aesthetics is in the spiritual beliefs of a man who thinks of himself not only as a Catholic, but also as a Catholic Musician, and even a Theologian-Musician. In effect, the purpose of the impossibilities is to lead the listener, by seducing and charming him or her, towards that "sorte 'd'arc-en-ciel théologique' qu'essaie d'être le langage musical dont nous cherchons édification et théorie"[3] [that sort of 'theological rainbow' which attempts to be musical language in which we search for edification and theory]. This theological music seems to want to avail itself of compositional technique to transmit both the wonder of faith and theological speculation on its foundations. In the wake of the ambivalence between abandonment and reason, seduction and argumentation, faith and intellect—in a word, between charm and impossibility —the profound relationship of the *restrictive* compositional process and the spiritual domain is fairly blurred.

It is probably an automatic reflex to associate the generalized meaning of the word 'restriction' with elements of prohibition in Catholic doctrine. It is sufficient to think of the various dogmas, of concepts like Truth and Predestination, which present absolute restrictions, of the twin concept of sin and virtue restricting the range of possible human behavior that may be considered legitimate; of values such as obedience, sacrifice, chastity, or renunciation, of moral precepts, monastic rules, etc. But Messiaen was a problem-conscious Catholic; deeply immersed in the world, he did not underrate the discrepancies between faith and life. Although firm and undoubting in his faith, he was a brightly intellectual musician. Therefore, compositional restrictions and religious restrictions are much more than mere precepts, and the relationship between them is not one of simple analogy.

It would, for example, be highly misleading to consider the composer's restrictive musical processes as a kind of compositional temperance, or as a renunciation of sound possibilities, or as an exclusion on 'moral' grounds of 'illicit' or 'sinful' musical behavior. Messiaen was by no means a temperate, doctrinaire, or ascetic musician.[4] On the religious level, his restrictions permitted him to create an image of the world in relation to a concept of transcendence with a much stronger tendency to assimilate than to exclude, and, for this reason, alien to fundamentalism and bigotry. Beginning with the primary restriction to One (monotheism), every aspect of human experience is viewed as a manifestation of the divine: nature, science, love, time, birds, numbers, colors, and music. Every aspect of tangible or non-tangible reality is affected by a descending chain of interpretative restrictions that renders it assimilable. In music, a parallel but not necessarily analogous action is applied to the sound material. The restrictive idea thus underlies two different orders of things: a group of compositional techniques and a theological vision of the world.

So far, I have offered a preview of the themes with which this article intends to deal. In what follows, I examine Messiaen's technical devices, beginning with those that are conditioned by impossibilities and proceeding with others, along the full length of his creative career. Many matters are already well known and Messiaen himself was often the first to draw attention to them; it is not my intention to describe them yet again (although this is, to some extent, inevitable), but to provide a point of view and a possible interpretation. I try to go beyond a detached recording of the technical aspects in an attempt to identify the common denominator that, below the surface, determines what I like to call a genetic affinity among different sound manifestations. Once this affinity has been defined, I then attempt to describe its relationship

—provided that such a relationship exists—with Messiaen's spiritual and religious world.

COMPOSITIONAL PROCESSES

I

Messiaen developed three techniques that are affected by the phenomenon of impossibility: modes of limited transposition, non-retrogradable rhythms, and symmetrical permutations (or interversions). Although these processes are different from one another, their specific internal constitutions each impose a mathematical limit on duration and/or pitch, forcing certain behavior patterns. With the modes, the transposition possibilities are greatly reduced (involving the parameter of pitch), with rhythms, retrogradation is hindered (involving the parameter of duration, and on rare occasions, that of pitch), and with the permutations, the combinatory possibilities of a series of durations are drastically limited (but any parameter may be affected).

The modes of limited transposition represent the earliest phenomenon among the three mentioned. They already appear in compositions of the late twenties—*Le Banquet céleste* for organ, the eight *Préludes* for piano—when Messiaen was still a twenty-year-old student at the conservatory. They bear no relation to historical or folkloristic modes. They are artificial modes, of which there is a total of seven. The octave is divided into two, three, four, or six equal parts, which are in turn subdivided by a pattern of intervals which repeats itself. Mode 3, for example, is one of the most frequently used:

W = Whole-tone - H = Half-tone

EXAMPLE 1

The octave is divided into three equal segments here, each of them encompassing a major third. Each segment is in turn subdivided into the sequence tone-semitone-semitone. This mode has only four possible transpositions since the fifth is identical with the first, the sixth with the second, and so on. The transposition of these modes is limited because of the recurrence of identical interval segments. [Advancing a semitone at a time with the transpositions produces scales with different sounds only as far as the new segment, which necessarily reverts to the original scale shifted by the same interval as the interval by which the octave is divided.]

To state it in mathematical terms: the number of possible transpositions (T) depends on the number of segments contained in the octave (S) in relation to the octave as expressed in semitones (12): $T = 12/S$. Thus mode 1, which is divided into 6 equal segments (whole tones), has $12/6 = 2$ possible transpositions. Mode 2, divided into four equal segments (minor thirds), allows for $12/4 = 3$ transpositions. Modes 4, 5, 6, and 7, which are all divided into two equal segments (tritones) but which obviously have different subdivisions, exist in $12/2 = 6$ transpositions.[5]

Despite such mathematics, music composed using modes of limited transposition sounds anything but severe. The use of the modes is mainly harmonic, but the intrinsic recurrence of the same intervals produces an antifunctional tonal ubiquity which subtracts dynamic-motor tension from the harmony. Thus the chords form textures of colors and timbres that follow one another without pursuing any particular direction, and with a sort of spell-binding force that resides in the latent and obligatory cyclicity of the scale structures. Because of a neurophysiological condition known as anastomosis (a connection between the neural centers of sight and hearing), Messiaen was gifted with synaesthesia, which means he saw colors whenever he heard sounds. While such correspondences remain out of the reach of most listeners, we cannot objectively deny the visual, spatial, and in general, metaphorically colored nature of his harmony. In theory and in practice, impossibility limits transposability, but the tangible restrictive effect is something more complex, consisting in the subtraction of a directional temporal dimension from harmonic phenomena. Later on, we will see how this same effect and more accentuated forms of it can be obtained through forms of restriction other than mathematical.

Non-retrogradable rhythms appear in Messiaen's work from the mid-thirties onwards, for instance in his *Poèmes pour Mi* for soprano and piano as well as in *Les Corps glorieux* for organ. These rhythms are the same if read from left to right or from right to left. They consist of two wings that mirror one another symmetrically and are arranged around a central value that is common to both halves; see, for example, this rhythm: The pattern (expressed in sixteenth-notes) is 8-3-4-1; it finds its retrograde in the pattern 1-4-3-8, whereby 1 functions as a shared central value. This kind of rhythm is "not retrogradable" insofar as it contains its own retrograde. The restriction connected with non-retrogradability does not, therefore, represent a prohibition, but an obligation, in the sense that these rhythms are blocked temporal units. This sort of restriction also affects the ways in which the patterns can be modified. In order to maintain their non-retrogradability, modifications can only consist of additions or subtractions applied to both halves of the rhythm, in equal measure and in a specular fashion. The only type of variation possible is, therefore, dilation and/or contraction.

There is, in all this, a clear metaphysical aspiration to overcome the unidirectional nature of the flow of time. But this aspiration must also deal with the fact that non-retrogradability is not perceptible as such to the listener. In this case, too, the effectiveness of the process does not reside—or at least it does not only reside—in the mathematical impossibility taken literally, but in the concrete conception of the rhythm that is implicit in the idea. This, again, is not the result of an isochronous division of the time into beats, but of an irregular extension of durations in time. By means of a restriction that prohibits regular pulsation, i.e., our common notion of time, time simulates space, and so even a space arranged in a specular fashion (non-retrogradable). All of Messiaen's rhythmic techniques are based on various spatializations of time.

The third technique that is affected by the charm of impossibilities is the most recent of the three. Symmetrical permutations (or interversions) first appear in 1950, in *Île de feu II* for piano. The term 'permutation' indicates the free shuffling of the order within a series of objects. A small increase in the number of objects leads to an enormous increase in the number of possible permutations: 4 objects have 24 permutations (4 factorial = 1 x 2 x 3 x 4); 12 objects have 479,001,600 (12 factorial) permutations. Symmetry drastically reduces the permutational possibilities: once a series is given, it is a matter of always applying the same permutational law to each new sequence that is obtained. In this manner, after a reasonable number of permutations, the original sequence returns. The so-called 'open fan' interversion shown below, from the center towards the ends, is one of the most frequent; it reduces the number of permutations, for example, of four durations, from a possible 24 to 3. (Note that the law of permutation is always 3-2-4-1.)

♪	♪	♪.	♩	Original series
1	2	3	4	
♪.	♪	♩	♪	1st interversion
3	2	4	1	
♩	♪	♪	♪.	2nd interversion
4	2	1	3	
♪	♪	♪.	♩	3rd interversion
1	2	3	4	(identical to the original)

The same type of interversion, when applied to 12 durations, reduces the number of possible permutations from the astronomical figure mentioned above to a mere 10. Other permutations include the 'closed fan' interversion, which moves from the ends to the center, and yet others that have different symmetries but are always fixed and repeated. This process is mainly applied to 'chromatic series' of durations, obtained by means of the progressive addition of a unit which is established as the minimum duration (in the chart, the sixteenth-note). The rhythmical chromaticism of the original series constitutes a *rallentando* (its retrograde motion, an *accelerando*), and intrinsically annuls any possibility of equal pulsation. The process accentuates this characteristic by generating maximum variety, both within each interversion, where the same duration is never repeated, and between the interversions, which are fairly dissimilar. This means that impossibility does not restrict the available combinations indiscriminately, but restricts them by automatically selecting sequences with maximum differentiation. In this way, rhythm really does seem to acquire the pliability of space; it is, as it were, atomistic rhythm, articulated through the multiplication of a minimum durational unit. Where different interversions overlap (and this occurs often), polyrhythms are generated, which seem also to acquire the polydimensional nature of space.

Although the three processes considered in this article are objectively different, there are affinities below the surface. Modes of limited transposition and non-retrogradable rhythms share a structure that is divided into repeating segments, thus resulting in impossibilities; the former produce in the vertical dimension of harmony that which the latter produce in the horizontal dimension of rhythm.[6] The intrinsic, not necessarily visible, cyclicity of harmony/color and rhythms unleashed in this way create that visionary and spell-binding quality that constitutes Messiaen's 'charm.' The symmetrical permutations produce the maximum rhythmic variety, but follow a rigid generative principle. The result is a very deep, concealed cyclicity that is imperceptible, or only subliminally perceptible (consider the fixed position of the eighth-note in the above chart). But the main characteristic, which provides the point at which the three different processes converge, is their invariable tendency to project all kinds of sound behavior into a virtual spatiality. In this sense, they are restrictive, because they force a way of being onto these behavior patterns; although, let it be clear, this way of being is phenomenologically rich and anything but 'restricted.'

II

In his writings, with the exception of the realm of the *charme des impossibilités*, Messiaen normally expresses himself in terms of possibility rather than impossibility, of enlargement rather than restriction. It should by now be clear that the words 'impossibility' and 'restriction,' in this context, have nothing to do with the concept of hostility towards whatever may be new or as yet unheard, or towards experimentation. On the contrary, in the main body of this article I intend to highlight not only how restrictive processes affect many other compositional techniques, but also how they are not incompatible with the objective of expanding one's perception of music.

Messiaen's use of harmony is by no means limited to the modes of limited transposition. There is a variety of techniques covering thousands of chord types that do not necessarily fit into a particular system and that vary in density, dissonance, and complexity, from simple patterns of thirds to the clangor of clusters, with all imaginable shades in between. How can the idea of restriction persist amidst so much variety? Whatever its external form may be, Messiaen's harmony adheres to a basic principle, which can be more or less visible, but is immutable— the natural resonance of vibrating bodies.

There is a chord that is expressly defined in these terms, the *accord de la résonance* [chord of resonance]. It consists of all the notes of the harmonic series, up to the fifteenth, arranged as shown here:

EXAMPLE 2

(Note that all the pitches belong to mode 3.)

Practically all of Messiaen's triadic harmony, more or less disturbed by added notes, can be considered as an infinite refraction of natural resonance, reconfigured according to need. In this context, consonance and dissonance lose their traditional function of tension/relaxation, and contribute to produce color-chords operating as static timbral entities. But this is not enough to satisfy Messiaen's eagerness for color. The complex harmony that first makes its appearance in his work during the fifties, and which takes on its most elaborate forms in some of the bird songs (and elsewhere), is not obviously connected with modes, overlapping thirds, or the harmonic series. And yet, it is an expansion of these principles. An intermediate stage in the development towards Messiaen's complex harmony can be identified in the so-called 'chords with added resonance.' In short, this technique consists in the addition of a second chord above or below a first, where the second chord is foreign to the first and sounds in a clearly distinct register. This produces an effect that is similar to an interference between two different spectra of harmonics. If the resonance is close, i.e. the two chords mingle in the same registral range, the interference increases and, with it, the amalgamation of color-timbres.

The extreme results of this transfiguration of harmony into timbre reach such an intense state of poly-resonance that it becomes practically impossible to distinguish the different constituent parts of the chordal agglomerations. A chord like the one shown here (from *Le Merle de roche*, p. 19, fourth staff, third chord)

EXAMPLE 3

is open to at least a half dozen legitimate interpretations. It seems like a cluster of ten sounds, which do not quite create an indistinct noise because of their masterly internal organization. It can be perceived as a sort of 'modal integral' arranging all the notes of a scale that excludes C and F, or as a bi-pentatonic mode (black keys for the right hand, white keys for the left). It could derive from a series of perfect fourths: A♯-D♯-G♯-C♯-F♯-B♮-E♮-A♮-D♮-G♮. But even as far as overlapping thirds are concerned, it can be viewed in various ways and is tonally ubiquitous; I will limit myself, here, to pointing out five interlacing simultaneous dominant seventh chords: $D♯^7$, $E♮^7$, $F♯^7$, $A♮^7$, and $B♮^7$. These five fundamentals in turn constitute a dominant seventh ($B♮^7$) that contains its own 'tonic' (E♮). Finally, one could put an end to the discussion by deciding that, all things considered, a ten-note chord is necessarily an atonal chord, whose internal relationships cannot be distinguished.

The fact that all these interpretations, however contradictory they may be, are plausible and well founded is an indication of their inadequacy. None of them takes into account the real position of each pitch within the agglomeration and the effect created by specific interval interference. Pitch position is a distinguishing feature to the extent that two chords composed of the same pitches, but with different internal arrangements, can sound very different. In the example, the highest and lowest pitches, A♮/A♯, which relate to one another in the manner of a distorted octave, enclose other octave-interfering encounters. Taken together, the pitch agglomeration shapes natural acoustic space—by deforming it. Harmony of this kind, which explores its own timbral possibilities empirically, cannot be reduced to a system.

In a context in which interference becomes the norm, harmony becomes artificial resonance through distortion of acoustic space, synthesized in a vertical, octave-avoiding agglomeration that alters the interval rapports according to complex timbral demands. Hence the use of 'falsifying' intervals: seconds, sevenths, and ninths, employed as unison and octave interferences, tritones as interferences of fourths and fifths, and so on. Intervals, therefore, are no longer consonant or dissonant, but a combination of harmonics with more or less interference. In the bird songs, in the rock-and-jem musics, in the color-musics, in the landscape-musics, each of the thousands of different and unclassifiable chords (or, in Messiaen's words, "invented chords"[7]) that one comes across is a sophisticated sound synthesis, a planned dislocation of timbral components, an *ex-novo* creation of unheard sound spectra.

Harmony as timbre simulation is the effect of an idea of restriction that goes beyond the rigid and predetermined forms of mathematical impossibility. The chord structures are now subject to flexible restrictions: no longer obligatory interval symmetries, but demarcations of the modalities of interval relationships, which serve to mold a microcosm of timbre out of vertical sound space. No sound or interval is impossible; any sound or interval is subject to a functional restriction that endows it with its own fixity of resonance.

Messiaen's color-harmony has finely honed tools, immersed, as it is, in ever greater complexity, transforming a technical 'device' (impossibility) into a technical 'mentality' (restriction). In this way, it preserves or, to be more accurate, it accentuates its distinctive and intrinsic, spatial and a-temporal essence: static chordal agglomerations progress by addition, and not by logical concatenation. Free association of ideas replaces consistent discourse. By blocking the flow of discourse, restriction produces movement with no final destination, along with a loss of temporal finality in harmony (resolutions, cadences, keys), thereby stimulating a vivid perception of each chord as a color-timbre experience, each time new and unrelated to whatever follows or precedes it.

III

As with Messiaen's harmony, impossibility does not account entirely for the great variety of rhythm in his music. Once again, the challenge is to find the common factor that unites numerous different processes under the banner of the idea of restriction.

Although it does not involve impossibilities of a mathematical nature, the technique of the *personnages rythmiques* [rhythmic characters], used for the first time in a complete manner in the *Turangalîla-Symphonie* (1946–48), imposes a fairly evident restriction. This technique is applied to three rhythmic groups that are repeated, whereby the first increases with every repetition, the second decreases, and the third remains unchanged. (The curious name of this technique derives from an analogy with three characters on a stage, of whom one is active, one passive, and one indifferent).[8] Increase can mean augmentation or the addition of new values; in a specular fashion, decrease can mean diminution or the subtraction of values. So there is an obligatory route, a path that is signposted, along which enlargement, elimination, and repetition intersect one another in accordance with a kind of 'conceptual symmetry' that is not interested in given forms, but in how they mutate.

In the rhythms of the Indian countryside (*deçî-tâlas*), and in the rhythms adapted from ancient Greek meter (feet), both of which are frequent in all of Messiaen's compositions starting from the forties, the presence of the idea of restriction is less obvious. These do not constitute techniques so much as preformed rhythms that Messiaen selected and reinterpreted according to his own personal ideas on rhythm. For example,

- the *tâla dhenkî* (♩ ♪♩) or the Cretic foot (♩ ♩♩) are frequently used on account of their non-retrogradability;
- the four Greek epitrites (I: ♩♩ ♩ ♩, II: ♩ ♩♩ ♩, III: ♩ ♩ ♩♩, IV: ♩ ♩ ♩ ♩) on account of their permutational symmetry;
- the *tâla simhavikrîdita* (♪♩. ♩ ♩. ♩. ♩. ♩ ♩. ♪♩.), which alternates fixed durations (♩.) with durations that first increase, and then decrease, is seen as an embryonic manifestation of *personnages rythmiques*.

Other organizing principles of rhythm that are typical of Messiaen can be found in

- the *tâla lakskmîça* (♪♪. ♩ ♩ = 2-3-4-8), where the added value (in this case the dot) offsets the regular pulsation;
- the rhythmic chromaticism (2-3-4);
- the inexact increase (4-8 in relation to 2-3);
- the overall value corresponding to a prime number (2 + 3 + 4 + 8 = 17), which is a cause of irregularity.

In Hindu and Greek rhythms,[9] as used by Messiaen, the same characteristics can be found as are produced elsewhere by impossibilities or restrictions: absence of pulsation, irregularity with more or less manifest elements of symmetrical repetition, multiplication of a minimum durational unit, and the simulation of space.

Ornithological rhythm is a chapter in its own right, especially in its more complex manifestations, which appear from the fifties onwards. Rhythms in the bird songs are agitated, unequal, and unexpected, as the agogic component becomes a conscious factor in the organization of durations. Each bird song—sometimes, each phrase within the same song—has its own speed: i.e. the value of the basic durational unit changes continually (and continually returns). For example, in the first eighteen measures[10] of *La Bouscarle* (the ninth piece in the *Catalogue d'oiseaux* for piano, 1956–58), which last approximately thirty seconds, there are three different, alternating bird songs and twelve changes of metronome indication: ♪ = 108, ♪ = 138, ♪ = 126, ♪ = 160, ♪ = 126, ♪ = 200, ♪ = 108, ♪ = 138, ♪ = 108, ♪ = 160, ♪ = 108, ♪ = 138. In the first indication, the duration of an eighth-note is equal to 0.5555... seconds, in the second indication, 0.4347... seconds, and so on, with changes of value that are not only frequent, but also reflect irrational mathematical ratios. The human ear is unable to perceive these ratios, just as the performer is unable to reproduce them precisely. But the effect of recurring rhythmic contraction and dilation can certainly be perceived and reproduced. The rhythm is thus freed from the constraint of a constant unit of measurement; it acquires the plastic characteristic of space as well as the capacity to expand and withdraw with infinitesimal subtlety. By the same token, absolute time is negated in favor of a multiplicity of roaming and recurring relative temporal schemes, as in a deformed spiral.

As harmony simulates timbre, so rhythm simulates space. As Messiaen's harmony distorts in interference from harmonics, so his rhythm deforms itself in the irrationality of the durations' ratios. To paraphrase Messiaen,[11] one can say that the restrictions generate similar phenomena both in the horizontal and in the vertical dimension.

IV

There is a category of compositional techniques that do not refer to specific parameters so much as to an indivisible integration of different sound parameters.[12] This is the case with "modes of pitches, durations, intensities, and attacks." They appear rarely in Messiaen's work and are always limited to brief passages, with the sole exception of *Mode de valeurs et d'intensités* for piano (1949), which is entirely based on a mode of this kind. The word "mode" in this context does not have the normal meaning of a division of an octave into particular intervals, but refers to a multi-parameter technique that is serial and not serial at the same time. It is serial in that the material is predetermined: from four series—of pitches (12 sounds with fixed register), durations ('chromatic' series), intensities, and attacks—a synthetic series is created. This, then, is the 'mode.' It consists of what I would like to call four-dimensional entities, each of which is determined by an indissoluble combination of four parameter values. It is not serial, on the other hand, at the compositional level, as the material is organized in free sequences that are permuted only occasionally. With few exceptions, if the combination C³ / ♩. / *f* / *tenuto* has been established, it remains stable for as long as the mode applies, and the four parameter values do not re-appear within the series. The multi-parameter serial mode, thus defined, represents a total diversification in which repetition and regularity simply cease to exist. One or more 'modes' are always superimposed, but the result bears no resemblance to counterpoint. What is obtained is a simultaneity of polyrhythm, polyphony, polydynamics, and poly-agogics, an irretrievable loss of the sense of the vertical and horizontal dimensions, whereby the sound entities appear as suspended in an oblique and fluctuating space-time dimension. The use of restrictions that fix the four-dimensional 'position' of each entity makes convention-al musical 'discourse' quite impossible. This time, all the parameters work together to simulate abstract space, which has no connection whatsoever with any 'figurative' dimension.

The so-called *langage communicable* [communicable language], which was conceived and used for the first time in 1969, in the *Médi-tations sur le Mystère de la Sainte-Trinité* for organ, avails itself of a different type of multi-parameter combination. The minimum option is a 'two-dimensional' combination of duration and pitch, used in the *Méditations*; another combination is one of duration, pitch, harmony-color, and fixed instrumentation, used, for example, in *Des Canyons aux Étoiles...* for orchestra (1972–74). The combinations conceal a code that 'translates' words and entire sentences into music through a set of fixed correspondences between the letters of the alphabet and sound entities.[13] In this way, for example the word *Saint* generates, letter by letter, the following sequence of sounds+durations:

EXAMPLE 4

The code system constitutes the criterion for establishing the shape and rhythm of the melodies. But since the logic behind the order of letters in words is unpredictable and totally foreign to any logic of melody, to all effects and purposes it is as if the criterion were casual. The bizarre, spiky, and capricious nature of the brief example given above is sufficient to demonstrate this. Behind the pseudo-casual ordering of the entities, however, there are the entities themselves with the combinatory restriction that determines them once and for all. For this reason, the *langage communicable* should not really be considered as an aleatory technique, but rather as a technique that uses aspects of chance as tools to simulate characteristics of space, which, although still within conventional melodic guidelines, are disproportionate and deformed.

While we are in the area of the multi-parameter, some attention should be paid to the *neumes rythmiques* [rhythmic neumes]. The term is paradoxical in that neumes are rhythmically undefined or, at least, not precisely measurable. When Messiaen quotes directly from plainsong motifs—a frequent occurrence—he preserves the bare contours of the melody, altering the pitches according to his modes. (He never uses antique ecclesiastical modes.) In this manner, he implicitly conceives the neumes as geometrical abstractions, broken rising and falling segments with characteristic shapes and lengths. Thus, the 'rhythmic neumes' come to represent a total reinvention of the idea of the neume on a multi-parameter basis, which is quite distant from the antique idea. Each neume is thickened with a fixed color-chord that has a fixed duration and intensity; the line segment (melodic neume) thus becomes a segment of band (rhythmic neume) with variable thickness, unequal articulation (the effect of the rhythm), and changing perspective (the effect of the intensities). Although they appear only in Messiaen's piano composition bearing the same name (1949), the rhythmic neumes cannot be considered marginal, because they anticipate the sound behavior of the bird songs.

So far, timbre-harmony and space-rhythm in the bird songs have been discussed separately, and the greater complexity of each has been noted. At this stage, it can be understood how the two aspects, together with dynamics, are joined in a multi-parameter combination in a way similar to the rhythmic neumes. The notable difference is that in the 'ornithological neumes,' if they can be so defined, complexity is heaped upon complexity, in an escalation that puts the tools of analysis to a hard test. A rhythmic neume is established once and for all according to clearly defined morphological contours; by contrast, an ornithological neume is usually constitutionally unstable, as its morphological contours—its parameter components—are subject to continuous micro-variations. Among the hundreds of neumes in any single ornithological composition, when one neume (or phrase composed of more than one neume) recurs, it is not literally the same; yet each recurrence has a kind of perceptible equivalence. The identity of a neume, therefore, is not jeopardized by its instability: it remains equivalent to itself while varying its own parameters within a margin whose limits cannot be defined, except empirically. With his ornithological neumes, Messiaen gives shape to a space whose variable geometry is no longer 'Euclidean.'

V

So far, I have dealt with the various technical processes individually for two reasons: an obvious necessity of exposition, and, above all, the fact that, in the works, they effectively present themselves as distinct phenomena generating distinct sound objects. It is precisely this circumscribability which is responsible for a central feature in Messiaen's music: 'additivity.' This works both as juxtaposition and superimposition, as well as both ways at the same time.

Juxtaposition, being a succession of events that are enclosed in themselves, generates macroforms consisting in segments that are usually devoid of any cause/effect relationship, in accordance with logical principles that are alien to models of organic growth or structural consistency. The underlying idea of form is based on an elementary logical principle of the alternation/recurrence of sections (A-B, A-B-A, rondo form, strophe-refrain, or the like). However, by multiplying the basic binary/ternary models and by substituting relationships of equality between sections with relationships of similarity or equivalence, Messiaen succeeds in inventing more complex, concise articulations. Examples include the kaleidoscopic forms of *Reveil des oiseaux*, *Oiseaux exotiques*, and *Couleurs de la Cité céleste*, or the absolutely unpredictable, centrifugal forms of *Catalogue d'oiseaux*. The overall form also simulates space: it delimits areas, it does not generate evolving organisms.

Superimposition is a multi-faceted phenomenon: it includes the simultaneous coexistence of color-harmonies (polymodality, polyharmony), of heterogeneous rhythms (polyrhythm), of multi-parameter entities (heterophony), and of various combinations of all these things. It can involve any number of simultaneous events from two to more than a dozen, in a progressive continuum of complexity that goes from a relatively decipherable state to a state of organized chaos. Here are two typical examples.

In the first measures of *Amen de la Création* (the first piece in the *Visions de l'Amen* for two pianos, 1943), the second piano plays in the lowest register a theme in chords that is very simple, short, homophonic, in 4/4 time, mainly consonant, and that establishes the key of A major, albeit in a modal context. At the same time, the first piano plays, in the high and very high register, two layers of chords in non-retrogradable rhythms of differing lengths (and, therefore, constantly out of phase), dissonant and in two different modes. Three simultaneous, independent and non-communicating events—three musics!—generate polymodality, polyrhythm, polyphony of homophonies, as well as a vast distance between registers, with dissonance on top, consonance in the bottom register, and a huge void in between.

Conversely in the so-called 'bird concertos,' the sound space tends towards saturation. In *Les oiseaux de Karuizawa* (sixth piece in *Sept Haï-kaï* for orchestra, 1962) from number 9 to number 14—twenty-two measures for a few seconds of music—ten simultaneous events are superimposed: the piccolo, flute, piccolo clarinet, first and second clarinet play five independent lines of different bird song in melodic form; the group composed of two oboes and English horn, that composed of bass clarinet and two bassoons, that composed of xylophone and marimba, and the piano play four independent lines of different bird songs in complex neumatic form; the percussion instruments (*cencerros*, crotales, tubular bells, cymbals, gong, and tam-tam) play Greek rhythms. The overall effect is a very dissonant, animated whirling of sounds, lines, color-harmonies, clusters, and near-noise. The rhythms—each of which is, on its own account, irregular, discontinuous, and epileptic—join together in a tangle of contractions and dilations, where different basic durational units coexist. (They are achieved through irrational groups, as it is clearly impossible to change metronome indications vertically.) The result is interfering polyharmony, polyrhythm of polyrhythms (polytemporality), polyphony of polyphonies: heterophony. In this magma-like, saturated, distorted, and non-Euclidean space-time, the different elements remain distinct because of their individual differences of timbre: woodwind, the striking of strings, the striking of wood, and the striking of metal. There is a layering of timbre, while the registers cross wildly.

Between the two extremes illustrated above there is a notable variety of superimposition methods. The constant feature is the combination of different speeds, of simultaneous processes, each of which moves forward independently. (In late works like *Saint François d'Assise* and *Éclairs sur l'au-delà*, this mutual indifference of relative times is sometimes expressed by parts written "hors-tempo" [outside the tempo], in a measured rhythm not synchronized with what is going on concurrently.)

As Messiaen would have expressed it: plurality of musics; plurality of times projected onto a plural space; heaps of spatio-temporal events, each of which is distinct and yet constrained within its portion of perceptual reality. This changeably 'additive' form presupposes the impermeability of the materials, their inability to interact, i.e. the restrictions that underlie their construction.

VI

If one views Messiaen's work as a whole, it becomes clear that his different techniques, even when decades passed between their inventions, do not point to a linear development, where the new replaces the old. Rather, they settle down beside each other in a repertoire that grows and grows, at times coexisting in the same composition without conflict.

Despite the composer's own words, according to which many Messiaens have already died,[14] one is tempted to say that none of the many Messiaens ever died and that, on the contrary, the many hypothetical Messiaens are, in fact, one and the same person. The joint presence in his work of the modern and the traditional, the theoretical and the pragmatic, the antique and the avant-garde, of western, exotic, natural, and artificial elements, does not result in contamination or hybrid style. The variety of his historic influences, from plainsong to his pupil Boulez, via Claude Le Jeune, Berlioz, Debussy, and Stravinsky, never results in dispersion or eclecticism. In other words, although Messiaen immersed himself in the vastness of human and non-human musical history and geography, his work as a composer has an extraordinary conceptual unity. The influences, however heterogeneous they may be, are subjugated to the highly personal and totalizing acoustic language of their manipulator. Messiaen's perspective is restrictive on a wide scale: he extracts and isolates pieces of music or musical ideas from their specific historical, stylistic, and cultural context, he gives them a decontextualized acoustic identity, which he incorporates his own acoustic universe, whose ultimate aspiration is totality.

Once again, the image of 'additivity,' in the restrictive sense of indifferent coexistence, can be useful to describe Messiaen's music on all levels, from the smallest morphological detail to the complete works as a whole. From the small to the large, it is always the same phenomenologic model that reappears: circumscribed micro-worlds group together in circumscribed small worlds, which group together in circumscribed medium-sized worlds, which group together in circumscribed large worlds... the simulation of portions of space that characterizes the individual compositional techniques, viewed globally, becomes simulation of the universe.

In order to represent schematically what has been said so far, I attempt to define certain principles (and combinations thereof) that the restrictions follow:

- *Limitation*: of transposition, of symmetrical permutations (impossibility).
- *Selection*: of symmetrical permutations (impossibility), pseudo-casual.
- *Impediment*: of the rhythmic pulsation, functional harmony, and interaction of materials.

- *Imposition*: of retrogradation (impossibility), of multi-parameter associations, of symmetries, of contractions/dilations.
- *Fixation*: of color harmonies, of interference-resonances,
  of sound-entities, of spatialized tempos.
- *Segmentation*: formal, horizontal, vertical (stratification),
  'non-Euclidean.'
- *Incorporation* (subjugation of heterogeneous material): of
  different times and spaces, of styles, genres, acoustic worlds.

It is apparent that the idea of restriction cannot be reduced to a prohibition or a system of prohibitions, nor to a renunciation, a preclusion, or self-limitation of experience. In this case, it would be a 'restricted mentality' rather than a 'way of thinking based on an idea of restriction.' This 'way of thinking,' this 'idea of restriction' is the underlying thought structure which, despite its manifold action that shapes and assembles multi-faceted sound materials, binds everything together in a single, totalizing conception of the world.

THEOLOGICAL IDEAS

I

Messiaen was a devout Catholic. Seventy to eighty per cent of his work is explicitly inspired by Catholic doctrinal truths, as is evident from the titles and subtitles fashioned after or taken from the Scriptures, the comments quoted from the Church Fathers, and his own wordings. On the basis of lucid and speculative theological knowledge, and a predisposition for the visionary, Messiaen worked the themes of faith into his music: the Trinity, the Ascension, the Apocalypse, the Trans-figuration, the Resurrection, of Christ, of men, etc. He made his music a vehicle, in symbolic terms, for theological visions. In this sense, his work has no comparison, at least not in the modern era. The salient features of his musical language—its static essence, its 'visual' and spatial qualities—are naturally suited to a symbolic function.

There are symbols which have some form of analogy with the music. The best-known example occurs in the *Quatuor pour la fin du Temps* (*Quartet for the End of Time*, 1941). The preface to the score contains a quotation from the *Apocalypse* of Saint John that culminates in the prophesy "Il n'y aura plus de Temps" [There will be no more Time] (X, 4). In musical symbolism, this corresponds to a rhythmic conception which, as we have already seen, implies a block, a spatial-ization: 'end of time' as an absolute. A similar correspondence can be observed with regard to the supernatural 'colors of the heavenly

City'—another apocalyptic location (XXI, 19–20). The precious stones with which it is built are symbolized by the complex color-harmonies of the composition by the same title. At times, a theological concept is supported by the music in greater detail, to the extent that the concept constitutes a summary description of the music's morphology. This is the case with the articulated concept that recurs in many of Messiaen's works, in relation to the characteristics of the spiritual bodies of those who rise from the dead: *clarté, joie, force, agilité, subtilité* [luminosity, joy, strength, agility, fineness]. *Subtilité des Corps glorieux*, the first piece of *Les Corps glorieux* (1939), is a monody; this needs no comment. In the fourth piece of *Et exspecto resurrectionem mortuorum* (1964), 'luminosity' corresponds to plainsong motifs, thickened in parallel color-harmonies by a the shining halo of harmonics; 'joy' and 'agility' in the song of the *Alouette Calandre* [Calandra Lark] correspond to rhythmical-motor frenzy. The biblical quotation that opens this piece is "Ils ressusciteront, glorieux, avec un nom nouveau... dans le concert joyeux des étoiles et les acclamations des fils du ciel"[15] [They will rise from the dead, glorious, with a new name... amid the glorious concert of the stars and the acclamation of the children of heaven]. It is hard to resist the temptation to read these words as an anticipation of the musical material of which the piece is composed, even if this does not exactly coincide with the interpretation furnished by Messiaen in his preface to the score. The isolated, mysterious, and recurring beats of the tam-tam correspond to the no less mysterious 'new name,' the already mentioned color-harmonies to the 'glorious concert of the stars,' the song of the Calandra Lark, the winged child of the sky, to the 'acclamation of the children of heaven.'

The relationship between music and underlying concept is not always one of such obvious analogy; this is only to be expected of a symbolic mechanism, since such a mechanism does not necessarily have to *allude*, as it is sufficient for it to *substitute*. This is the case with many themes such as *Thème de la Création* [Theme of Creation] in *Vision de l'Amen*, all the themes in *Vingt regards sur l'Enfant-Jésus* of 1944—the *Thème de Dieu* [Theme of God], *Thème d'amour* [Theme of Love], *Thème de l'Étoile et de la Croix* [Theme of the Star and of the Cross], the themes in *Saint François d'Assise*: *Thème de l'Ange* [Theme of the Angel] and *Thème de la Vérité* [Theme of Truth], and with many others. It is also the case with the enigmatic, fleeting, pianistic scrawl, reminiscent of an ornithological neume, in *Couleurs de la Cité céleste*, which is indicated in the score as "l'étoile qui a la clef de l'abîme" [the star that possesses the key to the abyss] (*Apocalypse*, IX, 1). In the *Quartet*, again, a fact that could appear to be little more than accidental, such as the number of movements of which the work is composed (eight), is invested with a numerical symbolic value. As Messiaen explains: "Sept est le nombre parfait, la création de 6 jours sanctifiée par le sabbat divin; le 7 de ce repos se prolonge dans l'éternité et devient le 8 de la lumière indéfectible, de l'inaltérable paix"[16] [Seven is the perfect number, the creation of 6 days sanctified by the divine Sabbath; the 7 of this rest extends into eternity and becomes the 8 of indefectible light and unalterable peace].

The application of symbolism to music is most solemnly explicated in a paraphrased quotation from Thomas Aquinas, which Messiaen often recalls. Its fullest enunciation appears in *Saint François d'Assise*, where the dying Francis pronounces the following prayer:

> "*Seigneur! Musique et Poésie m'ont conduit vers Toi: par image, par symbole et par défaut de Vérité. Seigneur, illumine-moi de ta Présence! Délivre-moi, enivre-moi, éblouis-moi pour toujours de ton excès de Vérité...*"[17]

> [Lord! Music and Poetry have led me towards You: through image, through symbol and by default of Truth. Lord, illuminate me with your Presence! Free me, inebriate me, dazzle me forever with your excess of Truth].

In theological terms, symbols function 'by default of Truth,' in that they represent a tending towards something that is by definition unreachable —or, that can only be reached through death and beatitude: 'excess of Truth,' God. From a musicological point of view, the symbols also act by default of truth (with a small 't'), in that the same 'tending towards something' distances them from the concrete substance of which they avail themselves: music. There is the tendency inherent in all religious symbolism to transform objects "into something different from how they appear in the profane experience,"[18] as well as to make them meaningful within a consistent and totalizing cosmo-theological system, which in this case is Christian.

Admittedly, the relationship between music as an autonomous form of expression responding to its own sense horizons, and the 'other' horizon to which the symbolic system refers, is somewhat problematic. This relationship, which is of an extra-rational nature, pertains to a sensibility and a faith that escape reason. Moreover, the cultural matrix of the contemporary world—especially in the West, dominated as it is by technology and often disconnected from a sense of the sacred—is not particularly conducive to an understanding and sharing of the language of religious symbolism.[19] That, however, is territory beyond the scope of this article. This small digression was only meant to draw attention to the fact that the relationship between music and religious symbolism is neither banal nor obvious: the surface analogies which it sometimes produces (some of which have been listed above) are neither indicative of its full complexity, nor do they solve its problematic nature.

II

Messiaen subjugates extra-musical references and superstructures, be they religious or not, to a vision of the world that can be called total-izing: a theology that not only expresses itself in its own terms, but also extends to all aspects of human knowledge. Scientific and philosophical theories, exotic cultures and arts, the natural world, non-Christian myths, cosmogonies, symbolism, and religions, all are seen as a mani-festation of the divine, all are incorporated and absorbed into a theocentric image of the universe. Conversely—which here come to the same—Messiaen theologically espies all possible human and natural phenomena in the mysteries and dogmas of faith.

At the beginning of the *Credo*, the official, doctrinal formulation of the articles of faith, the omnipotent God is declared "creator of things visible and invisible." For Messiaen, the expression 'things invisible' "contains everything, the world of the stars, the world of the atoms, the world of the angels, the world of the demons, the world of our own thoughts, and the world of all that is unknown to us, particularly the world of what is possible, which is only known to God."[20] One returns to the same conceptual image pertaining to formal musical 'additivity': a simulation of the universe through the aggregation of circumscribed worlds, and the same intention to subjugate.

The ways in which the variety of the world is absorbed and reduced (restriction) to a theological perspective are numerous and diversified. Human love is treated symbolically and often poetically (since four of the following five works have a text) in *Poèmes pour Mi*, *Chants de Terre et de Ciel* and—through that great story of sensual and fatal love-death, the myth of Tristan and Isolde—in the trilogy comprising *Harawi*, the *Turangalîla-Symphonie,* and *Cinq rechants*. But the com-plete, terrestrial union of two beings is but "a pale reflection of the only authentic love, divine love." Messiaen establishes a hierarchy of love, which is basically theological, from trivial love (*à la* Don Giovanni), through human love of the Tristan variety, to maternal love... "but it is divine love which is at the peak of the pyramid."[21]

Nature with its colors, noises, and, of course, its bird song, pervades a large part of Messiaen's work; it is certainly his greatest inspiration after religion. For an entire decade (1952–1962), he dedicated himself totally to nature. During this time he made no use of explicit religious symbolism, as can be seen, for example, in the purely ornithological and geographical descriptions that introduce the thirteen pieces of *Catalogue d'oiseaux*. For a composer like Messiaen, this is an exceptional event, but it should not be interpreted as a move away from religion. Nature, like human love, is perceived as a manifestation of divine love,[22] and has its place in the same theological hierarchy. In his compositions between 1952 and 1962, this subjugation is not explicit; nature seems to be drawn from its own independent imagery which, almost pantheistically, exists autonomously. Later on, however—as if a kind of precautionary naturalistic investigation had been necessary—it is totally and explicitly reabsorbed into religious symbolism.

At this point, all manifestations of nature have their collocation, and nothing is what it seems. For example, the desert in *Des Canyons aux étoiles...* is the "vide de l'âme qui lui permet d'entendre la conversation intérieur de l'Esprit" [emptiness of the soul which allows it to listen to the inner conversation of the Spirit]. The canyons of Utah, their high points and their abysses, are seen from the New Testament viewpoint of St. Paul: "...vous comprendrez la hauteur et la profondeur..." [...you will comprehend the loftiness and the depth...].[23] The birds hovering between the earth and sky become, in this cosmology, intermediaries between the terrestrial and the divine.[24] They have the same role in *Saint François d'Assise*, the spiritual tale of the saint who, by definition—in hagiography, iconography, and in the collective imagery —was the saint who 'spoke with the birds.'

Behind nature of a human dimension, which is friendly and immediately perceivable, there is a second nature, which is distant, unknown, and inaccessible to the senses. It is the reality of physics, observable with the tools of science: the infinitely large and the infinitely small, that which is far from common feeling. According to Messiaen, scientific research has increased our ignorance by continually showing us new realities, which are illusory.[25] Nevertheless, he is fascinated by scientific research and uses it, imposing upon it the restriction that subjugates it to his own theology. His own theories on time and space-time as a multiple and changing reality that is neither objective nor absolute, find theoretical support in Albert Einstein's theory of relativity,[26] in quantum microphysics,[27] as well as in biological[28] and psychological theories,[29] the latter of which are reinforced by Henri Bergson's philosophy.[30] The validity of these theories for Messiaen consists in the confirmation they find, for example, in the famous passage in *Ecclesiastes* III, 1–8: "There is a time for everything. A time for everything under the heavens: a time to be born, a time to die; a time to sow and a time to reap, a time to kill, a time to heal..."[31] The multiplicity of time schemes is, according to Messiaen, a symptom of their illusory nature, which is totally different from the true, immutable reality of eternity: "Time is the measure of the created, eternity is God himself."[32] The value of the truth of scientific knowledge is accepted as a restriction which is hierarchically inferior to theological Truth, which includes it, comprehends it, and transcends it. The 'big-bang' theory confirms the divine act of creation,[33] the undulatory activity of the quasars confirms that the 'stars sing' (*Book of Job*, XXXVIII, 7)...[34]

III

Messiaen's interest in extra-European cultures is well known. The religious and musical aspects of Hindu culture fascinated him particularly. Yet even where the exotic is concerned, the restrictive intention is active, and the heterogeneous is drawn within his own vision. Although Messiaen almost always abstained from attaching precise values of Christian symbolism to Hindu rhythms, these normally appear in compositions with religious themes. Significantly, they even play an important role in the only specifically liturgical composition he ever wrote, the *Messe de la Pentecôte* for organ (1950). In rare cases, the original Hindu symbolism is coopted into Christian symbolism. In the second piece of *Et exspecto resurrectionem mortuorum*, Messiaen imposes his own interpretation on the *tâla simhavikrama*, which in its original context stands for the "force of the lion" and is dedicated to Shiva. Shiva— a divinity who is foreign to the Christian sensibility, ambiguous, as much a bearer of good as of evil, as much a creator as a destroyer— inasmuch as he is a symbol of the "death of death" here comes to represent the victory of Christ over death, as in the biblical quotation, "Christ, resuscitated from the dead, dies no more; death no longer has dominion over him."[35] The *tâla simhavikrama* (♩ ♩ ♩ ♪♩. ♩ ♩.) is analyzed by Messiaen as a combination of the fourth epitrite (♩ ♩ ♩ ♪) and the *tâla vijaya* (♩. ♩ ♩.). This is a historically arbitrary technical justification which, by mixing temporal and spatial distances, imposes the category of 'exotic' on history as much as on geography: an attitude that decontextualizes and de-historicizes, which is to say a restrictive attitude, that is necessary to the incorporating tendency. Messiaen also gives a Christian interpretation to the *tâla candrakalâ* ("the beauty of the moon:" ♩ ♩ ♩ | ♩. ♩. ♩. | ♪) and the complex symbolism it represents in Hindu astrology. The three segments of which this rhythm is composed have eighth-note values of 6, 9, and 1. These correspond, according to numerical symbolism, to conception, birth, and divinity respectively. Messiaen defines divinity as "l'infiniment un" [the infinitely one] and summarizes in a concise sentence: "Derrière la Vie, il y a Dieu"[36] [Behind Life, there is God].

Finally, there are the worlds of non-musical forms of artistic expression, and of painting in particular. Messiaen's preferences are invariably for artists and works that give a primary role to color and light: Mathias Grünewald (the Isenheim Altarpiece), Claude Monet (*Nymphéas*), Robert Delaunay (*Première fenêtre simultanée, Formes circulaires*), Marc Chagall, and the colorful stained-glass windows of the French Gothic cathedrals.[37] We have already seen the importance of color for Messiaen as a metaphor for harmony. What interests us here is how Messiaen's intense sensitivity to color is part of his spiritual perspective, which infuses the glare, brightness, layering, and light of color with a longing for the single immutable light of Truth, thus recalling once again Thomas Aquinas's image of being "dazzled by excess of Truth." It is no coincidence that one of the evangelical passages to which Messiaen most frequently refers, the Apocalypse, is characterized by the most unrestrained tornado of color. The type of reaction that Messiaen has to a work of art is well summarized in the following extracts from a letter to Chagall: "The sparkling of your blues and reds, your Faith in divine Love, unforgettable figures like the Moses whose robe is made of the crossing of the Red Sea, like the immeasurably white dress of the Betrothed in the Canticle of the canticles, remain in my memory as indelible archetypes."[38]

Here again, Messiaen carries out a decontextualization process that drastically delimits (restricts) the meaning and importance of art for him. Art essentially becomes a vivid visionary experience. There is little difference from other visionary experiences of color, like those stimulated by nature, dreams, synaesthesia, or the hallucinogenic effects of mescaline.[39]

The association of ideas and images that are ostensibly incongruous and in strong contrast is typical of the surrealist expressive mood. Messiaen availed himself of this on more than one occasion. Even more than in his specific references to paintings by, for instance, Roland Penrose[40] and Max Ernst,[41] it can be observed on the literary level. He incorporated his own poetry into several of his compositions: *Trois petites liturgies de la Présence divine, Poèmes pour Mi, Harawi,* and *Cinq Rechants.* Another instance of surrealist expressivity can be found in his choice of isolated, pseudo-surrealist passages from the Bible, like that of the vision of the chariot in *Ezekiel* I, 18–20, which opens the sixth piece in the *Livre d'orgue*: "Et les jantes des quatre roues étaient remplies d'yeux tout atour. Car l'Esprit de l'être vivant était dans les roues" [And the rings of the four wheels were full of eyes all around.

For the Spirit of the living being was in the wheels]. All this should, however, not be taken to imply that Messiaen sympathized with the movement that is historically defined as Surrealist, whose declared atheism and nihilism are about as far away from Messiaen's spiritual attitude as it is possible to imagine. Nevertheless, he adopts the expressive mood of this movement, as well as its capacity to organize 'syntactically' the realm of dreams and the subconscious, channeling these aspects to his own ends.

The poetic text of the third *petite liturgie* (*Psalmodie de l'ubiquité par amour*) is at once a profession of faith, an enunciation of Thomistic theological concepts, a *pot-pourri* of biblical quotations, a mass of Messiaen-like visions and... a piece of surrealist literature. The text is copyrighted with Éditions Durand (1952) and reprinted here with the kind permission of the editor. The English translation is by Paul Sears.

*Tout entier en tous lieux**	Whole in all places
Tout entier en chaque lieu,	Whole in every place,
Donnant l'être à chaque lieu,	Giving being to each place,
À tout ce qui occupe un lieu,	To all that occupies a place,
Le successif vous est simultané,	The subsequent is simultaneous to you,
Dans ces espaces et ces temps que	In these spaces and times you have
vous avez crées,	created,
Satellites de votre Douceur.	Satellites of your Sweetness.
Posez-vous comme un sceau sur mon cœur.	Alight like a seal on my heart.
Temps de l'homme et de la planète,	Time of man and the planet,
Temps de la montagne et de l'insecte,	Time of the mountain and the insect,
Bouquet de rire pour le merle et l'alouette,	Bouquet of laughter for the blackbird
Eventail de lune au fuchsia,	Fan of moon *à la* fuchsia, [and lark,
À la balsamine, au bégonia;	*À la* balsamine, *a la* begonia;
De la profondeur une ride surgit,	From the depths rises a crease,
La montagne saute comme une brebis	The mountain leaps like a sheep
Et devient un grand océan.	And becomes a great ocean.
Présent, vous êtes présent.	Present, you are present.
Imprimez votre nom dans mon sang.	Impress your name in my blood.
Dans le mouvement d'Arcturus, présent,	In the movement of Arthur, present,
Dans l'arc-en-ciel d'une aile après l'autre,	In the rainbow of one wing after another,
(Écharpe aveugle autour de Saturne),	(Blind scarf around Saturn),
Dans la race cachée de mes cellules,	In the hidden race of my cells,
présent,	present,
Dans le sang qui répare ses rives,	In the blood that shelters its banks,
Dans vos Saints par la grâce, présent	In your Saints through grace, present
(Interprétations de votre Verbe,	(Interpretations of your Word,
Pierres précieuses au mur de la Fraîcheur)	Precious stones on the walls of Freshness)
Posez-vous comme un sceau sur mon cœur.	Alight like a seal on my heart.

Un cœur pur est votre repos,
Lis en arc-en-ciel du troupeau,
Vous vous cachez sous votre Hostie,
Frère silencieux dans la Fleur-Eucharistie,
Pour que je demeure en vous comme une
    aile dans le soleil,
Vers la résurrection du dernier jour.
Il est plus fort que la mort, votre Amour.
Mettez votre caresse tout autour.

Violet-jaune, vision,
Voile blanc, subtilité,
Orangé-bleu, force et joie,
Flèche-azur, agilité,
Donnez-moi le rouge et le vert de votre
    amour,
Feuille-flamme-or, clarté,
Plus de langage, plus de mots
Plus de Prophètes ni de science
(C'est l'Amen de l'espérance,
Silence mélodieux de l'Eternité.)
Mais la robe lavée dans le sang de
    l'Agneau,
Mais la pierre de neige avec un nom
    nouveau,
Les éventails, la cloche et l'ordre des
    clartés,
Et l'échelle en arc-en-ciel de la Vérité,
Mais la porte qui parle et le soleil qui
    s'ouvre,
L'auréole tête de rechange qui délivre,
Et l'encre d'or ineffaçable sur le livre;
Mais le face à face et l'Amour.

Vous qui parlez en nous,
Vous qui vous taisez en nous,
Et gardez le silence dans votre Amour,
Vous êtes près,
Vous êtes loin,
Vous êtes la lumière et les ténèbres,
Vous êtes si compliqué et si simple,
Vous êtes infiniment simple.
L'arc-en-ciel de l'Amour, c'est vous,
L'unique oiseau de l'Eternité, c'est vous,
Elles s'alignent lentement, les cloches de la
    profondeur.
Posez-vous comme un sceau sur mon cœur.
(Tout entier en tous lieux,
Tout entier en chaque lieu...)

A pure heart is your rest,
Lily in a rainbow of the flock,
You hide beneath your Host,
Silent brother in the Eucharist-Flower,
So that I may reside in you like a wing
    in the sun,
Towards the resurrection of the last day.
It is stronger than death, your Love.
Put your caress all around.

Violet-yellow, vision,
White veil, fineness,
Orangy-blue, strength and joy,
Azure arrow, agility,
Give me the red and green of your
    Love,
Leaf-flame-gold, luminosity,
No more language, nor words
No more Prophets, nor science
(It is the Amen of hope,
Melodious silence of Eternity.)
But the robe washed in the blood of the
    Lamb,
But the stone of snow with a new
    name,
The fans, the bell and the order of
    luminosities,
And the rainbow ladder of the Truth,
But the door that speaks and the sun
    that opens,
The halo head of renewal that delivers,
And the indelible gold ink in the book;
But the face to face and Love.

You who speak in us,
You who are silent in us,
And guard the silence in your Love,
You are near,
You are far,
You are the light and the darkness,
You are so complicated and so simple,
You are infinitely simple.
The rainbow of Love is you,
The only bird of Eternity is you,
They slowly align themselves, the bells
    of the depths.
Alight like a seal on my heart.
(Whole in all places,
Whole in every place...)

Vous qui parlez en nous,	You who speak in us,
Vous qui vous taisez en nous,	You who are silent in us,
Et gardez le silence dans votre Amour,	And guard the silence in your Love,
Enfoncez votre image dans la durée de mes jours.	Plunge your image into the duration of my days.

This text is a poetic, aesthetic, philosophical and theological synthesis of a theocentric conception of the world. The primary monotheistic restriction to One, to a single God, who contains all truth, all eternity, and all that is possible, substantiates a transcendental theology that provides a framework for interpreting that which has been created, i.e. all that is accessible to the senses, to the intellect, to the imagination, to the tools of science and artistic expression. Messiaen does not shun multiplicity. On the contrary, he accepts the challenge of any diversification, no matter how extreme, making it comply with the oneness of the eternal, immutable principle, and the theology that attempts to explain it.

In brief, his theological restrictions *select-segment* reality, they *limit* its original sense and range, by decontextualizing and de-historicizing, they *impose* their own sense and symbolic system upon it, and, finally, they *incorporate* it by subjugating its heterogeneity, which, nevertheless, remains evident.

CONCLUSION

All of Messiaen's work is profoundly characterized by a yearning of 'something,' which is the music, towards 'something else,' an eternal Reality that is also *external*. As this supernatural destination involves "the leap outside Time,"[42] death and resurrection, it is unattainable for the living. But since music is the stuff of the living, it is what it is, precisely because what it yearns for is unattainable—the charm of a metaphysical impossibility.

Between its continual efforts to go beyond itself and its continual frustration, music ends up resembling Paul Valéry's ballerina, "who would cease divinely to be a woman, if she could obey the leap she took, as far as the clouds. But, as we cannot reach the infinite, either in our sleep or while we are awake, in the same way, she always becomes herself again; she ceases to be snowflake, bird, idea; to be all that is agreeable to the flute she was, for the same Earth that launched her, calls her back and returns her, panting, to her woman's nature..."[43]

What remains of a transcendence that cannot be experienced is the yearning for this very transcendence. The yearning is an immanent and concrete aesthetic quality of a music which, as it is incessantly compelled to re-become itself, incessantly recreates its *own* reality.

NOTES

I wish to express my gratitude to Paul Sears for having translated this article from Italian into English.

[1] Olivier Messiaen, *Technique de mon langage musical*, 2 vols. (Paris: Leduc, 1944), vol. I: p. 5.

[2] Olivier Messiaen, *Musique et couleur. Nouveaux entretiens avec Claude Samuel* (Paris: Belfond, 1986), p. 50.

[3] Olivier Messiaen, *Technique*, vol. I, p. 13.

[4] "Comme compositeur je ne veux renoncer à rien" [As a composer, I don't want to renounce anything]. Messiaen's words in: Brigitte Massin, *Olivier Messiaen: une poétique du merveilleux* (Aix-en-Provence: Alinéa, 1989), p. 182.

[5] The mathematics of the modes presented here is mine, based on the well-known properties of equal division of the tempered scale. I have adopted this scheme because it seems to me very concise and apt to reveal the inner mechanism of the modes in a very memorable way.

[6] Olivier Messiaen, *Technique*, vol. I, p. 13.

[7] Olivier Messiaen, *Musique et couleur*, p. 102.

[8] Olivier Messiaen, *Traité de rythme, de couleur, et d'ornithologie (1949-1992)*, 7 vols. (Paris: Leduc, 1994-...), vol. II, p. 112. At the time of writing (1997), only the first three volumes have been published.

[9] A complete treatment of these subjects can be found in the second volume of the *Traité de rythme*.

[10] These are not traditional measures, but serve only as reference points for the performer; they have no metrical significance, they are of unequal length, and have no time signature.

[11] Please refer back to note 6.

[12] "Doubtless, some unthinking musician could with some vestige of truth paraphrase Mallarmé's letter to Degas: 'Poetry is made with words,' and say, 'Music is made with sounds.' I say, No! Music is not made with sounds alone... it is also made with intensities and densities (dynamics), with timbres and attack (phonetics), with accents, arsis and thesis, and different tempi (kinematics), and last, ,and above all, with time, the division of time, numbers and durations (quantities)." Olivier Messiaen, *Conférence de Bruxelles. Texte français - Deutscher Text - English text* (Paris: Leduc, 1960), p. 11.

[13] Olivier Messiaen, "Neuf méditations sur le mystère de la Sainte-Trinité," *Hommage à Olivier Messiaen* (Paris: La recherche artistique), 1978, p. 90.

[14] Antoine Goléa, *Rencontres avec Olivier Messiaen* (Paris: Julliard, 1960), p. 249.

[15] A collage of quotations from *St Paul's first letter to the Corinthians* (XV, 43), *Apocalypse* (II, 17), *Job* (XXXVIII, 7). Composite quotations like this demonstrate an uncommon knowledge of the Bible. Without declaring it overtly, Messiaen carries out a detailed exegesis, finding concealed and bold concordances between parts of the Old and New Testaments.

[16] Preface to the score Durand.

[17] Olivier Messiaen, "Saint François d'Assise," [libretto] *L'Avant-scène opéra*, Hors série no. 4, 1992, p.98.

[18]Mircea Eliade, *Traité d'histoire des religions* (Paris: Payot, 1964), p. 379. "Ainsi, d'un côté le symbole continue la dialectique de l'hiérophanie, en transformant les objects en *autre chose* que ce qu'ils semblent être à l'expérience profane..."

[19]"Les auditeurs, qui sont athées, ou simplement indifférents et inavertis des questions théologiques, ne comprennent rien à cet aspect de mes œuvres" [Listeners who are atheists or simply indifferent or inattentive to theological questions, do not understand anything about this aspect of my work]; Olivier Messiaen, "Obstacles," *20ème siècle. Images de la musique française. Textes et entretiens*, réunis par Jean-Pierre Derrien (Paris: Sacem & Papiers, 1986), p. 168. We can add that even those pupils of Messian's who have become famous composers (and there are quite a few) have mostly ignored the symbolic and religious aspects of their Maestro's teachings. Another symptom of this difficulty in responding to these aspects lies in the continual necessity to explain the symbols and render them explicit; otherwise, they would not be transparent.

[20]Antoine Goléa, *op. cit.*, p. 38.

[21]Olivier Messiaen, *Musique et couleur*, pp. 32-33: "...mais c'est l'amour divin qui est au sommet de la pyramide."

[22]*Ibid.*, p. 39.

[23]*Letter to the Ephesians*, III, 18.

[24]Olivier Messiaen, "Des Canyons aux étoiles...," *Hommage à Olivier Messiaen*, p. 90; especially the comments on the first, seventh, and tenth pieces.

[25]Reproduction of an autograph manuscript of the composer in: *Ibid.*, p. 3.

[26]Olivier Messiaen, *Traité de rythme*, vol. I, pp. 14-17.

[27]*Ibid.*, vol. I, pp. 25-26.

[28]*Ibid.*, vol. I, p. 13.

[29]*Ibid.*, vol. I, pp. 20-22.

[30]*Ibid.*, vol. I, pp. 9-12, 31-36.

[31]*Ibid.*, vol. I, p. 8.

[32]*Ibid*, vol. I, pp. 7.

[33]Brigitte Massin, *op. cit.*, p. 101. And also: Jean-Christophe Marti, "Entretien avec Olivier Messiaen," *L'Avant-scène opéra*, p. 11.

[34]Brigitte Massin, *op. cit.*, p. 99. Also: Olivier Messiaen, *Musique et couleur*, p. 183.

[35]*St. Paul's Letter to the Romans*, VI, 9. Cf. the introductory note to the score Leduc.

[36]Olivier Messiaen, *Traité de Rythme*, vol. I, p. 311.

[37]*Ibid.*, vol. I, p. 66. And also: Olivier Messiaen, *Musique et couleur*, pp. 46-48.

[38]Letter dated 23 June 1974, published in: *Portrait(s) d'Olivier Messiaen*, sous la direction de Catherine Massip (Paris: Bibliothèque Nationale de France, 1996), p. 37. The original French wording reads: "Le flamboiement de vos bleus et de vos rouges, votre Foi en l'Amour divin, [...] figures inoubliables comme le Moïse dont la robe est faite de la traversée de la Mer Rouge, [...] comme la robe démesurément blanche de la Fiancée du Cantique des cantiques [...] restent dans mon souvenir comme des archetypes ineffaçables."

[39]Olivier Messiaen, *Traité de rythme*, vol. I, pp. 67-68. Messiaen recognizes the hallucinogenic effects of Mescalin as similar to his visions, on the basis of literary descriptions by Weir Mitchell.

[40]Antoine Goléa, *op. cit.*, pp. 155-156.

[41]Olivier Messiaen, *Traité de rythme*, vol. II, p. 42.

[42]"Le saut hors du Temps"; see the reproduction of an autograph manuscript of the composer in: *Hommage à Olivier Messiaen*, p. 3.

[43]Paul Valéry, *L'Âme et la danse* (Paris: Gallimard). Quoted in: Olivier Messiaen, *Traité de rythme*, vol. I: p. 58. The quotation from Valéry in *Traité* occurs in a completely different context, and concerns a generic vital quality of rhythm. In fact, Valéry compares his ballerina to Life.

Mystical Symbols of Faith: Olivier Messiaen's Charm of Impossibilities

Jean Marie Wu

One point will attract our attention at the outset: the charm of impossibilities. It is a glistening music we seek, giving to the aural sense voluptuously refined pleasures. At the same time, this music should be able to express some noble sentiments (and especially the most noble of all, the religious sentiments exalted by the theology and the truths of our Catholic faith). This charm, at once voluptuous and contemplative, resides particularly in certain mathematical impossibilities of the modal and rhythmic domains.[1]

INTRODUCTION

Olivier Messiaen's belief that "a technical process had all the more power when it came up, in its very essence, against an insuperable obstacle"[2] is the foundation for a phenomenon that dominated his whole life as a composer and which he beautifully called the *"charm of impossibilities."*[3] This inimitable term defines how, in his musical language, "certain mathematical impossibilities, certain closed circuits, possess a strength of bewitchment, a magic strength, a *charm*."[4] It describes the power he discovered in his three principal innovations: the modes of limited transposition, the non-retrogradable rhythms, and the symmetrical permutations.

The mathematical impossibilities that Messiaen associated with this effect of "magical enchantment"[5] are the musical impossibilities he established by creating structural symmetries in his musical language. The modes of limited transposition are modes created by dividing the octave into symmetrical groups; it is impossible to transpose them to all twelve notes of the octave without returning to the original notes of the first transposition. A non-retrogradable rhythm is a palindromically structured rhythm, which is the same whether one reads it forwards or backwards; it is impossible to play the rhythm in retrograde without repeating the original order of values. Symmetrical permutations are rhythmic permutations that are generated by following the same structural algorithm; it is impossible to generate an astronomical number of permutations without returning to the first permutation. These impossibilities form a closed circuit, bringing each musical innovation back to its origin. And therein, Messiaen found the power of his charm.

It is a power garnered by challenging an "insuperable obstacle"[6]—the compositional limitation established in each innovation. From Messiaen's metaphysical perspective, this "calculated ascendancy, in time and sound,"[7] gave his music an added dimension—beyond time and sound—opening up new expressive possibilities. As a Catholic composer, Messiaen was confronted by a temporal limitation: the impossibility of expressing, while still on earth, the ineffable truths of his faith. He often said, using the words of St. Thomas Aquinas, "Music brings us to God through 'default of truth', until the day when He Himself will dazzle us with 'an excess of truth'."[8]

For him, the phrase "default of truth"[9] represented the fact that the truths of his faith could only be expressed incompletely, through symbolic representation that anticipates their true expression and manifestation in heaven. With the power he perceived in his "charm of impossibilities," Messiaen attempted to transcend the temporal limitations of his music, to express his faith as he aspired towards eternity.

THE MODES OF LIMITED TRANSPOSITION

My passion for the sound-color relationship drove me to work with these modes of limited transposition, which people did not understand either, because they thought it had to be an arithmetical problem. But first and foremost it is a color phenomenon. Each mode has a precisely definable color, which changes every time it is transposed.[10]

The first manifestation of Messiaen's "charm of impossibilities" harnesses the power of sound-color: the modes of limited transposition were founded on his unique perception of color. Sound and color were synaesthetically connected in Messiaen's perception because he saw colors in his mind's eye when he heard music.[11] For him, it was a case of "inner vision"[12] cultivated by a sensitivity to color and a childhood

FIGURE 1: The Stained Glass Windows
of the Sainte Chapelle, Paris

imagination nurtured by fairy tales, poetry, and Shakespearean plays. His extraordinary perspective of color was also intrinsically linked to his first experience of dazzlement. When Messiaen was ten years old, he saw the magnificent stained glass windows of the Sainte Chapelle in Paris (Figure 1). The ensuing experience of dazzlement, of being over-whelmed by the beautiful colors, was a "shining revelation."[13] This "first colored emotion"[14] remained with him for the rest of his life and is the key to his use of sound-color in his music.

> The Sainte Chapelle... for me that was a shining revelation, which I have never forgotten, and this first impression as a child—I was ten years old—became a key experience for my later musical thinking.[15]

Appearing in his earliest compositions, the modes of limited trans-position are a systematized description of Messiaen's use of sound-color in his musical language. Messiaen claimed that he started to use them instinctively, guided by the colors they evoked; each mode posses-ses its own characteristic colors, which change with each transposition. These colors are formed by symmetrical formulas in the modal domain, and when he initially explained his modes to the public, it was the sym-metrical aspect he emphasized.[16] Based on the fact that the octave is composed of twelve semitones and the number twelve is divisible by various numbers, Messiaen formed his modes by segmenting the octave into different recurring groups—tiny transpositions themselves. Each group comprises an identical order of intervals, whereby the last pitch of one group serves simultaneously as the first pitch of the next. The original form of each mode, called the first transposition, always begins on C; successive transpositions begin on subsequent chromatic steps. Owing to the identical construction of each group within a mode, only a limited number of transpositions generates results that are genuinely different from the original form. (After that, further transpositions will only differ in terms of enharmonic notation.) Hence, Messiaen's term: "modes of limited transposition"[17] (see Example 1, next page).

Messiaen found seven such modes, but he primarily used the colors of four of them: modes 2, 3, 4, and 6. Mode 2 is the one that appears most frequently in his music. Allowing only three transpositions, it possessed for Messiaen a strong sense of the power of impossibilities, and its first transposition evoked different shades of violet, his favorite color. Mode 2 is composed of four groups of three notes (4 x 3 = 12); each group contains a half step followed by a whole step. The first transposition of mode 2 begins on C,[18] the second transposition on C♯, and the third on D. The fourth transposition, beginning on E♭, brings us back to the original notes of the first transposition.

Ex. 1: Messiaen's Seven Modes of Limited Transposition

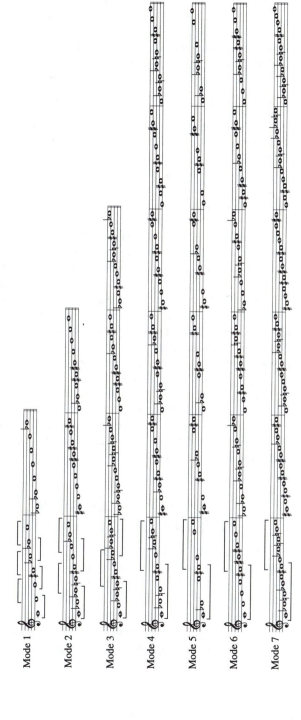

Mode 1

Mode 2

Mode 3

Mode 4

Mode 5

Mode 6

Mode 7

Unlike the diatonic scales, which can be transposed to all twelve semitones, the modes thus permit only a very limited number of transpositions. This is the impossibility that Messiaen loved. He was fascinated by this limitation—a limitation created by the tiny transpositions used to construct the mode. For him, the charm of these modes lay in the impossibility of further transpositions: their power sprang "from the impossibility of transpositions and also from the color linked to this impossibility."[19]

In his conversations with Claude Samuel, Messiaen described his colors for mode 2. Mode 2 in its first transposition evokes the following colors: "blue-violet rocks, speckled with little gray cubes, cobalt blue, deep Prussian blue, highlighted by a bit of violet-purple, gold, red, ruby, and stars mauve, black, and white. Blue-violet is dominant."[20] Mode 2 in its second transposition contains a different color picture: "gold and silver spirals against a background of brown and ruby-red vertical stripes. Gold and brown are dominant."[21] And the color scene for the third transposition is "light green and prairie-green foliage, with specks of blue, silver, and reddish orange. Dominant is green."[22]

These elaborate color descriptions possess a surreal, mystical sense; perhaps Messiaen's color tableaux are not to be found in the real world. Although he believed that it was possible to convey these colors to his listeners,[23] his sound-color perception seems to be highly subjective. In the pantheon of classical composers, Messiaen found traces of mode 2 in the works of his immediate predecessors; in his first treatise, *Technique de mon langage musical* (*The Technique of My Musical Language*), he points out its undeveloped use by Rimsky-Korsakov, Scriabin, Ravel, and Stravinsky.[24] Yet solely in his conception and use of it, did mode 2 evoke specific color connotations—colors that can be seen only through the imagination of his color hearing and are invisible to the naked, physical eye.

MODAL COLOR IN
"THE KISS OF THE INFANT JESUS"

The mystical colors of mode 2 permeate Messiaen's musical language throughout his career—from his earliest published work, *Préludes* (1928–1929) for piano, to the crowning achievement of his only opera, *Saint François d'Assise* (1975–1983). For the religious masterpiece of his piano literature, the *Vingt regards sur l'Enfant-Jésus* (1944), Messiaen often utilized mode 2 with F♯ major, as he sought "a language of mystical love... in multicolored arrangements."[25] One of the most beautiful examples of mode 2 and F♯ major is the fifteenth *regard*, "Le baiser de l'Enfant-Jésus" (The Kiss of the Infant Jesus), arguably one of Messiaen's most exquisite and sublime slow pieces.

"Le baiser de l'Enfant-Jésus" was inspired by an engraving of the Infant Jesus kissing Sister Theresa, which Messiaen, in his accompanying text for the *regard*, reveals is symbolic of Divine Love and Holy Communion. To illustrate this symbolic kiss from Jesus, Messiaen uses the color palette of mode 2. As he explained in *Technique*, the modes of limited transposition are "in the atmosphere of several tonalities at once, *without polytonality*, the composer being free to give predominance to one of the tonalities or to leave the tonal impression unsettled."[26] Consequently, in its first transposition, mode 2 "can hesitate between the four major tonalities of C, E♭, F♯, and A."[27] In "Le baiser," Messiaen chose to emphasize F♯ major with mode 2; the three transpositions of mode 2 correspond with the primary chords of F♯ major. Here, like a painter, he mixes the colors of mode 2 with the colors of the key of F♯ major, which for him was "a sparkling of all possible colors."[28] Mode 2 in its first transposition, with a dominating color of blue-violet, contains all the notes of the tonic chord with an added sixth in F♯ major. Mode 2 in its second transposition, with dominant colors of gold and brown, possesses all the notes of the dominant seventh chord in F♯ major. And mode 2 in its third transposition, with the dominant color of green, comprises all the notes of the subdominant with an added sixth chord in F♯ major.

The opening of "Le baiser" (Example 2) establishes this color relationship with the Theme of God (*Thème de Dieu*) in a lullaby. Over an F♯ tonic pedal, Messiaen creates the gentle rocking motion of the berceuse by alternating between the two axes of the tonic added sixth / mode 2 (first transposition) sonority and the dominant seventh / mode 2 (second transposition) sonority. Each color entity is created, over an F♯ pedal point, solely by the notes from mode 2. To illustrate: in measure 3, all seven notes that color the tonic are taken from the first transposition of mode 2; in measure 4, all eight notes of mode 2, second transposition, are used in conjunction with the dominant. After establishing this color dynamic, Messiaen adds the color combination of the subdominant function with mode 2 in its third transposition; in measure 12, six notes from the third transposition of mode 2 suffuse the subdominant. By using mode 2 in conjunction with F♯ major, shifting between the color scenes in each transposition, Messiaen adds his signature color and tonal complexity to the otherwise classically simple tonic, subdominant, dominant, harmonic underpinning that is the basis for most of this beautiful *regard*.

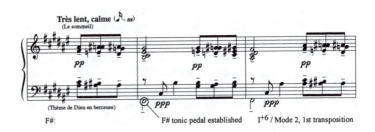

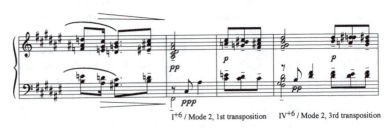

EXAMPLE 2: *Vingt regards sur l'Enfant-Jésus*,
"Le baiser de l'Enfant-Jésus," mm. 1-12
© 1949 by Éditions Durand, Paris. Reprinted with permission.

The highlight of this piece is a section marked *Le baiser*, "The Kiss" (Example 3, see next page). Leading up to the divine kiss of love, Messiaen departs from the peaceful mode 2/F♯ major melange and begins to build up chromatic chord clusters for his musical representation of the arms reaching out towards love. At the height of the chromatic buildup, he presents "The Kiss," *fortissimo*, with mode 2 and F♯ major. The effect of this change from intense chromaticism to the sparkling spectrum of colors found in mode 2 with F♯ major is a feeling of fulfillment—the chromaticism has been absorbed and transformed into the mode 2 / F♯-major sonority. Musically, Messiaen has represented his belief in communion, where "we are absorbed by Christ."[29]

The ending of this piece (Example 4) shimmers like Messiaen's beloved stained glass windows. Over a sustained F♯ with an added sixth chord, which is held down by the pedal for eight measures, the left hand outlines the C♯ and A♯ of the F♯ tonic chord while the right hand has arpeggiated F♯ with an added sixth chords cascading down the upper keyboard. The sonority of mode 2 in its first transposition is now created simply by the notes that form the tonic added sixth chord in F♯ major. The result is a sparkling wash of sound easily evoking and reminding one of the colors of blues and violets—the colors Messiaen saw when he heard mode 2 in its first transposition.[30]

With this sparkling ending, Messiaen reinforces the color center of the piece: the color combination implied by mode 2, first transposition, and the tonic triad of F♯ major. In the mystical sound-colors of "violets, blues, and violet-purples,"[31] highlighted by the luminous "sparkling of all possible colors"[32] of F♯ major, Messiaen seems to convey his own spiritual color symbolism. Like the effect of the stained glass windows where, as he observed, we are taught by images and symbols and the overall effect is an immense dazzlement of color,[33] in "Le baiser" we hear and are dazzled by the musical colors of blue-violet that dominate the piece. According to Messiaen's understanding of the color symbolism used by the medieval stained glass artisans, blue-violet symbolized the Truth of Love.[34] In "Le baiser," with the sound-colors of mode 2 emulating the religious color symbolism of the stained glass windows, Messiaen exquisitely portrays the Holy Communion, the Kiss of the Baby Jesus, as a Truth of Love.

And so, we return to the image of the beautiful stained glass windows and dazzlement—the key to Messiaen's passion for color. Through the sound-colors of his modes of limited transposition, Messiaen dazzles the listener, as he was dazzled by the colors of the stained glass windows of the Sainte Chapelle in Paris. Messiaen believed that this effect of dazzlement occurs when colors and sounds combine in a

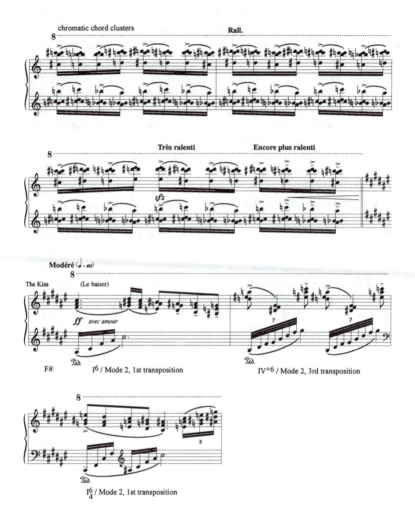

EXAMPLE 3: *Vingt regards sur l'Enfant-Jésus*,
"Le baiser de l'Enfant-Jésus," mm. 92-97
© 1949 by Éditions Durand, Paris. Reprinted with permission.

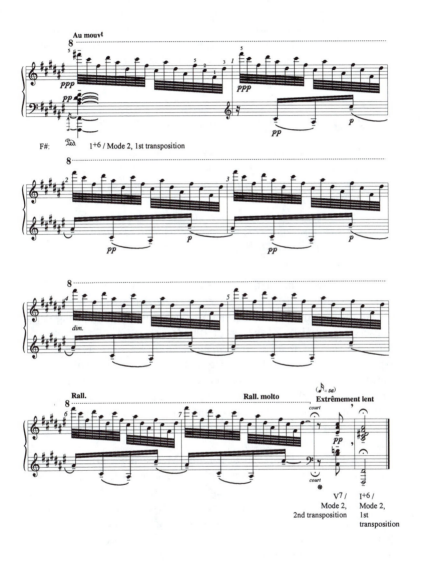

EXAMPLE 4: *Vingt regards sur l'Enfant-Jésus,*
"Le baiser de l'Enfant-Jésus," mm. 127-136
© 1949 by Éditions Durand, Paris. Reprinted with permission.

colored emotion to form a new reality, a reality closer to eternity.[35] His sound-colors reach beyond the temporal world to anticipate the "perpetual dazzlement"[36] of heaven, which he envisioned as "an eternal music of colors, an eternal color of musics."[37] Contained in the modes of limited transposition, the earliest realization of his sound-color reality, is a symbol of eternal life, where the separation of the senses no longer exists.[38]

THE NON-RETROGRADABLE RHYTHMS

It is one of my favorite discoveries. As in the case of many discoveries, I simply found something that already existed, potentially, if not in fact. However, in spite of the very ancient Hindu "dhenkî" ... and the antique Greek "amphimacer"... which are, in date, the first known non-retrogradable rhythms, no one thought of establishing a musical theory of these rhythms and even less of putting them into practice.[39]

The second manifestation of Messiaen's "charm of impossibilities" utilizes the power of time: Messiaen uncovered the non-retrogradable rhythm in his study of ancient Hindu rhythms. His find, as a young Paris Conservatory student, of the list of 120 *deçî-tâlas* from Sharngadeva's thirteenth-century treatise, the *Samgitaratnakara*, was as Messiaen expressed it, "a stroke of luck."[40] He studied these ancient rhythms from North India from "every possible angle."[41] By applying the technique of retrogradation to them, he discovered what was for him the primordial element of these ancient Hindu rhythms—the existence of a special type of rhythm that was the same whether one read it forwards or backwards: "the non-retrogradable rhythm."[42]

Among the list of 120 *deçî-tâlas*, Messiaen identified what he considered to be the first known non-retrogradable rhythm—the *dhenkî*, *deçî-tâla* number 58: S I S. Messiaen translated the Hindu notation for the *dhenkî*—S I S—into the rhythm ♩ ♪♩. According to his understanding,[43] S, representing the Hindu time value *guru*, is equivalent to the quarter-note and I, representing the Hindu time value *laghu*, to the eighth-note; the entire rhythm contains five *mâtras*, the Hindu unit for counting these rhythms, which corresponds with five eighth-notes. His description for this non-retrogradable rhythm appears in the first volume of his second treatise, *Traité de rythme, de couleur, et d'ornithologie* (Treatise of Rhythm, Color, and Ornithology):

Dhenkî is a Bengali word designating a device for the shelling of rice. This device is generally maneuvered by two women, the one on the right, the other on the left, the device between them, just as here the laghu is placed between the two gurus. Our tâla maybe also reproduces the movement imparted to the device by the two women, during the shelling.... It is without doubt very old, like all the rhythms based on the number five, the number of fingers of the hand. The Dhenkî (I emphasize this) is the oldest, the simplest and the most natural of the non-retrogradable rhythms.[44]

Messiaen found the same rhythmic proportion and phenomenon, in his study of Greek meters, with the Amphimacer or Cretic rhythm, which he translated into the rhythm ♩ ♩ ♩. Finally in his own music, he often presented the *dhenkî* in the form of ♪ ♪♪.

From his study of the Hindu *deçî-tâlas*, Messiaen derived his principle for non-retrogradable rhythms. In simple rhythms containing only three values, such as the *dhenkî*, the non-retrogradable principle is upheld if the two outer values are identical and surround a "free central value."[45]

EXAMPLE 5: two identical values
flanking a free central value

free central value

For complex rhythms containing more than three values, Messiaen's principle is extended: "All rhythms divisible into two groups, one of which is the retrograde of the other, with a *common central value*, are non-retrogradable."[46] The following is an example using the *dhenkî* as the common central value (Example 6):[47]

EXAMPLE 6

The power of these rhythms lay, for Messiaen, in their philosophic and symbolic importance; they "draw their strength from a temporal impossibility"[48] just as the modes "draw their strength

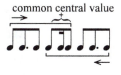

common central value

from a resonant impossibility."[49] In the second volume of the *Traité*, he identified three sources of such strength. The first comes from the closed circuitry caused by the relationship of the two outer groups of values—identical or symmetrical retrogrades of each other— which when linked by a common central value form a non-retrogradable rhythm. The rhythm is now identical whether read from left to right or right to left and, in essence, a retrograde no longer exists. The second source resides in the irreversibility of time. Just as it is impossible to go back in time and change past events, the non-retrogradable rhythm does not change when played backward, it merely repeats itself. And the third source links the rhythmic force with our temporal life. Messiaen's metaphysical view identifies the qualities of the free central value, which joins the two outer groups of the non-retrogradable rhythm, as analogous to the present, which, in life, links the past and future. Inasmuch as it is impossible to distinguish past and future without the freedom of the present, so it is impossible to distinguish the outer groups of the non-retrogradable rhythm without the freedom of the common central value. Messiaen believed that these sources of strength, created by temporal impossibilities, endowed the non-retrogradable rhythm with "great power, a kind of explosive force . . . a magical strength."[50]

It is a power that Messiaen found not only in the Hindu rhythms, but saw affirmed everywhere in the world around him. He detected non-retrogradable rhythms in the decorative arts (architecture, glaziery, tapestry, flower parterres) with their use of symmetrical motifs. Marvelous living non-retrogradable rhythms could be discerned in nature in the leaves of trees and the wings of the butterfly. The occult power of ancient magic spells using palindromic words was the power of the non-retrogradable rhythm. The symmetry of the non-retrogradable rhythm was the symmetry of the human body. And finally, applied in his own life, Messiaen perceived the non-retrogradable rhythm as a symbol of life and eternity: "A final symbol—this moment which I live, this thought which crosses my mind, this movement which I accomplish, this time which I beat, before and after lies eternity: it is a non-retrogradable rhythm."[51]

NON-RETROGRADABILITY AND "THE CHURCH OF LOVE"

Messiaen utilized the power and strength of the non-retrogradable rhythm throughout his career. The *dhenkî* can be heard in his early works, from the *Quatuor pour la fin du temps* (1940–1941), where he first explained, in the preface, the presence of the non-retrogradable rhythm, until the works at the end of his life, most notably his opera *Saint François d'Assise*, which he considered a synthesis of all his musical researches. In the *Vingt regards*, it forms one of the compositional building blocks of the piano cycle, culminating in the final *regard*, "Regard de l'Eglise d'amour" (Glance of the Church of Love).

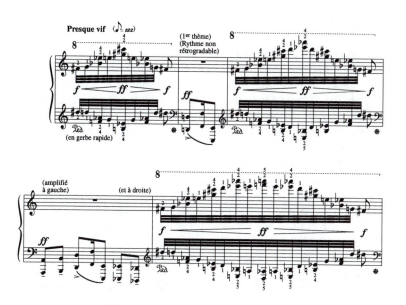

EXAMPLE 7: *Vingt regards sur l'Enfant-Jésus,*
"Regard de l'Eglise d'amour," mm. 1- 6
© 1949 by Éditions Durand, Paris. Reprinted with permission.

The "Regard de l'Eglise d'amour" is the glorious summation of Messiaen's monumental piano cycle. This final contemplation of the Infant Jesus in the manger is from the collective and timeless perspective of all Christians who form the Church, the mystical Body of Christ. The dramatic opening harnesses the power of the non-retrogradable rhythm (see Example 7).[52]

Creating the power for this brilliant opening, the *dhenkî* first appears in measure 2, where Messiaen labels it the first theme and identifies it as a non-retrogradable rhythm. It appears *fortissimo* in the bold declamatory octaves of the left hand. Along with its non-retrogradable strength, the *dhenkî* endows the first theme with the power of the prime number, seen in its total duration of five sixteenth-notes. The indivisibility of the prime number gives the rhythm an occult power symbolic of the divinity, which is indivisible.[53] In volume II of the *Traité*, where he explained the force of the non-retrogradable rhythm, Messiaen noted that one never repeats a non-retrogradable rhythm in succession (because repetition does not reveal anything new and consequently does not increase its power), unless one develops it by augmentation or diminution.[54] Therefore, when presenting the power of the *dhenkî* again in measure 4, he augments it on either side by two eighth-notes.[55] The new rhythm keeps the strength of the non-retrogradable rhythm: the *dhenkî* acts as the common central value and the two eighth-notes on each side are identical or symmetrical retrogrades. The power of the prime number is represented by a new total duration of thirteen sixteenth-notes. In measure 6, Messiaen continues his augmentation, adding another eighth-note and a dot to each side. The resulting rhythm maintains the power of non-retrogradation with the *dhenkî* still serving as the common central value. In addition, the outer groups of ♪ ♪. ♪ are non-retrogradable rhythms within themselves—the dotted eighth-note acting as the common central value surrounded by an eighth-note on either side. The power of the prime number is retained with a new total duration of nineteen sixteenth-notes. By these means, Messiaen is able to repeat the *dhenkî* three times in the opening—the number three representing the Holy Trinity of God the Father, Son, and Holy Spirit—while ever increasing its power and strength.

What makes this opening even more compelling is that Messiaen has intensified the strength of these non-retrogradable rhythms by extending the principle of non-retrogradation to the other musical elements in the section. In the opening measure, we hear the melodic counterpart of the non-retrogradable rhythm—the non-retrogradable melody.[56] The non-retrogradable melody, which Messiaen instructs the performer to play "in a rapid burst,"[57] illustrates "the bursts of night"[58]

presented in his text for this *regard.* In measure 1, the right hand starts
with the second finger on F♯ and ascends with the fingering 1-4/2-1-4/2
to the double notes G♯-C♯ and then descends exactly in reverse. The left
hand, a free reflection of the right hand, starts with the second finger on
D♯ and descends with the fingering 1-2/4-1-2/4 to the double notes B♮
and E♭ and ascends exactly in reverse. Thus we have two superimposed
non-retrogradable melodies in the horizontal sense, which also contain
by virtue of their contrary movement between the hands, emphasized by
symmetrical fingering, the power of the non-retrogradable rhythm in the
vertical sense.[59] A final non-retrogradable correspondence can be found
in the dynamic marking for this rapid burst. The dynamic marking of f <
ff > f reproduces the non-retrogradable strength in volume and shading.
In principle, each note of the melodic burst ascending in the *crescendo*
has its corresponding dynamic intensity in the descending *diminuendo.*

Like the development of the non-retrogradable rhythm of the first
theme, which builds up and amplifies its strength of non-retrogradation
by augmentation, the non-retrogradable melody has its corresponding
augmentations. Messiaen alternates the development of this non-retrogradable melody with the development of the first theme. Just as the
augmentations of the first theme from measure 2 appear in measures 4
and 6, the augmentations of the palindromic burst from measure 1
appear in measures 3 and 5. The palindromic bursts develop their augmentations by enlarging the inner or middle values in contrast to the
first theme, which develops its augmentations by enlarging the outer
values. Accordingly, in measure 3, Messiaen augments the palindromic
burst in the middle, the highest part of its wave and the melodic corre-
spondent to the non-retrogradable rhythm's common central value. All
the powers of its non-retrogradation in the areas of melody, ambit, and
dynamics remain intact with the exception of the symmetrical fingering
effect, which is slightly adjusted.[60] In the augmentation, another palindromic feature is evident: the melodic intervals between the right hand
fingers 1-4 and the left hand fingers 1-2 are progressively shortened in
each displacement and correspondingly lengthened in their retrograde.
The right hand ascends with the melodic intervals sixth, sixth, fifth; the
left hand descends with the melodic intervals fourth, third, third. In
measure 5, the palindromic burst is further augmented, using the same
procedure. All aspects of the previous augmentation apply to this bigger
augmentation. The palindromic contraction and expansion of the melodic intervals of each hand is continued: the right hand has the ascending melodic intervals of sixth, sixth, fifth, fourth; the left hand has the
descending melodic intervals of fourth, third, third, second.

FIGURE 2: The Royal Portal of the Cathedral of Chartres

The architectural symmetry that gives strength and grandeur to the great French cathedrals he loved—Sainte Chapelle, Notre Dame, Bourges, Chartres (Figure 2)—is captured in the opening of Messiaen's musical representation of the Church. In the "Regard de l'Eglise d'amour," through the principle of non-retrogradation, Messiaen re- creates the powerful Catholic symbolism embodied in the awe-inspiring Gothic and Romanesque arches, the beautiful arrangements of stained glass windows, the crux-based floor plan.

> *It is maybe in architecture that we will find the most beautiful, the simplest and the most powerful non-retrogradable rhythms. ... Here is the Gothic art: one magnificent example taken from the Cathedral of Chartres: the Royal portal and its three doors. All together, the ensemble of the three doors is non-retrogradable.*[61]

Captivating the listener, capturing the sacred grandeur of the great French cathedrals, and introducing the feeling of grand summation needed to complete the monumental *Vingt regards*, the mesmerizing effect of this magnificent opening stems, for Messiaen, from the "charm of impossibilities" found in his non-retrogradable rhythms. This phenomenon leads the listener "out of temporal things"[62] into a new reality; its "spellbinding"[63] effect acts as a *"theological rainbow,"*[64] bridging the divide between the temporal and spiritual worlds. As Messiaen himself explained the effect of his charm:

> Let us think now of the hearer of our modal and rhythmic music; he will not have time at the concert to inspect the nontranspositions and the nonretrogradations, and, at that moment, these questions will not interest him further; to be charmed will be his only desire. And that is precisely what will happen; in spite of himself he will submit to the strange charm of impossibilities: a certain effect of tonal ubiquity in the non-transposition, a certain unity of move-ment (where beginning and end are confused because iden-tical) in the non-retrogradation, all things that will lead him progressively to that sort of *theological rainbow* which the musical language, of which we seek edification and theory, attempts to be.[65]

And so Messiaen was able to evoke a mystical experience of eternity, reflecting his paraphrase of the angel's statement of eternity from the biblical book of Revelations: *"There will be no more time."*[66] In the symmetry of the non-retrogradable rhythm, temporal parameters are blurred and the experience of time is nonprogressive; there is no development. Contained in the non-retrogradable rhythm, the point of departure for nearly all of his rhythmic researches,[67] is a symbol of eternity, where there is no longer a succession of time and thus beginning and ending are the same.

THE SYMMETRICAL PERMUTATIONS

The musician possesses a mysterious power: by means of his rhythms, he can chop up Time here and there, and can even put it together again in the reverse order, a little as though he were going for a walk through different points of time, or as though he were amassing the future by turning to the past, in the process of which, his memory of the past becomes transformed into a memory of the future. The "symmetrical permutations" and the "non-retrogradable rhythms" utilize this power, nevertheless working against it.[68]

Completing the trinity of musical innovations embracing Messiaen's "charm of impossibilities" are the symmetrical permutations. Like the non-retrogradable rhythms, the symmetrical permutations exploit the power of time. This third innovation represents a deliberate, perhaps less natural, realization of his charm; Messiaen's hand as the composer manipulating time is more clearly seen. The modes of limited transposition were a color-guided discovery for him. With his non-retrogradable rhythms, he merely recovered a strength that he found in the Hindu *deçî-tâlas* and saw affirmed in the world around him. For the final manifestation of his "charm of impossibilities," Messiaen developed, in the rhythmic domain, his own original, mature response to the symmetrical manipulation of musical elements to achieve an effect of impossibility—rhythmic permutations that are linked by the same generating formula: the "symmetrical permutations."[69]

The procedure for his symmetrical permutations starts out with what Messiaen calls "a chromatic scale of durations."[70] An outgrowth of his earlier work with serialization, the chromatic scale of durations is a sequential arrangement of durations using a common denominator. Much as the chromatic scale using pitch is based on the lowest common denominator of the half step, Messiaen's chromatic scale of durations is based on increments of a tiny duration. Using the example of a chromatic scale of durations based on the thirty-second note, ranging from ♪ (1 thirty-second note) to o (32 thirty-second notes)—which Messiaen uses with great success in *Chronochromie* (1959–1960)—we then get the following ascending durations, numbered 1 to 32 (Example 8):[71]

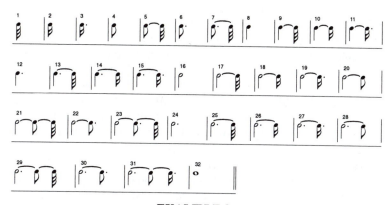

EXAMPLE 8

To generate his symmetrical permutations, Messiaen chooses a reading order for his scale. In *Chronochromie*, he uses the following order:[72]

3	28	5	30	7	32	26	2	25
1	8	24	9	23	16	17	18	22
21	19	20	4	31	6	29	10	27
11	15	14	12	13				

EXAMPLE 9

By applying the reading order to the scale of durations, he obtains his first interversion[73] or permutation:[74]

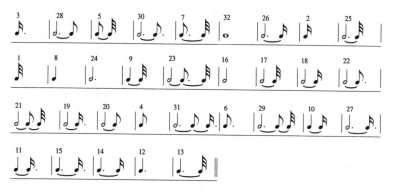

EXAMPLE 10

This result is then renumbered 1 to 32 and the process is repeated. Subsequent permutations are thus generated symmetrically by employing the same algorithm: the reading order is sequentially applied and the result then renumbered. By using this symmetrical procedure, Messiaen avoids what would amount to an astronomical number of possible permutations (for this thirty-two-note selection the number would be an astounding 263130836933693530167218012160000000!).[75] Using his process, the thirty-sixth interversion recreates the initial chromatic scale of durations, bringing the thirty-seventh interversion back to the original permutation. The impossibility here is that of generating any more than a fairly limited number of permutations.[76]

This procedure offered Messiaen an additional opportunity to manipulate time, infusing supplementary rhythmic power into the overall inevitability of the entire rhythmic flow. In addition to limiting his permutations, the above reading order (Example 9), chosen for *Chronochromie*, provides fascinating numerical details that add to the procedure's rhythmic strength.[77] Starting with the initial chromatic scale of durations (Example 8), Messiaen formulates this order by instilling certain rhythmic movements: retrograding, alternating, and sequential patterns. For the initial six units of his interversion, he takes three values from the beginning and three from the end of the original scale. From the beginning, he uses every other unit starting with the number 3 (3, 5, 7); from the end, he chooses three corresponding values, also skipping every other unit, starting with the number 28 (28, 30, 32). Placing these values in alternation, he forms the beginning of his reading order: 3, 28, 5, 30, 7, 32. He chooses the next four units by continuing in retrograde on both sides of the scale. From the left side, he uses the numbers 26 and 25; from the right side, he chooses 2 and 1. Alternating these values, he constructs the next four units of his interversion: 26, 2, 25, 1. By reading from left to right (the right sense) at the beginning of the scale and right to left (the retrograde sense) at the end, he obtains the numbers 8, 9, 24, 23. Again, he alternates the values as follows: 8, 24, 9, 23. The next three units are three consecutive chromatic values, which he places directly without alternation: 16, 17, 18. He continues by choosing numbers immediately above the center of the scale, using the retrograde on one side with numbers 22, 21 and the right movement on the other side for numbers 19, 20. Without alternation, he places them into his order: 22, 21, 19, 20. Using every other unit, he then selects two values from the left side (4, 6) and two values from the right side, but in the retrograde sense (31, 29). He places them by alternation: 4, 31, 6, 29. His last jump within the scale adds the values 10 and 27 to the series. He finishes his permutation order by going from the extremes to the center of the scale, alternating between a forwards movement (11, 15) and a retrograde movement (14, 12): 11, 15, 14, 12.

With the numerical choices for his reading order, Messiaen could add certain rhythmic effects, manipulate certain outcomes—not relying solely on chance, but taking power and control over the destiny of his rhythmic manipulations. One such striking effect is caused by his deliberate placement of the number 27. Because it is placed at the twenty-seventh spot in his reading order, it also coincides with the duration of twenty-seven thirty-second notes in his initial chromatic scale of durations. As a result, this duration never changes its position; it appears in all thirty-six permutations immutably at the same twenty-seventh spot. This control by the composer over the rhythmic process is the key to the power that Messiaen perceived in his symmetrical permutations. Displaying his calculated application of the principles behind the modes of limited transposition and the non-retrogradable rhythms, the symmetrical permutations use an artistically-imposed algorithm to produce different rhythmic permutations. The number of permutations is limited, and that for Messiaen is the charm embodied in his symmetrical permutations: his compositional procedure has created a power and strength by relentlessly drawing the rhythmic permutations back to the beginning, circumventing the natural process of possibilities.

SYMMETRICAL PERMUTATIONS IN *CHRONOCHROMIE*

The power of impossibilities found in the symmetrical permutations first appeared in *Île de feu 2* (1950) and is utilized in *Chronochromie* (1959-1960), *Couleurs de la cité céleste* (1963), the "Le baiser au lépreux" from *Saint François d'Assise*, and *Éclairs sur l'au-delà* (1987–1991); in *Chronochromie* (Color of Time), Messiaen felt he was the most successful with this procedure. The title of the orchestral work *Chronochromie* comes from the Greek *kronos* "time" and *kroma* "color" and its form is based on his idiosyncratic assimilation of the Greek poetic triad of strophe, antistrophe, and epode.[78] Messiaen's musical adaptation presents seven continuous sections: Introduction – Strophe I – Antistrophe I – Strophe II – Antistrophe II – Épôde – Coda. It is the two strophes that highlight the symmetrical permutations and give the piece its title.

For the two strophes of *Chronochromie*, Messiaen presents his symmetrical permutations in superimposition. Using the thirty-two-note scale of durations and reading order examined above (Examples 8 and 9), he unfolds three lines of symmetrical permutations simultaneously. In the first strophe, he uses permutations 1, 2, 3; in the second strophe, he uses permutations 22, 23, 24. For this rhythmic scheme, Messiaen gathers the permutations into a 4/8 time signature, rewriting values with ties across the barline. While this imposed time signature makes the rhythmic pattern less evident to the eye, he felt that it was necessary in order to facilitate a simple beat for the conductor and promote the exact execution of the values by the orchestra.[79] Each permutation will now take thirty-three measures. Here is the beginning of the rhythmic scheme for the three superimposed interversions that are used in the first strophe (Example 11), followed by Messiaen's unparalleled realization of it in *Chronochromie* (Example 12, next two facing pages):[80]

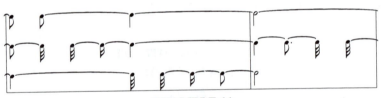

EXAMPLE 11

Although easily seen and understood in the abstract, in his music the aural effect is less clear. Messiaen's grand time scheme, his fascination with the particular rhythmic patterns he creates through a formula that has the power of impossibilities, is probably better understood mentally and felt subliminally than consciously perceived aurally. The "charm of impossibilities," when applied in his symmetrical permutations, has a less visceral effect than the modes and non-retrogradable rhythms. Can the listener sense the power behind his rhythmic manipulations? Hear the unfolding of the permutations? Perhaps it is as Messiaen himself described, wherein the listener "in spite of himself... will submit to the strange charm of impossibilities."[81] For *Chronochromie*, to assist the listener in hearing the unfolding of these permutations, Messiaen colored the note-values in three ways: "by 'minting' [*le monnayage*],[82] by timbre, and by strains of chords."[83]

The first method, by minting, emphasizes and highlights the longer durations sounding the rhythmic permutations by realizing the tiny durations that compose them, enabling the listener "to appreciate the tiny differences between the long durations."[84] For this method, Messiaen mints the durations through different counterpoints of birdsong, highlighting the lowest common denominator of the thirty-second note. In the opening of the first strophe (Example 12), we hear a panoply of song from four French birds. The first bird to burst into song is the marsh warbler (*Rousserolle verderolle*) with the clarinet in B♭. Its song displays the thirty-second notes that create the rhythmic permutations. The wren (*Troglodyte*) follows in the glockenspiel, presenting its song with different triplet and sextuplet realizations of the thirty-second note. A second marsh warbler enters with the second clarinet in B♭. Its song motif, characterized by a repeated *staccato* pattern, also reveals the thirty-second note. And the great tit (*Mésange charbonnière*) and the icterine warbler (*Hypolaïs ictérine*) enter together. Presented by the flute, the great tit expresses the sixteenth note in a repeated two-note call using a leap of an ascending augmented fourth. Sharing the melodic line of its song in the opening bars with four different instruments—the English horn, the oboe, the bass clarinet, and the clarinet in E♭—the icterine warbler exhibits different variants of sixteenth-note and thirty-second note durations. The second method, through timbre, is realized by the metallic percussion instruments that present the permutations. The first interversion is presented by three gongs and begins *pianissimo* with the high gong. The second interversion is revealed simultaneously by a set of bells, which, in contrast, are sounded *forte*. The third interversion is concurrently unfolded *pianissimo* by a suspended cymbal, a Chinese cymbal, and a tam-tam; in the opening bars, the tam-tam sounds the first duration, the suspended cymbal the second, the Chinese cymbal the third, and the suspended cymbal the fourth. And the third method, which Messiaen considered the most effective, is through the sound-colors of his chords.[85] His strings present the sound-colors of various chords while emphasizing the rhythmic attacks of the percussive instruments by playing *non vibrato* and enunciating each new duration with a *mf* accent followed by a *subito pianissimo*. Eight violins articulate and color the first interversion, creating the following colors with opening chord: "pale yellow, mauve,—brassy rose, pearly gray."[86] Seven violins likewise sound and color the second interversion, evoking a different color drama. And three violas and four cellos realize and color the third interversion with the following color scene for the beginning chord: "bright yellow gold, purple violet tinged with whiteness, gold and black."[87]

EXAMPLE 12: *Chronochromie,*
"Strophe I," mm. 1-2
Reprinted with kind permission of Alphonse Leduc & Co.

EXAMPLE 12 continued: *Chronochromie*,
"Strophe I," mm. 3-4
Reprinted with kind permission of Alphonse Leduc & Co.

The free counterpoint of the birdsong meshes with the calculated counterpoint of the permutations: our ears hear a vibrant panorama of colorful textures as the symmetrical permutations are revealed by the timbre and dynamics of the metallic percussion instruments, colored by the accentuation and sound-colors of the strings, and defined by the fleet rhythms of the bird's swift song. The resultant effect is, as Messiaen explained to Claude Samuel, "durations and permutations of durations made perceptible by sound colorations (one type explaining the other)—this is truly a 'color of time,' a *Chronochromie*."[88]

And so, the symmetrical permutations of *Chronochromie* illustrate the mystical experience of eternity that was behind Messiaen's exploration of time. In his words: "Time makes Eternity comprehensible to us by contrasting with it."[89] The symmetrical permutations are another nonprogressive way to experience time, revealing Messiaen's search for an understanding of temporal limitations that reaches to the eternity of everlasting life. Contained in the symmetrical permutations is a symbol of eternity, where there is no progression of time and in an infinitely continuous sense, one is always at the beginning.

CONCLUSION

This is the charm of impossibilities—they possess an occult power, a calculated ascendancy, in time and sound. It has been said that some of my works had a spellbinding power over the public. There is nothing of the magician in me, and this spellbinding power is not achieved crudely through repetition, as has been claimed, but perhaps results from those impossibilities enclosed within such and such a formula.[90]

The "charm of impossibilities" created by the modes of limited transposition, non-retrogradable rhythms, and symmetrical permutations gave Messiaen's music mystical power to express the truths of his faith. Manifested in each innovation is his belief that "a technical process had all the more power when it came up, in its very essence, against an insuperable obstacle."[91] This belief is not only the foundation for the mystical power in his music, but also a reflection of the conflict in his own life as a Catholic believer. For Messiaen the devout believer, true reality was in the realm of faith—"the one sole reality"[92] of eternity. The "insuperable obstacle"[93] he faced in his life was how to experience the truth of eternity, while still on earth, bound by temporal limitations. As a composer, Messiaen searched for this truth through his musical language. He believed that music could prepare us for eternity "as a picture, as a reflection, as a symbol."[94] Incomparably, the "charm of impossibilities" in his music brings us to God by the "default of truth."[95] The modes of limited transposition, non-retrogradable rhythms, and symmetrical permutations serve as mystical symbols of faith, revealing his aspiration towards eternity.

The truth of eternity at the heart of his Catholic faith guides Messiaen's musical language in "an unbroken sequence,"[96] all the parts fitting into a glorious whole. While the modes of limited transposition, non-retrogradable rhythms, and symmetrical permutations utilize different musical elements, create divergent musical effects, and represent musical discoveries from different points of departure, all are unified by the same symmetrical model, a prototype that affirms Messsiaen's faith in eternity by creating a "charm of impossibilities." Accordingly, each innovation is created by establishing symmetrical groups.[97] In addition, the symmetrical groups in each innovation share a common central element.[98] And contained in the symmetrical groups of each innovation is the musical possibility that engenders the innovation's compositional impossibility.[99] Constructed upon the same symmetrical foundation, the modes realize in the vertical sense (transposition) what the non-retrogradable rhythms and symmetrical permutations realize in the horizontal sense (retrogradation and permutation). For all three innovations, the limitations created by this symmetrical formula form a closed circuit— the resultant impossibilities always lead the innovation back to the beginning, just as in the Catholic faith, one always returns to the truth of eternity.

It is in the Catholic faith that Messiaen found his exemplar of closed circuitry: for the believer, there is only one eternal God and only one infinitely continuous reality—eternity. Thus, embodied in the closed circuitry of each innovation, Messiaen found expressions of eternal life. The absence of progression and development caused by the closed circuitry mirrors his belief in the unchanging truth of eternity. The unifying effect of the closed circuitry reflects his belief in the unity of eternity, where man will be united with God. And from this circular construction, Messiaen beautifully harnessed the power of time and sound to convey his mystical experience of heaven. With the sound-colors of his modes, he reaches beyond the boundaries of our visual sense to create the mystical color experience found in the dazzlement of heaven. Through the rhythmic force embedded in the non-retrogradable rhythms and symmetrical permutations, he goes beyond the conventional understanding of time to evoke the mystical experience of eternity, where there is no more time.

Above all, Messiaen wanted "to rejoin the eternal durations and the resonances of the above and beyond, to apprehend that inaudible which is above actual music."[100] Through the "charm of impossibilities" he transports his music beyond the temporal boundaries of the world into the spiritual realm of his faith. Forming a trinity of mystical symbols, the modes of limited transposition, non-retrogradable rhythms, and symmetrical permutations emulate his aspiration for eternal unification with the perfect triumvirate—the Holy Trinity of God the Father, Son, and Holy Spirit. The compositional limitations of his three innovations reflect the temporal limitations he faced in his life on earth—limitations that he believed would dissolve in eternity. Like the truths of his Catholic faith, the power of his "charm of impossibilities" is fulfilled in heaven. The "charm of impossibilities," at the heart of Olivier Messiaen's musical language of mystical love, is ultimately a reflection and symbol of the final "insuperable obstacle"[101]—death—and the transcending power of God's love, which gives man eternal life.

NOTES

[1] Olivier Messiaen, *The Technique of My Musical Language*, trans. John Satterfield (Paris: Alphonse Leduc, 1956), p. 13. "Un point fixera d'abord notre attention: le *charme des impossibilités*. C'est une musique chatoyante que nous cherchons, donnant au sens auditif des plaisirs voluptueusement raffinés. En même temps, cette musique doit pouvoir exprimer des sentiments nobles (et spécialement les plus nobles de tous, les sentiments religieux exaltés par la théologie et les vérités de notre foi catholique). Ce charme, à la fois voluptueux et contemplatif, réside particulièrement dans certaines impossiblités mathématiques des domaines modal et rythmique" (Messiaen, *Technique de mon langage musical* [Paris: Alphonse Leduc, 1944], p. 5).

[2] Olivier Messiaen, *Music and Color: Conversations with Claude Samuel*, trans. E. Thomas Glasow (Portland: Amadeus Press, 1996), p. 47. "Un procédé technique possédait d'autant plus de force qu'il se heurtait davantage, dans son essence même, à un obstacle infranchissable" (Messiaen, *Musique et couleur: Nouveaux entretiens avec Claude Samuel* [Paris: Pierre Belford, 1986], p. 50).

[3] Messiaen, *The Technique of My Musical Language*, p. 13. "*Charme des impossibilités*" (Messiaen, *Technique de mon langage musical*, p. 5).

[4] "Certaines impossibilités mathématiques, certains circuits fermés, possèdent une puissance d'envoûtement, une force magique, un *charme*" (Olivier Messiaen, *Traité de rythme, de couleur, et d'ornithologie (1949-1992)*, vol. III [Paris: Alphonse Leduc, 1996], p. 7).

[5] "Enchantement magique" (*Ibid.*).

[6] See note 2 above.

[7] *Ibid.*, p. 48. "Une emprise chiffrée, temporelle et sonore" (*Ibid.*, p. 51).

[8]Almut Rössler, *Contributions to the Spiritual World of Olivier Messiaen*, trans. Barbara Dagg and Nancy Poland (Duisburg: Gilles & Francke, 1986), p. 10. Messiaen's words initially appeared in a handwritten introduction for the Messiaen festival program book, *Hommage à Messiaen: novembre-décembre 1978* (Paris: La recherche artistique, 1978), p. 3, which is reproduced in Rössler, *Contributions*, pp. 8-9: "La musique nous porte à Dieu, 'par défaut de vérité', jusqu'au jour où Lui-même nous éblouira, 'par excès de vérité'."

[9]*Ibid.* "Défaut de vérité" (*Hommage à Messiaen*, p. 3). Messiaen's explanation for this phrase, which can also be translated as "absence of truth," appears in *Musique et couleur*, p. 256; the English translation appears in *Music and Color*, p. 233: "It's in that sense that music expresses the beyond with its absence of truth, because it isn't inside the actual framework of reality. God alone is the single true reality . . . 'Absence of truth' doesn't signify falsehood. It's the symbolic representation of an event that isn't really visible, whereas celestial meditation is no longer symbolic: it's reality."

[10]*Ibid.*, p. 76 [slightly edited for clarity].

[11]Messiaen noted in *Musique et couleur*, p. 42, that he saw colors in his mind and did not have physiological synesthesia like his friend Blanc-Gatti.

[12]Rössler, *op. cit.*, p. 43.

[13]*Ibid.*, p. 78.

[14]*Ibid.*, p. 60.

[15]*Ibid.*, p. 78 [slightly edited]. Messiaen's original words are not available; Rössler's book first appeared as *Beiträge zur geistigen Welt Olivier Messiaens* (Duisburg: Gilles & Francke, 1984).

[16]Messiaen first cataloged his seven modes of limited transposition in *Technique de mon langage musical*; an earlier explanation of some of his modes appeared in the preface of his organ work *La nativité du Seigneur* (1935).

[17]Messiaen, *The Technique of My Musical Language*, p. 58. "Modes à transpositions limitées" (Messiaen, *Technique de mon langage musical* p. 51).

[18]Messiaen also used enharmonic equivalents.

[19]Messiaen, *Music and Color*, p. 49. "L'impossibilité des transpositions est aussi de la couleur qui est d'ailleurs liée à cette impossibilité" (Messiaen, *Musique et couleur*, p. 52).

[20]*Ibid.*, p. 64. "Rochers bleu-violet, parsemés de petits cubes gris, bleu de cobalt, bleu de Prusse foncé, avec quelques reflets pourpre violacé, or, rouge, rubis, et des étoiles mauves, noires, blanches. La dominante est: bleu-violet" (*Ibid.*, p. 68).

[21]*Ibid.* "Spirales d'or et d'argent, sur fond de bandes verticales brunes et rouge rubis. Dominante: or et brun" (*Ibid.*).

[22]*Ibid.* "Feuillages vert clair et vert prairie, avec des taches de bleu, d'argent et d'orangé rougeâtre. Dominante: vert" (*Ibid.*).

[23]Rössler, *op. cit.*, p. 54.

[24]Messiaen, *Technique de mon langage musical*, p. 52. Stravinsky's use of the arrangement of intervals found in Messiaen's mode 2 is often referred to as the octatonic scale.

See Richard Taruskin, "Chernomor to Kashchei: Harmonic Sorcery; or, Stravinsky's 'Angle'," *Journal of the American Musicological Society*, XXXVIII, no. 1 (Spring 1985): 72-142.

[25]"Un langage d'amour mystique . . . aux ordonnances multicolores" (Messiaen, *Vingt regards sur l'Enfant-Jésus* [Paris: Durand, 1947], p. i).

[26]Messiaen, *The Technique of My Musical Language*, p. 64. "Dans la atmosphère de plusieurs tonalités à la fois, *sans polytonalité*—le compositeur étant libre de donner la prédominance à l'une des tonalités, ou de laisser l'impression tonale flottante" (Messiaen, *Technique de mon langage musical*, p. 57).

[27]*Ibid.*, 64. "Peut hésiter entre les quatre tonalités majeures de do, mi bémol, fa dièse et la" (*Ibid.*, p. 57).

[28]Rössler, *op. cit.*, p. 118 [slightly edited].

[29]Messiaen, *Music and Color*, p. 31. "Nous sommes absorbés par le Christ" (Messiaen, *Musique et couleur*, p. 33).

[30]Messiaen has not described the exact colors that he saw for this particular use of the notes which form the tonic added sixth chord in F♯ major. More information will be available upon the publication of the seventh volume of his *Traité de rythme, de couleur, et d'ornithologie*, which is currently being published posthumously by Leduc under the direction of his widow, Yvonne Loriod (vol. 1, 1994; vol. 2, 1995; vol. 3, 1996). Volume seven will be devoted to Messiaen's explanation of his sound-color perception in his music.

[31]Messiaen, *Music and Color*, p. 42. "De certains violets, de certains bleus et du pourpre violacé" (Messiaen, *Musique et couleur*, p. 45).

[32]Rössler, *op. cit.*, p. 118.

[33]Messiaen, *Musique et couleur*, pp. 150-151.

[34]Claude Samuel, *Entretiens avec Olivier Messiaen* (Paris: Pierre Belfond, 1967), p. 43.

[35]Messiaen, *Conférence de Notre-Dame* (Paris: Alphonse Leduc, 1978), p. 14.

[36]Rössler, *op. cit.*, p. 66. "Éblouissement perpétuel" (Messiaen, *Notre-Dame*, p. 15).

[37]"Une éternelle musique de couleurs, une éternelle couleur de musiques" (*Ibid.*).

[38]Rössler, *op. cit.*, p. 79.

[39]"C'est une de mes découvertes préférées. Comme cela se passe dans beaucoup de découvertes, je n'ai fait que retrouver une chose qui existait déjà, en puissance sinon en fait. Cependant, malgré le très ancien *"dhenkî* " hindou . . . et l'antique *"amphimacre"* grec . . . qui sont, en date, les premiers rythmes non rétrogradables connus—personne ne pensait à établir une théorie musicale de ces rythmes et encore moins à les mettre en pratique" (Messiaen, *Traité de rythme, de couleur, et d'ornithologie (1949-1992)*, vol. II [Paris: Alphonse Leduc, 1995], p. 7).

[40]Messiaen, *Music and Color*, p. 77. "Un coup de chance" (Messiaen, *Musique et couleur*, p. 82).

[41]"Tous les sens" (*Ibid.*).

[42]"Le rythme non rétrogradable" (Messiaen, *Conférence de Kyoto* [Paris: Alphonse Leduc, 1988], p. 2).

[43]Messiaen, *Traité de rythme, de couleur, et d'ornithologie (1949-1992)*, vol. I (Paris: Alphonse Leduc, 1994), pp. 288-289.

[44]"Dhenkî est un mot bengali désignant un appareil pour le décorticage du riz. Cet appareil est généralement manuvré par 2 femmes, l'une à droite, l'autre à gauche, l'appareil entre les deux comme ici le laghu est placé entre les 2 guru. Notre tâla reproduit peut-être aussi le mouvement imprimé à l'appareil par les 2 femmes, pendant le décorticage. . . . Il est sans doute très ancien, comme tous les rythmes basés sur le chiffre 5, nombre des doigts de la main. Le Dhenkî (je le répète avec force) est le plus ancien, le plus simple et le plus naturel des rythmes non rétrogradables" (*Ibid.*).

[45]"Valeur centrale libre" (Messiaen, *Technique de mon langage musical*, p. 12).

[46]"Tous les rythmes, divisibles en 2 groupes rétrogradés l'un par rapport à l'autre, avec '*valeur centrale commune*', sont non rétrogradables" (*Ibid.*).

[47]This rhythm is taken from m. 6 of the "Regard de l'Eglise d'amour" in the *Vingt regards* and will be examined further in the next section. In *Traité*, vol. II, pp. 26, 29, Messiaen shows other non-retrogradable rhythms which use the Hindu *dhenkî* as the common central value.

[48]"Tirent leur force d'une impossibilité temporelle" (Messiaen, *Traité*, vol. II, p. 7).

[49]"Tirent leur force d'une impossibilité sonore" (*Ibid.*).

[50]Rössler, *op. cit.*, p. 42.

[51]Messiaen, *Music and Color*, p. 77 [slightly edited]. "Dernier symbole: ce moment que je vis, cette pensée qui me traverse, ce mouvement que j'accomplis, ce temps que je frappe: il y a l'éternité avant, l'éternité après: c'est un rythme non rétrogradable" (Messiaen, *Musique et couleur*, p. 82).

[52]Messiaen's analysis of the opening of the "Regard de l'Eglise d'amour" appears in *Traité*, vol. II, p. 30; his analysis of the entire *regard* appears in the same volume, pp. 492-509.

[53]Messiaen, *Musique et couleur*, p. 84.

[54]Messiaen, *Traité*, vol. II, p. 8. Messiaen does occasionally repeat a non-retrogradable rhythm in succession in his music (e.g. "Regard de l'Esprit de joie" in the *Vingt regards*). Presumably, he does so for other musical reasons.

[55]In *Traité*, vol. I, pp. 331-332, Messiaen compares this process of augmentation to the *Mátsya* found in the Karnatic theory of South India. Although this theory was unknown to him when he was composing the *Vingt regards*, he often felt that he was able to in-stinctively use different aspects of Indian rhythms in his music. This view followed his belief in a higher truth which guided destiny, a belief which included a fascination with coincidences.

[56]Note that this motive is non-retrogradable in the melodic sense and not in the rhythmic sense because the last note of the measure is an eighth note, which thus cancels the sym-metrical rhythmic balance necessary for the non-retrogradable rhythm.

[57]"En gerbe rapide" (Messiaen, *Vingt regards*, p. 158).

⁵⁸"Les gerbes de nuit" (*Ibid.*, p. iv).

⁵⁹In their physical movements, although the notes they play are not exact inversions of each other, the hands are mirror images of one another, adding a kinetic aspect of non-retrogradability.

⁶⁰Messiaen meticulously fingered these passages to reflect his palindromic intentions and points out the symmetrical fingerings in his analysis in *Traité*, vol. II, p. 30. In the development of the non-retrogradable melody (mm. 3, 5), he is only able to approximate this effect because the left hand must occasionally use the fingering 2/5 as the counterpart to the right hand fingering of 4/2.

⁶¹"C'est peut-être en architecture que nous trouverons les plus beaux, les plus simples et les plus puissants rythmes non rétrogradables.... Voici l'art gothique: un seul magnifique exemple tiré de la Cathédrale de Chartres: le portail Royal et ses trois portes. Grosso modo, l'ensemble des trois portes est non rétrogradable" (Messiaen, *Traité*, vol. II, p. 11).

⁶²"Hors du Temps" (*Hommage à Messiaen*, p. 3).

⁶³Messiaen, *Music and Color*, p. 48. "Incantatoire" (Messiaen, *Musique et couleur*, p. 51).

⁶⁴Messiaen, *The Technique of My Musical Language*, p. 21. "*D'arc-en-ciel théologique*" (Messiaen, *Technique de mon langage musical*, p. 13).

⁶⁵"Pensons maintenant à l'auditeur de notre musique modale et rythmique: il n'aura pas le temps, au concert, de vérifier les non-transpositions et les non-rétrogradations, et, à ce moment-là, ces questions ne l'intéresseront plus: être séduit, tel sera son unique désir. Et c'est précisément ce qui se produira: il subira malgré lui le charme étrange des impossibilités: un certain effet d'ubiquité tonale dans la non-transposition, une certaine unité de mouvement (où commencement et fin se confondent parce qu'identiques) dans la non-rétrogradation, toutes choses qui l'amèneront progressivement à cette sorte '*d'arc-en-ciel théologique*' qu'essaie d'être le langage musical dont nous cherchons édification et théorie" (*Ibid.*).

⁶⁶"*Il n'y aura plus de Temps*" (Messiaen, *Traité*, vol. I, p. 8).

⁶⁷Messiaen, *Conférence de Kyoto*, p. 2.

⁶⁸Rössler, *op. cit.*, p. 41.

⁶⁹"Permutations symétriques" (Messiaen, *Traité*, vol. III, p. 7).

⁷⁰"Une gamme chromatique de durées" (*Ibid.*, p. 13).

⁷¹Example 8 is taken from *Traité*, vol. III, p. 14.

⁷²Example 9 is taken from *Traité*, vol. III, p. 14.

⁷³The term interversion is an earlier version of the later, more specific, term permutation; Messiaen seems to use both terms interchangeably when referring to the symmetrical permutations.

⁷⁴Example 10 is taken from *Traité*, vol. III, p. 15.

⁷⁵The number of possible permutations for a set of 32 elements can be calculated by the following formula: 32! or 1 x 2 x 3 x ...32 = 263130836933693530167218012160000000.

Messiaen shows the mathematical process for this calculation for the numbers 2-12 in *Traité*, vol. III, p. 7.

[76]Messiaen presents all 36 permutations in *Traité*, vol. III, pp. 16-38.

[77]Messiaen explains his numerical choices in *Traité*, vol. III, p. 14.

[78]Messiaen's analysis of *Chronochromie* appears in *Traité*, vol. III, pp. 79-120.

[79]Messiaen, *Traité*, vol. III, p. 38.

[80]Example 11 is taken from *Traité*, vol. III, p. 39. [The typographical omission of the tie over the first two values in m. 2 of the second permutation has been corrected.]

[81]See note 65 above.

[82]"Le monnayage" is Messiaen's own term which seems to translate into a coining or minting of longer values into subdivided smaller ones.

[83]Messiaen, *Music and Color*, p. 135. "Par le monnayage, par le timbre, par les races d'accords" (Messiaen, *Musique et couleur*, p. 146).

[84]*Ibid.*, 136. "Pour apprécier les petites différences entre les grandes durées" (*Ibid.*, p. 147).

[85]Messiaen presents a brief explanation of these chords and their colors in *Chronochromie* in *Traité*, vol. III, pp. 84-88. A more detailed description will appear in the forthcoming vol. VII.

[86]"Jaune pâle, mauve,—rose cuivré, gris perle" (Messiaen, *Traité*, vol. III, p. 85).

[87]"Or jaune éclatant, violet pourpre taché de blancheur, or et noir" (*Ibid.*, p. 88).

[88]Messiaen, *Music and Color*, p. 136. "Les durées et les permutations de durées rendues sensibles par des colorations sonores (les unes expliquant les autres): c'est bien une 'couleur du temps', une *Chronochromie*" (Messiaen, *Musique at couleur*, p. 147).

[89]Rössler, *op. cit.*, p. 40. This is an English translation of Messiaen's address at the conferring of the *Praemium Erasmianum* on June 25, 1971, in Amsterdam.

[90]Messiaen, *Music and Color*, p. 48 [slightly edited]. "C'est là le charme des impossibilités... Elles possèdent une puissance occulte, une emprise chiffrée, temporelle et sonore; on a dit que certaines de mes uvresavaient sur le public un pouvoir incantatoire: je n'ai rien d'un magicien et ce pouvoir incantatoire provient non pas bêtement des répétitions comme on l'a prétendu, mais peut-être de ces impossibilités encloses dans telle ou telle formule" (Messiaen, *Musique et couleur*, p. 51).

[91]See note 2 above.

[92]Rössler, *Contributions*, p. 10. "La seule réalité" (*Hommage à Messiaen*, p. 3).

[93]See note 2 above.

[94]Rössler, *Contributions*, p. 10. "Comme image, comme reflet, comme symbole" (*Hommage à Messiaen*, p. 3).

[95]See note 9 above.

[96]*The Messiaen Companion*, ed. Peter Hill (Portland: Amadeus Press, 1995), p. 303.

[97]This analogy focuses on the symmetrical groups in each innovation and follows Messiaen's own analogy for the modes of limited transposition and the non-retrogradable rhythms in *Technique de mon langage musical*, p. 13. The modes of limited transposition are composed by dividing the octave into symmetrical groups (groups composed of identical intervallic relationships); the non-retrogradable rhythms are formed by two symmetrical groups (the symmetrical relationship here is a retrograde symmetry); the symmetrical permutations are composed of symmetrical rhythmic interversions (permutations generated sequentially by the same procedure).

[98]In the groups which form the modes, the last note of each group is common with the first of the following group; in the non-retrogradable rhythms, the two outer groups frame a central value common to each group; with the symmetrical permutations, each interversion is a permutation of a common chromatic scale of durations.

[99]It is impossible to transpose the modes beyond a certain number of transpositions because they contain, with each symmetrical group, tiny transpositions within themselves; it is impossible to play the non-retrogradable rhythms in retrograde because these rhythms contain, in their two groups, small retrogradations within themselves; it is impossible to generate all the possible permutations with the symmetrical permutations because they contain, in the procedure of sequentially renumbering and reapplying the reading order to each interversion, small permutations within themselves.

[100]Bernard Gavoty and Olivier Messiaen, "Who are you, Olivier Messiaen?" *Tempo* 58 (Summer 1961), 36. This is an unsigned translation of an interview previously published in the *Journal Musical Français* (1961).

[101]See note 2 above.

Rhythmic Technique and Symbolism in the Music of Olivier Messiaen

Robert Sherlaw-Johnson

INTRODUCTION

Let us not forget that the first, essential element in music is Rhythm, and that Rhythm is first and foremost the change of number and duration. Suppose that there were a single beat in all the universe. One beat; with eternity before it and eternity after it. A before and an after. That is the birth of time. Imagine then, almost immediately, a second beat. Since any beat is prolonged by the silence which follows it, the second beat will be longer than the first. Another number, another duration. That is the birth of Rhythm.[1]

An important point emerges from this statement by Messiaen: that he regarded rhythm, not as a division of time, but as an addition of time-durations. As we do not know whether to expect another beat after the second, or whether it is to be extended indefinitely, this beat must remain undefined. It could be argued, therefore, that the situation that he describes does not give us the birth of rhythm, but simply the birth of duration: a duration that is terminated by the second beat. One could conceive it as being a very simple piece of music consisting of nothing but a beginning and an end: a duration defined in time by two beats. In order to define rhythm, therefore, it would be necessary either to divide this time duration in some way by another beat, or to extend it by adding a third beat after a certain interval of time, which would then provide the termination of the music. The 'piece of music' would now consist of a simple rhythm.

For Messiaen, music, although it exists in time, has the power to bring the listener into contact with eternity. The way in which he organizes and thinks about rhythm is evidence of this—bringing about the end of (musical) time, as he describes it in connection with his *Quatuor pour la fin du temps*. Before discussing the philosophical nature of Messiaen's attitude to rhythm, however, we must first examine the theory and technical aspects.

THE DEVELOPMENT OF RHYTHM
IN MESSIAEN'S MUSIC

French composers from the time of the Middle Ages have had a particular interest in the rhythmic aspects of music. The breaking up of Gregorian chant into rhythmic patterns to form a tenor, or *cantus firmus*, against a free part in the music of the School of Notre Dame in the twelfth century led to the development of the isorhythmic motet, which reached its peak in the work of Guillaume de Machaut at the end of the fourteenth century. At the beginning of the seventeenth century Claude le Jeune was setting poetry following the principles of Greek meter in what was called *vers mesuré*. This was a reaction against the use of regularly occurring accents, and was based not on regular meters, but on the classical principle of long and short feet. Accented syllables were therefore given durations twice the length of short ones. Messiaen acknowledges the influence of Le Jeune's *Printemps* (1603), especially in his work for twelve voices, *Cinq rechants* (1948), but it was Marcel Dupré and Maurice Emmanuel, two of Messiaen's teachers at the Paris Conservatoire, who first introduced him to Greek poetic meters.

In 1924, Lavignac published his *Encyclopédie de la musique et dictionnaire du conservatoire,*[2] which contained in volume 1 an article on Indian music at the end of which was printed a table of 120 *deçi-tâlas* (rhythms of the provinces), collected by the thirteenth-century Indian musician Sharngadeva.[3] It was while he was at the Conservatoire that Messiaen first discovered these rhythms, although they did not appear in his music until *La Nativité du Seigneur* for organ (1935). Another early rhythmic influence was Stravinsky's *Sacre du printemps*, which he first analyzed in 1930. In this work, the expansion and contraction of rhythmic cells breaks up the regularity of metrical pulse; this provided the basis for Messiaen's treatment of rhythmic patterns from this time onwards.

Each of these *deçi-tâlas* in Sharngadeva's table is given a name in Sanskrit and they range from the basic number 1 (*aditâla*), consisting of a single value, to the longest, number 35 (*simhanandana*). In practice, Messiaen used less than half the number of rhythms on the table and initially selected a few with special characteristics, which formed the basis of his own rhythmic technique in general. His rhythmic theories are set out more fully in *Technique de mon langage musical,*[4] which he published in 1944 to explain his compositional methods up to that time. The most important features were the concepts of added values, irregular augmentations and diminutions, and non-retrogradable (palindromic)[5] rhythms; all of these relate to particular features of Sharngadeva's rhythms.

The three *deçî-tâlas* that Messiaen uses most frequently are number 93 (*râgavardhana*), number 22 (*candrakalâ*), and number 88 (*lakskmîça*).[6]

EXAMPLE 1

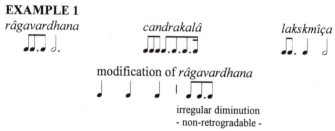

The first of these appears more often in a modified form by turning it backwards and dividing the resulting first long value into three equal values. In this form, the rhythm consists of a cell of three equal values, followed by a cell of three half-values, with a short value added to the second duration of the second cell to make an irregular diminution of the first cell. The second cell is also a non-retrogradable rhythm. *Candrakalâ* is formed by taking three equal values, following them by an augmentation by 1½, and adding a final value, this time in the form of a sixteenth-note. *Lakskmîça* shows a more irregular form of augmentation, the first two values, 2:3 units, being augmented irregularly to form 4:8 units. Another feature of *lakskmîça* is the successive addition of a unit value to form the first three durations: 2:3:4. Messiaen extends this principle in some pieces by creating a rhythm consisting of arithmetically increasing or decreasing values (1:2:3:4..... etc.). He was not the first to use this device, however, as there is an earlier isolated use of it at the beginning of Stravinsky's *Les Noces* (1914–15), where the cymbal part begins with a value of seven units, which is then reduced progressively by one unit at each successive stroke. Stravinsky also made use of non-retrogradable rhythms in *Sacre du printemps* (1913). A notable example occurs in the trumpet part in the Introduction to the Second Part, by expanding a non-retrogradable rhythm from the center, a treatment that was also much used by Messiaen in connection with these rhythms.

EXAMPLE 2:   Stravinsky, *Le Sacre du printemps*, seconde partie, introduction

(This example has been renotated to clarify the rhythm by eliminating the ties.)

The use of added values often gives a flexibility and sense of time-stretching in Messiaen's melodies. Some early examples appear to start from a more regularly metrical basis but achieve a sense of freedom without losing their sense of rhythmic shape. In the following example from *Chants de terre et de ciel*, the use of added values enhances the dance-like nature of the music, which would otherwise sound very four-square:

added values at *; without added values, showing the basic 2/4 meter:

EXAMPLE 3:   *Chants de terre et de ciel*, III "Danse du bébé-Pilule"

On the other hand, in a melody that already has the ametrical characteristics of Gregorian chant, they enhance the sense of timelessness and prolongation into eternity, as in the following example from the same work:

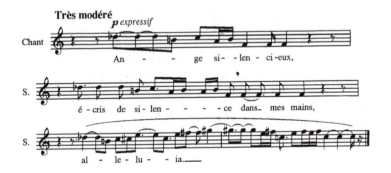

EXAMPLE 4:   *Chants de terre et de ciel*, II "Antienne du silence"

In the *Quatuor pour la Fin du Temps*, composed in a prisoner-of-war camp in 1940, Messiaen's use of rhythm took on a new degree of sophistication. The work was written during what must have been the most stressful period of his life; it is natural, therefore, that it should evoke in its symbolism the book of the Apocalypse and a vision of the end of time. For Messiaen, the title centers around a quotation from the seventh chapter of the Apocalypse: "And the angel which I saw stand upon the sea and upon the earth lifted up his hand to heaven, and sware by him that liveth for ever and ever.... that there should be time no longer."[7] There is a double meaning intended here as Messiaen also applies it to the end of musical time (i.e., regular metrical time), which has been destroyed by means of his use of rhythm. This work is the first to make considerable use of superimposition of different rhythmic patterns and to combine these with harmonic sequences that do not coincide in length with the rhythmic sequences. The first movement, *Liturgie de cristal*, uses, in the piano part, the three rhythms quoted above in succession forming 17 durations, defined by a sequence of 29 chords. On each repetition these overlap; to complete the sequence back to its starting point would take $17 \times 29 = 493$ chords, much longer than the actual movement. The resemblance between what Messiaen does here and medieval isorhythmic techniques is striking, but Messiaen himself, while emphasizing the importance of the dissociation of rhythm from harmony and melody in this work, denied any knowledge of the work of medieval composers at the time of its composition.[8] In addition he superimposes in the cello part a complex non-retrogradable rhythm of eighteen values and a melodic sequence of five notes. When the rhythm is extended by repetition throughout the movement, it is found to contain two other non-retrogradable rhythms embedded in it. The following example, on the next page, quotes the beginning of the piano and cello parts from this movement.

In the last movement of *Visions de l'Amen* for two pianos (1943), Messiaen introduces rhythmic canons, a technique that he extends further in *Regard du Fils sur le Fils*, the fifth movement of *Vingt regards sur l'Enfant-Jésus* for piano (1944), in which he uses a mensural canon where each hand has the same rhythmic sequence as in *Liturgie de cristal*, but the left hand values are 1½ times those of the right hand. In this case the chord sequences in each hand coincide with the rhythmic sequence. The process of superimposition of rhythmic and harmonic sequences reaches a very high degree of complexity in the first movement of the *Turangalîla-Symphonie* (1946–48) where *râgavardhana*, combined with a sequence of thirteen chords in the strings, is superimposed on *lakskmîça*, combined with fourteen chords in the woodwind.

EXAMPLE 5: *Quatuor pour la Fin du Temps*, 1. *Liturgie de cristal*

These two strands are heard simultaneously with a complex non-retro-gradable rhythm on the side drum, built up of cells of 7 and 17 six-teenth-note units and a 'chromatic' rhythm on the cymbal, contracting and expanding in lengths of seventeen to seven and back by the sub-traction or addition of a sixteenth-note unit.

For the composer, a problem arises in the use of such complex overlays of rhythms and harmonies: how is the process to be termina-ted? If the combination of rhythm and harmonies in the piano part of *Liturgie de cristal* were allowed to continue to its logical conclusion to coincide with the completion of a non-retrogradable sequence in the cello, the music would last over two hours at the tempo indicated (about ♪ = 54); the example from *Turangalîla* would last considerably longer. In fact, in each case Messiaen relegates the rhythmic process to the background and arbitrarily cuts it short, regardless of whether a particu-lar sequence or even an individual duration has reached its full conclu-sion. In *Liturgie de cristal* the cello rhythm is completed, but the piano finishes on the twenty-third chord of the sequence and the fourteenth rhythmic value is prolonged from three to five units. As a result, Messiaen's isorhythm (if one may borrow the medieval term) forms a 'modal' background to the texture, and plays no structural part in the composition. The course and duration of the movement is determined by what is happening in the foreground: bird song in the clarinet and violin in *Liturgie de cristal*, and a free expansion and contraction of rhythmic cells in the first movement from *Turangalîla*.

The background rhythm in *Liturgie de cristal*, taken to its logical conclusion, can be taken as symbolic of eternity (especially if one considers that it could then be subject to endless repetition); in using only an incomplete portion of the whole process, Messiaen is giving us a glimpse into eternity. The eternal is brought into the world, into time, to afford a glance at what is to become the ultimate destiny of mankind.

Another rhythmic feature to which Messiaen draws particular attention in his early music is that of the *personnages rythmiques* or rhythmic characters. He cites the example of three characters on a stage, one (the protagonist) acts by striking the second (the antagonist) and a third looks on, remaining inactive. Transferring this example to rhythm, he takes one value that expands, a second that decreases, and a third that remains constant. By 1950, the process was extended from single values to complete rhythmic groups. In *Offertoire*, the second movement of *Messe de la Pentecôte* (1950), and in *Reprises par interversion*, the first movement of *Livre d'orgue* (1952), it is applied to Sharngadeva rhythms with a resulting distortion of their durations—although the relative relationships of their values (long, medium, short) remain constant. At the same time the three *personnages* are permutated so that each time they occur in a different order. There are twelve different pitches in each group and these retain their durational values throughout the movement.

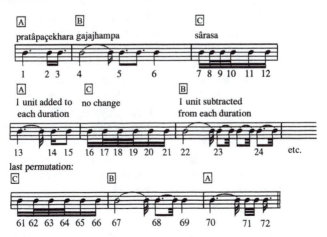

EXAMPLE 6: *Livre d'orgue*, 1. *Reprises par interversion*

A further permutation is applied in the second section of *Reprises par interversion*, where the values (and pitches) of the first three permutations alternate with those of the last three in retrograde, so that one is moving from the extremes of the passage to the center—a process which Messiaen compares to the closing of a fan.

EXAMPLE 7: *Reprises par interversion*
(Même musique, en éventail fermé, des extrèmes au centre)
(The same music, in the form of a closed fan, from the outside to the center)

The principle of *personnages rythmiques* is sometimes extended to apply to whole phrases or entire sections of a piece. One of the *Préludes* (1929) for piano, *Instants défunts*, consists of a simple ABABA-Coda form in which the A sections decrease and the B sections increase in duration. The coda, which uses different music from the rest of the piece, provides the stabilizing element which is not repeated, and therefore does not change.

Following the composition of *Turangalîla*, Messiaen's experimentation with rhythm took a different direction. In 1949 and 1950 he composed four piano pieces called *Études de rythme*, the most influential of which was the second, *Mode de valeurs et d'intensités*. This piece arose from his dissatisfaction with Second-Viennese-School serialism, which he considered illogical in that the serial technique was only applied to pitch, leaving rhythm, dynamics, timbres, and textures unaffected.[9] Although only durations and intensities are mentioned in the title of this work, the *'mode'* actually consists of 36 pitches arranged into three 12-note series, each pitch being fixed at a particular register within each series. One of 24 durations, 7 intensities, and 12 modes of attack are then assigned to each pitch, and this combination is retained whenever the particular pitch appears in the piece. Although the order in which pitches appear in the piece is free (there is no overall attempt to regard any of the pitch-series as 'rows' in the Schoenbergian sense), the rigidity by which each parameter is assigned to each note creates greater restrictions for the composer than did serial practice before or since. While Messiaen does make a limited use of similar techniques in his later music, it was left to his pupils, principally Boulez and Stockhausen, to develop the idea further.

The notes of the first three rhythmic cells form a twelve-note series. Messiaen, however, was never really interested in manipulating such series in the manner of the Second Viennese School. It was more important for him that methods of systematic permutation of such pitches should be employed, rather than strict interval relationships arising from the concept of serialism. The same applies to duration. By the time of *Chronochromie* for orchestra (1960), he was employing a limited closed set of permutations (interversions), which resulted from a combination of smaller sets of cyclic permutations. A cyclic permutation is one where elements change places in a fixed order. For example: 1234 - 3142 - 4321 - 2413 - 1234 is a cyclic permutation of four elements: the first element moves to second place, the second element to fourth place, the third element to first place, and the fourth element to third place, producing four permutations in all. Messiaen uses a simple combination of two cyclic permutations, one of two durations and one of ten (making twelve durations from 1 to 12 unit sixteenth-notes) in *Île de feu* 2, the fourth of the *Études de rythme* (1950). Since the values 5 and 10 simply interchange at each permutation, this makes a total of ten permutations, as determined by the set of ten durations:

TABLE 1

Initial series:	12	11	10	9	8	7	6	5	4	3	2	1
Permutations:												
I	6	7	5	8	4	9	3	10	2	11	1	12
II	3	9	10	4	2	8	11	5	1	7	12	6
III	11	8	5	2	1	4	7	10	12	9	6	3
IV	7	4	10	1	12	2	9	5	6	8	3	11
V	9	2	5	12	6	1	8	10	3	4	11	7
VI	8	1	10	6	3	12	4	5	11	2	7	9
VII	4	12	5	3	11	6	2	10	7	1	9	8
VIII	2	6	10	11	7	3	1	5	9	12	8	4
IX	1	3	5	7	9	11	12	10	8	6	4	2
X	12	11	10	9	8	7	6	5	4	3	2	1

In *Chronochromie* he creates a more complex set by dividing a series of 32 durations into five groups of 1, 3, 4, 6, and 18 values each. Because the different groups of permutations circulate only amongst themselves (19, 20, and 21 for instance), the total number of possible permutations becomes restricted to 36 (36 is the lowest common denominator of 1, 3, 4, 6, and 18). The value 27 always remains in the same place, forming the group of only one element (group 'a' in the following table); 19, 20, and 21, circulate between themselves, making the group of three ('b'); 2, 8, 11, and 28 form the group of four ('c'); 1,

3, 5, 7, 10, and 26 form the group of six ('d'); and the remaining values form the group of 18 ('e'). Only 4 is not a factor of 18, making it necessary to cycle twice through the group of eighteen elements to complete a cycle of 36 permutations. The following table shows the first three permutations of the complete set of 36. The remaining permutations can easily be deduced by moving the duration in third place to first place, the one in twenty-eighth place to second place and so on. The letters above the table indicate to which of the five groups each number belongs.

TABLE 2[10] (please read sideways)

	d	c	d	e	d	e	d	c	e	d	c	-	-	-	e	-	-	-	-	b	-	-	-e-	-	-	d	a	c	-	-e-	-	-
	1	2	3	4	5	6	7	8	9	10	11	12	13	14	15	16	17	18	19	20	21	22	23	24	25	26	27	28	29	30	31	32
I	3	28	5	30	7	32	26	2	25	1	8	24	9	23	16	17	18	22	21	19	20	4	31	6	29	10	27	11	15	14	12	13
II	5	11	7	14	26	13	10	28	29	3	2	6	25	31	17	18	22	4	20	21	19	30	12	32	15	1	27	8	16	23	24	9
III	7	8	26	23	10	9	1	11	15	5	28	32	19	12	18	22	4	30	19	20	21	14	24	13	16	3	27	2	17	31	6	25

There are seven movements in this work: *Introduction, Strophe 1, Antistrophe 1, Strophe 2, Antistrophe 2, Epode, and Coda.* Not all the possible permutations of the rhythmic series are used: the first, second, third, and twenty-second, twenty-third, and twenty-fourth series appear complete in *Strophe 1* and *Strophe 2* respectively; the thirteenth, fourteenth, and fifteenth series are divided into three parts and distributed throughout the *Introduction* and *Coda;* fragments of the seventh, eighth, ninth, and twenty-eighth, twenty-ninth, and thirtieth series are incorporated into each of the *Antistrophes*. In *Strophe 1* and *Strophe 2*, the three superimposed permutations are colored by different metal percussion instruments and different types of chord sequences in the strings. It is principally from these movements that the title of the work, which means *Color of Time*, is derived.

A further treatment of rhythm, which appears first in *Messe de la Pentecôte,* is the use of 'irrational values'. These are applied to Greek rhythms in the first movement of this work, to Sharngadeva rhythms in the second movement of *Livre d'orgue,* and again to Greek rhythms in the second movement of *Sept Haïkaï* (1962). The use of the term 'irrational' is analogous to, but not identical with, the mathematical concept of 'irrational numbers'. In the case of rhythm, it implies the division of a series of durations into different numbers of units, so that the rate of flow of the music is effectively subject to rapidly changing tempi. An irrational sequence might be five in the time of four, followed by seven in the time of six, followed by four in the time of three. Although it is always possible to find a smallest unit which would be common to a set of irrational values, this is often so short as to be virtually imperceptible. Examples of two Greek strophes used in this movement are given in example 8, showing the 'irrational' distortion of the original meters.

EXAMPLE 8: *Sept Haïkaï,*
2 *Le parc de Nara et les lanternes de pierre*

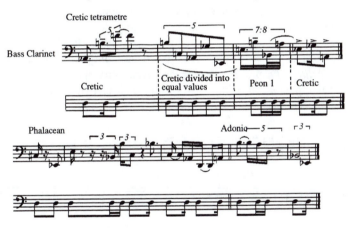

For many years, Messiaen was unaware of the meanings of the names of the rhythms in Sharngadeva's table, but by the 1960s, they take on a symbolic role in his music by virtue of an association between their Hindu meanings and Christianity. A striking example of this symbolism occurs in *Et expecto resurrectionem mortuorum* for wind and percussion (1964). In the second movement, rhythm number 8 is used, *simhavikrama* (example 9), which means "the power of the lion." This rhythm also contains rhythm number 51 in Sharngadeva's table, *vijaya,* meaning victory. *Simhavikrama* consists of fifteen unit values and, like all Sharngadeva rhythms consisting of five or multiples of five units, is dedicated to the Indian god Shiva. 15, then, equals 3 (the number of the Trinity) times 5 (the number of Shiva). Shiva represents the "death of death" and can therefore be taken as a symbol of Christ who conquered death on the Cross. *Simhavikrama*, for Messiaen, symbolizes the "power of the lion of the tribe of Judah who gained victory over death" (Apoc.5.5).

EXAMPLE 9: *Simhavikrama*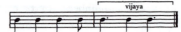

LARGE-SCALE RHYTHMIC CONSIDERATIONS

Messiaen's discussions of rhythm are generally concerned with the manipulation of small-scale durations: the building up of more complex rhythms by the addition of single values. There is evidence, however, from his music that he is concerned with rhythm on a larger scale, whether these are time-spans defined by rhythmic cells (see example 10) or whether they are complete sections (such as in *Instants défunts*, where a simple *personnage rythmique* is applied). The strict proportions of rhythms such as those of Sharngadeva are not used on a large scale, but their shape can play a part in proportioning successive sections. The phrase lengths of the first section of the first movement of *Trois petites liturgies de la Présence Divine* for women's choir, Ondes Martenot, piano, and strings (1943) show a clear rhythmic shape with a certain resemblance to *râgavardhana*:

EXAMPLE 10: *Trois petites liturgies de la Présence Divine,*
1. Antienne de la conversation intérieure

The symmetrical melodic cells of 7 - 8 - 7, 7 - 10 - 7 and 7 - 12 - 7 have the same non-retrogradable shape as the first cell of the Indian rhythm. Taking the three cells together with their rests and adding the longer section that follows, the shape of the whole of *râgavardhana* is formed, somewhat distorted it is true with the third duration only slightly shorter than the second. The total value of each of these sections (including rests) is 40, 54 and 52 quaver units and the following longer section is 80 units.

In his note to an early recording of this work,[11] Luc André-Marcel mentions that the threefold occurrence of symmetrical cell symbolizes the Trinity, and the eventual addition of the fourth longer value symbolizes the extension of the Godhead into the world. Also relevant is Messiaen's own interpretation of the rhythm *gajalîla* (ex. 11), to which the durations of this section also bear a resemblance. The word means 'the elephant's game', giving it an affinity to Ganesha, the Hindu elephant-god. Although Messiaen did not know the meaning of *gajalîla* at this time, in his conversations with Claude Samuel,[12] he says: "The number of the elephant-god: Ganesha - is ... the number 4. *Gajalîla* has four durations, and the fourth, which is dotted, [i.e. 1+ times the length of the previous durations] perhaps represents 'the enlightenment of the mind'.... it is a curious fact that I have always used this rhythm *gajalîla* in this sense; one is led to believe that this combination of durations contains a magic formula..."[13]

EXAMPLE 11: *Gajalîla*

The second section presents a counterpoint of rhythms in the phrase-lengths of the separate soprano, Ondes Martenot, and solo violin parts.

Soprano	51 - 51 - 84 |	51 - 51 - 84 |	51 - 51 - 72 |	51 - 51 - 65
Ondes Mt.	28 - 28 - 42 - 43 |	29 - 43 |	23 - 23 - 83 - 113	
Violin	45 - 45 - 67 -105 |	45 - 60 |	45 - 45 - 67 - 137	

EXAMPLE 12. *Antienne de la conversation intérieure*

Equivalent Sharngadeva rhythms:

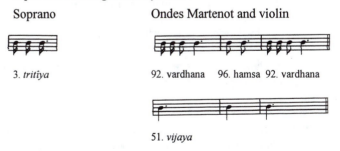

Soprano   Ondes Martenot and violin

3. *tritīya*   92. vardhana   96. hamsa   92. vardhana

51. *vijaya*

The first point to notice here is the repetition of the same rhythmic cell, consisting of three values, in the soprano, with the third value contracted at the third and fourth repetitions. More interesting, however, is

the resemblance between the two instrumental parts, the violin presenting the same rhythmic shape as the Ondes Martenot, but in augmentation. Again there is a resemblance between these various rhythms and
those of Sharngadeva as shown in example 10.[14]

A closer resemblance to *rāgavardhana* occurs in *Par Lui tout a été
fait*, the sixth movement of *Vingt regards sur l'Enfant-Jésus*. The whole
of the first main section of this piece is one long palindromic fugue,
followed by a climactic coda. The three sub-sections of the first main
section, taking the changes of tempo into account form a relationship of
almost exactly 2:3:2. The coda that follows, although not in proportion
to the long value of *rāgavardhana*, creates a sense of accent by virtue
of its climax that is analogous to the accentual effect of the final long
value of the Indian rhythm.

THE ROLE OF SILENCE

Like other composers in the twentieth century, Messiaen has been
aware of the role of silence in a composition. Occasionally silences may
be incorporated into the definition of a rhythm as in the following non-
retrogradable example from the sixth movement of *Turangalîla* where,
except for the first and last values, silences are substituted for sounds
and vice versa in the second half of the rhythm (a technique that was
exploited more by his pupil, Boulez):

(from figure ④ in the score).

EXAMPLE 13: *Turangalîla-Symphonie*:
VI Jardin du sommeil d'amour
Tails up show the original rhythm of the glockenspiel and harp.
Tails down clarify the non-retrogradable rhythm.

The role of silence becomes more important and apparent in later
music where it has an important role in providing a focus for the musical
events that it surrounds. In *Catalogue d'oiseaux* there are occasionally
very long silences, either creating in the mind of the listener a prolongation of what precedes them, or marking off an important event that
follows. In *La Bouscarle*, for instance, silences are used very effectively to offset fragments of chords (from a passage used earlier in the
piece) representing reflections of trees in the water. A three-second
silence divides the first two and a two-and-a-half second silence the

next two. At the end of a piece two long silences separate pairs of chords and the final burst of bird song, creating a greater sense of tension than sounds themselves would create at this point. The lack of rests after the final note of the bird song suggests that there should be no feeling of prolongation of the last chord into the silence that follows, as would be customary at the end of most pieces of music.

EXAMPLE 14a: *La Bouscarle: reflections*
(L'eau reflète les saules et les peupliers)

EXAMPLE 14b: *La Bouscarle: end*

The end of *L'Alouette-Lulu* (The Woodlark), on the other hand, prolongs the last sounds by means of the pedal for a further four seconds approximately. Messiaen adds a comment on the score: *mystérieux, rejoignant le silence*, implying that the piece does not end at the double bar-line, but carries on into silence.

The structural role of silences become more marked in *Et expecto resurrectionem mortuorum*, particularly in III "*L'heure vient où les morts entendront la voix du Fils de Dieu...*" ('The hour will come when the dead will hear the voice of the Son of God.' Jn.5.25). The musical material of this piece is very simple: a passage of bird song (the Uirapuru bird of the Amazon, of which legend says that one hears it at the hour of death), four notes on tubular bells played twice in permutation, a brief rising crescendo build up on a chord for the whole orchestra (3"), and the four bell-notes played on bass instruments out of which emerges a long crescendo and diminuendo on gongs and tam-tam (60"), the whole being repeated. Each of the four main events is offset by a silence and the long crescendo merges into a brief silence before the repetition as well as into the second silence at the end of the piece.[15]

The use of silences to mark out individual events creates a new and more subtle sense of rhythm in Messiaen's music. He returns to the idea again in later works such as the first movement of *Des canyons aux étoiles* (*Le désert*), which consists of a sparse texture of individual ideas, instruments, and sounds: the opening horn solo, various bird songs and calls, the sound of the wind-machine, and the representation of the hoopoe lark (*sirli du désert*), all offset by silences. The song of the hoopoe lark is made up of very high isolated notes, moving between a crotale played with a double-bass bow, piccolo, harmonics on a solo violin, and very short chords in the woodwind who are instructed to make a percussive effect with the keys of the instrument. Although these different sounds are not separated by silence, the effect is to create a sense of bird song against a background of silence of the desert, where nothing else can be heard.

DIEU PARMI NOUS

At the beginning of his *Traité de rythme, de couleur, et d'ornithologie*, the seven-volume treatise on which Messiaen worked from 1949 until his death,[16] he discusses, with the support of quotations from the work of Saint Thomas Aquinas, the difference between eternity and time. Time is not a part of eternity, time and eternity are two absolutely different measures of duration. Time is the measure of what is created, eternity is God himself and is indivisible as God is indivisible.[17] The end of time, a vision of eternity through the suspension of musical time was Messiaen's aim in the *Quatuor pour la fin du temps*, and in the works that immediately preceded it. A regular pulse draws the attention of the listener to an awareness of time, so the destruction of this regularity by the addition of short time values, or the creation of rhythms from the addition of different durations was to provide the contact between the listener and the eternal in order to illustrate the theological concepts involved in Messiaen's composition. It can be argued that, however one organizes rhythm, it is impossible for music to exist outside of time and that bringing about the 'end of musical time' through irregular rhythms is simply an illusion. Much music, however, depends on creating a sense of illusion in the listener—whether it is a vision of a submerged cathedral in a Debussy Prelude, a primitive ritual in *Le Sacre du printemps,* or simply the transporting of the listener from the physical world to a world of some musical experience as would be the case with music with no programmatic or pictorial content. In a certain sense, the illusion becomes the reality, if only for a short space of time.

This is also the aim of liturgy and liturgical music, and it is significant that the musical traditions of the older Christian churches should be ametrical in the sense of avoiding a sense of regular pulse, as for example in Old Roman and Gregorian chant and the liturgical polyphony of the High Renaissance. It is natural that the shape of Gregorian chant should form a constant basis of many of Messiaen's melodies. The use of the introit for the third mass of Christmas, *Puer natus est nobis*, or the gradual *Haec dies*, from the Easter Mass in *Regard de l'Esprit de joie* (no.10 from *Vingt regards sur l'Enfant-Jésus*) for instance, both freely transformed into his own modal language, are appropriate because of the association with the Nativity in the first case and with joy in the second, although the movement itself does not have a specific Easter association. Many other examples occur in all periods of his music.

Much of Messiaen's work takes on a ritual character, even when the content is not Christian. This aspect becomes particularly prominent in *Trois petites liturgies de la Présence Divine*, as the title suggests, and in *La Transfiguration de notre Seigneur Jésus-Christ* for chorus and orchestra (1963–69). These are literally 'liturgies of the concert hall', and his opera *Saint François d'Assise* must be thought of in the same way. Presented as a series of tableaux, rather than acts, the aim of the opera is a meditation on aspects of Saint Francis's life, rather than a dramatized biography. The three works of the mid-1940s—the song-cycle *Harawi*, the *Turangalîla-Symphonie*, and *Cinq rechants* for twelve solo singers—present three ritual presentations of the Tristan and Isolde myth. Again there is a total lack of narrative, but much use of symbolism —symbols of the cosmos, of love, and of death—which, together with the juxtaposition and superimposition of ametrical rhythms (in the sense of being free from a regular pulse), heighten the ritual aspect of these works. Messiaen can be described as a musical theologian since it is his intention to make the listener aware of the mysteries of the Godhead through his music. His aim, he maintained, was not to raise the listener into a mystical experience of God, but to bring God into contact with the listener. Nevertheless, can one really make such a distinction? In listening to his music, and especially perhaps the slow movements such as the second part of *Dyptique* (1930) or *Combat de la Mort et de la Vie* (from *Les Corps glorieux*, 1939), both for organ, or the nineteenth piece from *Vingt regards de l'Enfant-Jésus (Je dors, mais mon cœur veille)*, the latter described by Messiaen as a dialogue of mystical love, can the listener experience a certain degree of mysticism—not as intense as those of the great mystic saints—but at least the beginnings of such an experience? This is the aim of any liturgy of the Church.

When Vladimir, Prince of Kiev, sent emissaries to investigate various forms of worship, they went to the Great Church of the Holy Wisdom in Constantinople. They reported afterwards, "We knew not whether we were in heaven or on earth, for surely there is no such splendor or beauty anywhere upon earth. We cannot describe it to you: only this we know, that God dwells there among men, and that their service surpasses the worship of all other places." This quotation from the Russian Primary Chronicle is cited by Timothy Ware (now Bishop Callistos Ware of the Orthodox Church in Oxford) in his book on the Orthodox Church.[18] He goes on to say, "The Holy Liturgy is something that embraces two worlds at once, for both in heaven and on earth the Liturgy is one and the same—one altar, one sacrifice, one presence. In every place of worship.... as the faithful gather to perform the Eucharist, they are taken up into the 'heavenly places'." In spite of the emphasis on bringing God among men, the ultimate aim, as Bishop Callistos says, is to bring mankind into contact with the experience of heaven, to the contemplation of God, and so it is with Messiaen. The means by which the mystical experience is achieved, however, is not in itself mystical. The experience, if it happens at all, is for the individual worshipper or listener: it is not Messiaen who is the mystic.

NOTES

[1] Olivier Messiaen, from a lecture given at the Conférence de Bruxelles in 1958, published in French, German, and English by Leduc, Paris.

[2] Première Partie, Vol. 1 (Paris: Librairie Delagrave, 1921).

[3] Although the French spelling is Çarngadeva, the English transliteration is preferred here to conform to the spelling of his name in books on Indian music in English. Transliteration of the names of rhythms conform to the French convention of using 'ç' to represent 'sh' to avoid confusion with Messiaen's usage of his own writings. *Deçi-tâla* is therefore pronounced 'deshi-tahl'.

[4] (Paris: Alphonse Leduc, 1944). English translation by John Satterfield (Paris: Leduc, 1956-66).

[5] Although the correct English word for these rhythms would be 'palindromic' (the same forwards as well as backwards), it has become customary to use the Anglicized French word that Messiaen uses: non-retrogradable. There is a subtle extension in meaning as, for Messiaen, the word implies the impossibility of turning the rhythm backwards because it is the same and forms part of what he calls "the charm of impossibilities" in *Technique de mon langage musical*.

[6] It must be emphasized that Messiaen's use of these rhythms bears no relationship to the way they may have been used in Indian music. It would be wrong to talk of 'ethnic' in-

fluence in this connection, as Messiaen simply draws on features of the rhythms that he happens to find useful in connection with his own musical thought.

[7]The translation here is from the King James Bible, which corresponds to the version Messiaen quotes in French. Recent readings, however, replace the phrase "there will be time no longer" with "The time of waiting is over" (Jerusalem Bible, 1968), or a similar wording.

[8]Medieval isorhythm involved the arbitrary application of short rhythmic units to a section of plainchant, the number of rhythmic units (*talea*) not necessarily coinciding with the melodic (*color*). This overlapping sequence of *talea* and *color* was used in the tenor part as the basis of a 2, 3, or 4-part composition, each part having its own melody and rhythm and often a different text as well.

[9]This was not entirely true of Webern's work, but because of Nazi oppression, his later compositions only began to filter through to audiences from 1947 onwards, and little analytical work (if any) was done until the early 1950s.

[10]For the complete table see p. 177 of *Messiaen* by Robert Sherlaw Johnson (London: J.M. Dent and Berkeley, CA: University of California Press, 1974 and 1989; now Oxford: Oxford University Press).

[11]Decretet-Thomson, 270 C 075.

[12]Claude Samuel, *Entretiens avec Olivier Messiaen* (Paris: Editions Pierre Belfond, 1967), chapter III. This book was reissued in an expanded version in 1986 under the title *Olivier Messiaen: musique et couleur*, by the same publisher and in a translation by E. Thomas Glasow (Portland, OR: Amadeus Press, 1994).

[13]The author's own translation.

[14]In some cases there is a resemblance to more than one rhythm in the table when one considers only the relative proportions of the values, which occur elsewhere in Messiaen's work and are chosen because they do not fall into a strict regularly metrical shape.

[15]The timings are calculated from the metronome marks. Individual performances will vary. Although there is no silence actually marked in the score between the tubular bell event and the orchestral chord that follows, the bell sound quickly dies away, creating a silence.

[16]Published posthumously by Alphonse Leduc.

[17]"Le temps est la mesure du créé, l'éternité est Dieu lui-même. L'éternité est indivisible comme Dieu est indivisible. Le temps n'est pas une longueur finie qui rentrerait dans une longueur infinie (l'éternité): c'est un continu en face d'un indivisible (Dieu)." (*Traité de rythme...*, vol. I). There is a contradiction in the use of the word 'eternity' here, compared to its use in the quotation at the beginning of the chapter where he talks of a beat with eternity before and eternity after as being "the birth of time." Composers are not always consistent in the way they use language, and in discussing the philosophy of Messiaen's attitude to time, 'eternity' should be understood in the sense derived from Saint Thomas Aquinas.

[18]Timothy Ware, *The Orthodox Church* (Harmondsworth and Baltimore: Penguin Books, 1963), pp. 269-270. The passage from the *Russian Primary Chronicle* is also cited in *The Orthodox Liturgy* by Hugh Wybrew (SPCK, 1989), pp. 129-130.

PART THREE

**Praising God with
Saint Francis and the Song of Birds**

Saint Thomas Aquinas
and the Theme of Truth
in Messiaen's *Saint François d'Assise*

Camille Crunelle Hill

"God dazzles us by excess of Truth. Music leads us to God for lack of Truth."[1] With this paraphrase from the *Summa theologiae* of Saint Thomas Aquinas, Messiaen states the Theme of Truth in his opera *Saint François d'Assise*. In the course of the spiritual tests and miracles that François encounters, music leads him from lack of understanding toward the truth of God.

In 1975, Messiaen accepted a commission from Rolf Liebermann to compose an opera for the Palais Garnier. For Messiaen, the choice of a subject was not difficult, since he had for many years considered a work based on the life of Saint Francis, and he was thoroughly familiar with histories of the saint. Although he insisted that the work was not autobiographical, the composer identified with the humble saint who searched for the truth of God through his own poetry and music of praise, the songs of the birds, and the celestial music of an angel.[2] The work, entitled *Saint François d'Assise*, opera in 3 acts and 8 tableaux, was premiered in 1983, under the direction of Seiji Ozawa.

Sources for the libretto include the early biographies, the *Fioretti*, the *Considerations on the Holy Stigmata*, and two texts by Saint Francis: the *Cantique des créatures* [*Canticle to the Sun*] and *Louanges avant l'Office* [*Praises before the Office*]. From the Franciscan literature, Messiaen seeks aspects of the legends that bring out the *merveilleux* in the Catholic faith. To this end, he chooses eight tableaux from the saint's life and organizes them into three acts, each of which culminates in a miracle that demonstrates François's growing sanctity and the "progression of grace."[3] As he plots the drama to show the progressive revelation of grace that accompanies François's ascent to sainthood, Messiaen incorporates quotations from the Bible, the *Imitation of Christ*, and Saint Thomas's *Summa theologiae*.

The passage from Saint Thomas Aquinas demonstrates not only Messiaen's religious philosophy, but also his own creative process. He develops the notion of truth by means of a musical Theme of Truth based on his "modes of limited transposition," whose pitches evoke visual colors. From Messiaen's perspective, Saint Thomas's text and his own modes combine sacred truth with visual and tonal color to create a music of "éblouissement" [dazzlement].

TRUTH IN MESSIAEN'S WRITINGS

The subject of truth had emerged in Messiaen's writings long before it appeared in the opera. In 1936, Messiaen focused on the theme of truth in his analysis of Dukas's opera *Ariane et Barbe-Bleue* for an issue of *La Revue musicale* devoted to *hommages* for Dukas. At the outset, Messiaen quotes Ariane, who asks Bluebeard's wives why they demand liberation when they prefer darkness. Messiaen finds that Ariane brings deliverance and light, which he interprets as truth. As a universal symbol of truth, Ariane embraces many religions and philosophies when she offers enlightenment and freedom to Blue-Beard's wives.[4]

Messiaen also identifies a musical Theme of Truth that accompanies the heroine through the opera:

> Dukas paints Truth come to earth, bringing from above its
> infinite and multiform light to the dark depths of humanity,
> by an obstinate movement of descending fourths.[5]

According to Messiaen, the theme arrives with forceful rhythms in the first act and with calm and even rhythmic durations in the second act. In the third act, when Blue-Beard's wives refuse deliverance and truth, the theme first ascends by fifths, then descends by fourths. Messiaen believes that the theme pictures Truth as it ascends to the region of light and looks down with pity on the humans who prefer darkness.[6] Like Saint Thomas's passage, this thematic description shows truth as a light too dazzling to be comprehended by humans. Through his analysis, Messiaen also relates the philosophical idea of truth to a musical theme, a process he would later apply to his own opera.

In the introduction to *Technique de mon langage musical* (1944), Messiaen again explains the connection between truth and music. He states that he seeks in his composition "...a *true* music, that is, spiritual, a music that is an act of faith; a music that touches on all subjects without ceasing to touch on God."[7]

In a conversation with Claude Samuel that took place before the composition of the opera, Messiaen identified his goal as the expression in music of the truths of the Catholic faith.[8] From this faith he cherished since his childhood, Messiaen took delight in referring to sacred texts as "...de merveilleux contes de fées, vrais!" [wonderful, true fairy tales].[9] He continually affirmed his confidence in the miraculous events related in the Bible and Catholic tradition. In *Saint François d'Assise*, Messiaen expresses the idea of truth related both to the *merveilleux* in the Catholic faith and to the power of music.

THE TEXT OF SAINT THOMAS AQUINAS

Messiaen manifested a durable fascination with the writings of Saint Thomas Aquinas, and he had already used the *Summa theologiae* as a text source for *La Transfiguration de notre Seigneur Jésus-Christ* (1972). The passage Messiaen chooses for the opera comes from Part I-II of the *Summa theologiae*, a section that deals with religious ceremony. The original Latin reads:

> ...Sicut poetica non capiuntur a ratione humana propter defectum veritatis qui est in eis, ita etiam ratio humana perfecte capire non potest divina propter excedentem ipsorum veritatem. Et ideo utrobique opus est repræsentatione per sensibiles figuras.

> [...Just as human reason fails to grasp the import of poetical utterance on account of its deficiency in truth, neither can it grasp divine things perfectly on account of their superabundance of truth; and therefore in both cases there is need of representation by sensible figures.][10]

Messiaen interprets the dazzling effect God's "superabundance of truth" produces on human observers with the paraphrase: "Dieu nous éblouit par excès de Vérité." [God dazzles us by excess of truth.] This concept of dazzlement conforms with Saint Thomas's idea that the human eye is not capable of taking in the Truth and Light of God, which radiate a brilliance beyond man's capacity to perceive.[11]

In addition, Messiaen offers *music* as a sensible figure to represent truth: "La musique nous porte à Dieu par défaut de Vérité." [Music carries us to God for lack of Truth.] The original passage expresses Saint Thomas's belief that our minds are incapable of comprehending God except through *phantasms* we can grasp.[12] In the *Summa theologiae* II-II, Saint Thomas again emphasizes the idea that man must be led toward God through signs that can be observed in the world of the senses. Objects humans can touch and concepts they can understand bring about the spiritual actions that draw them toward God.[13] As Messiaen interprets the passage for the opera, music added to the deficient language of poetry represents God to Saint François's limited understanding. Through such celestial sounds as bird-songs and the music of an angel, God dazzles Saint François with a glimpse of truth.

Beyond demonstrating his knowledge of the writings of both Saint Thomas and Saint Francis, Messiaen does not explain the relationship between the great scholar and the simple mendicant. One significant link between the two thirteenth-century Christian leaders is found in a book from Messiaen's personal library, *Lire François d'Assise*, by Père Louis-Antoine. Messiaen mentioned this commentary on the poetry of Saint Francis in his interview with Samuel,[14] and Madame Messiaen listed it as one of the composer's sources for the opera.[15] Louis-Antoine's admiration of Saint Francis as poet-musician and his own reference to the Saint Thomas passage influenced Messiaen in his creation of the opera text. For Louis-Antoine, in the chapter "La beauté et l'art," images in the poetry of Saint Francis fulfill Saint Thomas's quest for phantasms that enrich man's understanding of God. Louis-Antoine also cites the *Summa theologiae* I-II, q 101, a 2, ad 2 as a source of Thomas Aquinas's notion concerning excess and lack of truth. Phrases from Louis-Antoine's French translation appear in Messiaen's opera text:

> Les réalités poétiques ne peuvent pas être saisies par la raison à cause d'un défaut de vérité qui est en elles; les réalités divines, à cause d'un excès de vérité. Par-là, les unes et les autres, pour des motifs opposés, sont obligés de faire appel à des images....[16]

> [Poetic realities cannot be grasped by reason because of the lack of truth in them, divine realities because of an excess of truth. Therefore both, for opposite reasons, are obliged to call up images.]

Louis-Antoine goes on to explain that man understands divine reality better through poetic images and symbols than through abstract concepts. As an example, he quotes Keats's *Endymion*, saying that a "thing of beauty" leads to God. Particularly in the *Cantique des créatures*, Louis-Antoine praises Saint Francis's personification of brother Wind, sister Water, brother Fire, mother Earth, brother Sun, sister Moon, and finally sister Death. He believes these images overpower humans and give them an appreciation of the beauty of the creation. Saint Francis's repeated "frère" and "sœur" in addressing the creatures

FIGURE 1: The Angel in Olivier Messiaen's *Saint François d'Assise*.
Mise en scène: Sandro Sequi, set and costumes: Giuseppe Crisolini-
Malatesta, Opéra Nationale de Paris, Palais Garnier, 1983.
Photo: Jacques Moatti.
Reproduced with the permission of l'Opéra National de Paris.

also adds a sense of ritual to the poem.[17] Moreover, for Louis-Antoine, poetry relates to music, since both produce images that communicate to the human mind. His ideas correlate with Messiaen's choice of *musique* to interpret the Saint Thomas text:

> It is therefore the superabundance of truth that the divine reality contains which requires the use of images and symbols by the human mind, incapable of expressing the infinite richness by the sole means of its concepts. Also, all the literary genres have found a place in the Bible, including lyricism. Poetry united to music has sung the praise of God.[18]

In the libretto of *Saint François*, Messiaen refers to three ideas from Louis-Antoine's commentary: the Saint Thomas Aquinas quotation, the words of Keats, and the interpretation that images and symbols lead to God. Relating these subjects to spiritual growth, Messiaen conceives of music and poetic images as phantasms that lead François toward the truth of God.

During an interview with Samuel, the composer explained his view of Saint Thomas's meaning, as he applies the quotation to his own views on faith and music expressed in the opera:

> The arts, and especially music, but also literature and painting, permit us to penetrate into domains that are not unreal, but beyond reality.... Now, I think that music, even more than literature and painting, is capable of expressing this aspect of the dream, fairy tales, the hereafter, this "surreal" aspect of the truths of faith. It is in this sense that music expresses all that for lack of truth, because it is not in true reality. God alone is the unique true reality, so true that it surpasses all truth.[19]

For Messiaen, music approaches the "true reality" of God.

AN OUTLINE OF THE TABLEAUX OF
SAINT FRANÇOIS D'ASSISE

The events in the eight tableaux of the opera provide the context for the exposition of the idea of truth. The topic of truth appears in Tableaux 3 and proceeds through the remaining scenes. In all tableaux, François's understanding of truth grows as a result of divine revelation, especially through the ministry of the angel.

Saint François d'Assise
Olivier Messiaen

Synopsis of the Acts

Act I. The Preparation of François for Sainthood.

Tableau 1. *La Croix.*

Scene: A road.
Personages: Léon, François, Chorus.

Léon approaches François three times with his fear of death. François's three answers concern perfect joy:
1) Perfect joy is not found in science.
2) Perfect joy is not found in knowledge of the languages of creation.
3) In a parable about acceptance of affliction, François explains that perfect joy is found in the Cross.

Conclusion: The chorus sings that those who wish to follow Christ must carry the Cross.

Tableau 2. *Les laudes.*

Scene: A small church in the cloister.
Personages: François, Sylvestre, Rufin, Bernard, Chorus.

François sings verses from his *Cantique des créatures*, praise to God for wind, water, fire, and earth; the three friars and the chorus respond.

Conclusion: In preparation for the next tableau, François prays that he may overcome his loathing of lepers.

Tableau 3. *Le baiser au lépreux.*

Scene: The leper hospital at Saint Sauveur des Murs.
Personages: Leper, François, Angel, Chorus.

1) The leper complains about his suffering, and François responds.
2) The angel, invisible, sings to the leper that God is greater than his heart.
3) François quotes verses of his prayer, asking that truth displace error. When he kisses the leper, the sick man is healed of his sores and François of his fear.

Conclusion: The chorus sings that those who show love are pardoned.

Act II. The Ministry of François.

Tableau 4. *L'ange voyageur.*

Scene: The mountain of La Verna.
Personages: Léon, Massée, Angel, Élie, Bernard.

While François is at prayer, the friars take charge of the convent.
Introduction: Léon sings a reprise of his verses about fear, and Massée serves as gate-keeper.
The angel in disguise arrives. He asks Élie and Bernard whether they have found their true visage, foreseen by God in the holiness of truth.
1) Impatiently, Élie refuses to answer the angel.
2) Bernard responds with wisdom.
Conclusion: Bernard questions the angel, who refuses to give his name. When the traveller departs, Bernard suggests that he was visited by an angel.

Tableau 5. *L'ange musicien.*

Scene: La Verna.
Personages: François, Angel, Léon, Bernard, Massée.

1) Continuing the *Cantique* begun in Tableau 2, François sings verses of praise to God for the sun and moon. He prays that he may taste the sweetness God has prepared for those who fear him.
2) The falcon alerts Saint François to the arrival of the angel. The angel sings the Theme of Truth and plays for François on his viol.
Epilogue: The three friars discover François, who has fainted from ecstasy.

Tableau 6. *Le prêche aux oiseaux.*

Scene: The hermitage of the Carceri.[20]
Personages: Massée, François.

1) Massée questions François about the birds he sees and hears near the Carceri. In his answers, François names the birds and calls them brothers and sisters. He subsequently describes the colors of foliage and exotic birds he has seen in a dream of a fantastic isle.

2) François preaches his sermon to the birds. He begins by saying that all beautiful things must reach the freedom of glory, and the birds await the day when Christ will reunite all creatures. When he finishes, the birds depart in the form of the Cross.

Conclusion: François sings that we must seek the kingdom of God and the rest will be given to us.

Act III. The Sanctification of François.

Tableau 7. *Les stigmates.*

Scene: La Verna.
Personages: François, Chorus.

François prays that he may share the suffering of Christ. The chorus answers that Christ is the true Word.
Conclusion: François is struck with the five wounds of Christ, in his hands, feet, and side.

Tableau 8. *La mort et la nouvelle vie.*

Scene: The church of the Porziuncola at Sainte Marie des Anges.[21]
Personages: François, Bernard, Massée, Léon, Sylvestre, Rufin, Bernard, Chorus, Angel.

1) In a reprise of Tableau 2, the litany continues between François, the three friars, and the chorus. From the *Cantique*, François sings the final verse of praise for sister Death. In a reprise of Tableau 3, the angel returns to report that the leper died a holy death.

2) François sings that music and poetry have led him to God; he prays for the eternal dazzlement of God's truth, and he dies.

Conclusion: Léon pronounces the eulogy, and the chorus closes with triumphant words of resurrection.

TRUTH IN THE TEXT OF
SAINT FRANÇOIS D'ASSISE

At the center of the opera, in Act II, Tableau 5, Messiaen gives the complete *Summa theologiae* text to the angel-musician, who quotes it to Saint François as a preface to the ecstatic music of his viol. Since Saint Thomas believes that angels possess a superior intellect as intermediaries between man and God, the angel fills an appropriate role as messenger to François in both words and music.[22] Messiaen prepares the idea of truth from the first appearances of the angel in Tableaux 3 and 4. In the tableaux that follow the announcement of the theme, he develops the importance of truth, building to its triumphant revelation at Saint François's death.

In the third tableau, Saint François introduces truth and light after the visitation of the angel, who appears behind a window and calls to the leper with the love François has not yet achieved. When the angel has left, Saint François quotes verses of the prayer attributed to him: "Où se trouve l'erreur, que j'ouvre la Vérité!... Où se trouvent les ténèbres, que j'apporte la lumière!" [Where error is found, let me open Truth!... Where darkness is found, let me bring light!] (Tableau 3, pp. 113, 119). In that setting, the angel has enlightened both Saint François and the leper, with the consequence that François makes a step toward truth and finds the courage to give the leper a healing kiss.

In Tableau 4, the angel-traveller begins his teaching of truth when he ministers to Frères Élie and Bernard. This time, the friars open the door to the angel after his knock of grace, but they fail to recognize his identity. First, the angel chastises Frère Élie for his impatience, saying that anger obscures truth (Tableau 4, p. 87). Then he asks each friar whether he has found the true countenance foreseen by God in "la sainteté de la Vérité" [the holiness of Truth] (Tableau 4, pp. 96, 148). The impatient Élie refuses to answer, but the enlightened Bernard receives the words of truth and responds with wisdom.

In Tableau 5, François first sings the verses to the sun and moon from the *Cantique des créatures*, then prays that he may taste a little of the feast that is found in the true light of God. In answer to his prayer, the angel appears, quoting the full paraphrase of the Saint Thomas passage on divine and human truth (Tableau 5, pp. 89, 91). On his viol, the angel plays a response to the *Cantique* François has offered to God. When the celestial music initiates François into the "secrets of Glory," the dazzlement causes the mortal listener to faint (Tableau 5, p. 103).

In Tableau 6, Messiaen does not mention the word *Vérité*, but introduces François's sermon to the birds with an expansion of Louis-Antoine's quotation from Keats: "Toute chose de beauté doit parvenir à la liberté, la liberté de la gloire." [Every thing of beauty must arrive at freedom, the freedom of glory.] These words identify the birds as images that lead toward God (Tableau 6, pp. 200–202).[23] In Tableau 7, the chorus sings in the first person that Christ is the epitome of truth: "Je suis la Vérité d'où part tout ce qui est vrai, la première Parole, le Verbe du Père..." [I am the Truth from whom all that is true emanates, the first Word, the Word of the Father...] (Tableau 7, pp. 89–91).

For Saint François's last words in Tableau 8, Messiaen adds his own interpretation to the Theme of Truth, referring to the images and symbols Louis-Antoine had also found in the poetry of Saint Francis:

> Musique et Poésie m'ont conduit vers toi: par image, par symbole, et par défaut de Vérité.... Délivre-moi, enivre-moi, éblouis-moi pour toujours de ton excès de Vérité....
>
> [Music and Poetry have led me toward you: by image, by symbol, and for lack of Truth.... Deliver me, intoxicate me, dazzle me forever with your excess of Truth....][24]

At the moment of death, François comprehends God's truth. For Messiaen, the meaning of the Saint Thomas text could be fulfilled only through music. To correct the deficiency in truth of the poetic words, the composer translates the Theme of Truth into his own musical language.

THE MUSICAL LANGUAGE OF DAZZLEMENT

In order to portray images that lead toward God, Messiaen offers a banquet of sound from the timbres of a large orchestra. In the foreground, three instrumental groups dominate: (1) a trio of electronic Ondes Martenot,[25] (2) a trio of xylophone, xylorimba, and marimba,[26] and (3) the woodwind choir. To add a spatial dimension at the Palais Garnier, Messiaen grouped the mallet percussion close together and placed the Ondes Martenot at the fringes of the orchestra. Strings, brass, and five sets of percussion serve as accompanists.

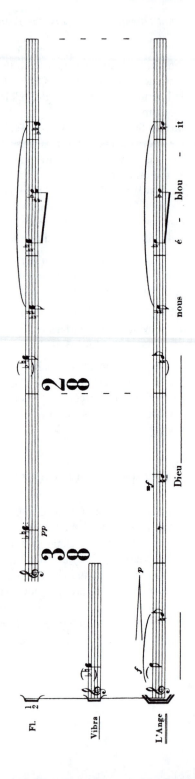

EXAMPLE 1: Olivier Messiaen, *Saint François d'Assise*, Theme of Truth
Reproduced with the kind authorization of Alphonse Leduc & Cie, proprietary editor worldwide.

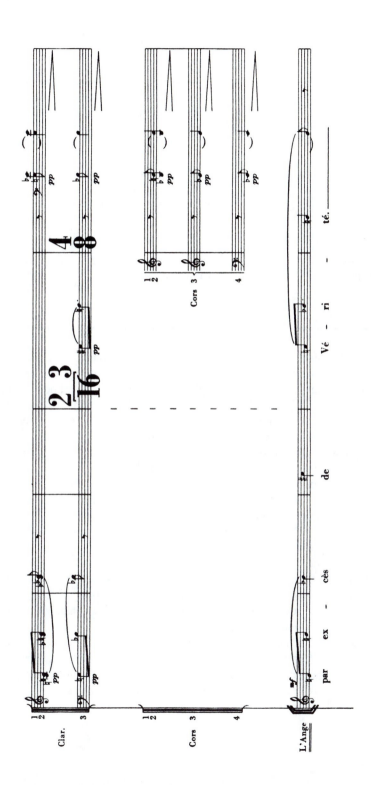

Palais Garnier

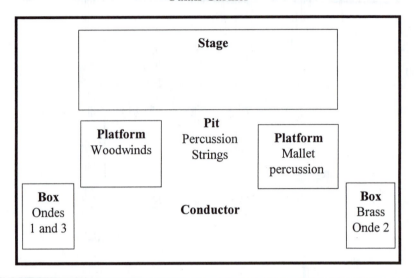

Messiaen exploits the capacity of the Ondes Martenot for extreme registers, symbolizing the distance between suffering on earth and the joy of heaven. A descending glissando played on the ribbon of the Ondes depicts the suffering of the leper, and the guttural bass prepares the monotone chant of the friars. The angelic choirs are represented by the ethereal high register. Ondes Martenot in an upper octave accompany the angel's call to François, and the three Ondes in their widely-spaced location evoke the heavenly strains of the angel's viol.

The birds, symbols of nature and eternity, appear as actual personages in the drama, and the xylos and woodwinds portray their primary songs. Bird-songs mark the progress of the tableaux, serving as overture, entr'actes, and interludes, and every human soloist is accompanied by the song of a distinct bird. Led by the woodwinds and xylos and enhanced by other instruments, bird-songs dazzle not only with their broad palette of instrumental colors, but also with the complexity of their rhythms and textures. When a single bird-song is heard, the homophonic texture broadens the melodic line with a complex of additional tones, moving in mostly parallel motion. The texture becomes more dense when xylo and woodwind skylarks combine at the conclusion of Tableau 1. Interrupting the angel's viol melody, the layers of bird-song increase, and the brilliant climax of texture follows François's sermon to the birds, where as many as twelve songs in seven octaves sound simultaneously.

MODES OF LIMITED TRANSPOSITION AND SOUND-COLOR

For the content of the melodies on truth that are sung by Saint François and the angel, and for their supporting harmonies, Messiaen turns to his seven "modes of limited transposition," which he had used from the outset of his composition.[27] Less dramatic materials than the rich timbres and layers of bird-song, the modes form the real basis for Messiaen's musical language of dazzlement. These patterns of tones (T) and semitones (s), each capable of a certain number of transpositions, divide the octave into symmetrical patterns. The angel's melodies are drawn from the first two transpositions of modes 2 and 3:[28]

Mode 2 (Octatonic Scale), First Transposition (2:1)

$$C\natural_s \; C\sharp_T \; E\flat_s \; E\natural_T \; F\sharp_s \; G\natural_T \; A\natural_s \; B\flat_T$$

Mode 2, Second Transposition (2:2)

$$C\sharp_s \; D\natural_T \; E\natural_s \; F\natural_T \; G\natural_s \; G\sharp_T \; B\flat_s \; B\natural_T$$

Mode 3, First Transposition (3:1)

$$C\natural_T \; D\natural_s \; E\flat_s \; E\natural_T \; F\sharp_s \; G\natural_s \; G\sharp_T \; B\flat_s \; B\natural_s$$

Mode 3, Second Transposition (3:2)

$$C\sharp_T \; E\flat_s \; E\natural_s \; F\natural_T \; G\natural_s \; G\sharp_s \; A\natural_T \; B\natural_s \; C\natural_s$$

Each mode determines certain pitch-complexes that support the melodies, and each contains the tones of particular major triads, which make reference to major-minor tonality without evoking cadential patterns in any key. In most cases, Messiaen prefers to keep the major triads in the second inversion, further separating them from any implication of tonality. In *Saint François*, as the meaning of truth is revealed in stages, Messiaen transforms the cadences from complex aggregates into pure major triads that embody static calm. Most important, Messiaen intended each moment of sound in the modal tone-complexes and triads to communicate visual color.[29]

In his lecture at Notre Dame Cathedral, delivered at the time he was composing the opera, Messiaen explained the relationship between the words of Thomas Aquinas that he selected for the opera and the phenomenon of *sound-color*. Music, he said, is filled with sound complexes that are constantly shifting. In his musical universe, specific visual colors correspond with each mixture of tones. Synchronized with the movement of the sound complexes, the color complexes remain in motion, taking the form of interlocked rainbows and spirals of color.

Visual color merges with spiritual dazzlement, on a level of perception
that is possible in the realm of truth described by Saint Thomas:

> ...le rapport...avec une autre réalité: rapport si puissant
> qu'il peut transformer notre ḥmoiï le plus caché, le plus
> profond, le plus intime, et nous fondre dans une Vérité plus
> haute que nous n'espérions pas atteindre....
> "Dieu nous éblouit par excès de Vérité", dit SAINT THOMAS
> D'AQUIN.

> [...the rapport...with another reality: a rapport so powerful
> that it can transform our most hidden, deepest, most inti-
> mate self, and dissolve us into a higher Truth than we could
> hope to reach....
> "God dazzles us by excess of Truth," said Saint Thomas
> Aquinas.][30]

For Messiaen, melody and chords evoke visual colors in a phenomenon
that he personally equates with sacred revelation. In his progression of
thought, the *éblouissement* produced by colored visions relates to faith
and faith to the knowledge that comes after death:

> "La vie éternelle, lisons-nous dans saint Jean, c'est de Te
> connaître, Toi, le seul vrai Dieu et Celui que Tu as envoyé,
> Jésus-Christ." / Cette connaissance sera un éblouissement
> perpétuel, une éternelle musique de couleurs, une éternelle
> couleur de musiques./ "Dans Ta Musique, nous VERRONS
> la Musique," / "Dans Ta Lumière, nous ENTENDRONS la
> Lumière"...

> ["Eternal life," we read in Saint John, "is to know Thee,
> Thou, the only true God and the One whom Thou has sent,
> Jesus Christ." / This knowledge will be a perpetual dazzle-
> ment, an eternal music of colors, an eternal color of
> musics. / "In Thy Music, we will SEE the Music," / "In
> Thy Light, we will HEAR the Light..."][31]

Although Messiaen's mystic visions of colored music cannot be
shared by listeners on his level of experience, he endeavored as far as
possible to communicate colors to the listeners. In his plans for the
Palais Garnier performance in 1983, the composer specified the colors
of sets, lighting, and costumes. In the first scene, he recommends a dark
green cypress tree and the projection of a large black cross on the blue
sky. In the score, he describes in detail the colors for the wings of the
angel: bands of red, blue, black, a series of yellow-blue-yellow-green-
yellow, and a large lozenge of blue in the middle.[32] When Saint Fran-

çois receives the stigmata in Tableau 7, the composer asks for a scene bathed in red-orange light and a gleaming golden cross. Still, Messiaen explains, the colors he outlines for the mise-en-scène could not begin to approach the myriad colors he sees in his own mind.[33]

Messiaen often attempted to demystify the phenomenon of sound-color by listing the colors he associated with each mode of limited transposition and its inversions. In mode 2, first transposition, he sees shades of violet, blue, and purplish blue, while mode 3:1 evokes orange with red and green, spots of gold, milky white, and even reflections like those from an opal.[34] For mode 2:2, the colors are gold and brown, and for mode 3:2, gray gold, and mauve.[35]

On occasions, the composer marked his scores with the colors he visualized. In *Couleurs de la Cité céleste*, the sound-colors represent precious stones that are the building-blocks of the holy city. The chord designated "orangé, or, blanc laiteux" consists of pitches of mode 3:1, and the following "violet" includes only members of mode 2:1.[36] Messiaen's complete written notebooks of sound-colors will be published in the final volume of the monumental *Traité de rythme, de couleur, et d'ornithologie,* left incomplete at the composer's death.[37] Messiaen kept these notebooks of sound-colors at hand when composing, assuring the precision and consistency of the visual colors of his tones.[38]

Major triads extracted from modes 2 and 3 also convey definite colors, although the colors do not always correspond to those indicated for the mode. In *Sept Haïkaï*, for example, the triad Bb-Eb-G in the violin is present in the "red" chord and E-C♯-A in the chord marked "blue."[39] Observing the general connection of the A-major triad (mode 2:1) with the color blue and the association of the Eb-major triad (modes 2:1 and 3:1) with red, Paul Griffiths surmises that the complementary colors of blue and red work with the complementary triads of A and Eb that symmetrically divide the octave at the distance of a tritone.[40]

In the Sixth Tableau of *Saint François d'Assise,* Messiaen illustrates François's dream-description of exotic birds and brilliant foliage by responding to each color with a specific triad or series of triads:

Là où les feuilles sont rouges...	E -major triad
...les pigeons verts.............	D -major triad
...les arbres blancs.............	C -major triad
...là où la mer change du vert au bleu......	A -major triad
...et du violet au vert comme les reflets d'une opale!......	D-major—Bb-major—F♯-major triads

[There where the leaves are red, the pigeons green, the trees white, there where the sea changes from green to blue and from violet to green like the reflections of an opal!][41]

The changing colors of the final triads are found in pitches of the three transpositions of mode 2, but those that represent green, the color of human love in the *Turangalîla-Symphonie*, appear in no other context close to the chaste Saint François. From this catalogue of colors, the E-major triad of mode 2:2 and the C and A-major triads of mode 2:1 play important roles in the final tableaux.

THE MUSICAL LANGUAGE OF
THE THEME OF TRUTH

In *Saint François d'Assise*, a number of motifs represent personages and abstract traits. Four themes chart the spiritual progress of the protagonist. (1) Saint François's leitmotif, introduced in Tableau 1 by strings in pure octaves, is a non-retrogradable melody (palindrome) that embraces the characteristic tritones G-C♯ and C-F♯.[42] (2) François's Theme of Decision, which first appears in Tableau 2 as he plans to visit the leper, signals the difficult choices that lead toward sanctity. The Decision Theme startles the listener with a descent to a low octave from a saturated chord in full orchestra, marked by the orchestral whip. (3) The Theme of Solemnity, which is also introduced in the second tableau, sets the saint's most profound words of wisdom. François proclaims these important words on the fixed pitches A♭-C. To announce his words, a *fortissimo* cluster demands attention, and a quartal chord of E-A-D-G-C responds with the *piano* cadence. (4) Although it is anticipated by a germinal motif in the first tableau, the fully-formed Theme of Joy appears only in the third tableau, when François succeeds in approaching the leper. In its tonic version, the joy theme comprises the four descending tones A-G-E-D, harmonized with triads.

Messiaen similarly transforms the idea of truth into a musical Theme of Truth. In the music for this theme, he avoids the fantastic rhythms and polyphony of bird-song and pares down the density of the shimmering timbres. Vocal durations are derived from the even rhythms of French speech, and the static harmonies lie in a middle register of the woodwinds, horns, and strings. Music of dazzlement in the Theme of Truth depends instead on sound-colors from the modes of limited transposition.

In Tableau 3, the angel first summons the leper over the static A-major triad of heavenly blue color, and in succeeding phrases the harmony is inflected toward its complementary E♭ triad. Saint François responds to the angel's appearance with the first music on the notion of truth. A harmonized transposition of the Saint François leitmotif prepares François's prayer that truth will replace error. The opening phrase, "Où se trouve l'erreur," continues the tritones of Saint François's leitmotif (B-G♯-C-F♯-G-C♯), doubled in octaves only by oboe and bassoon. The pitches of the first phrase fit into mode 3:2, while the answering phrase, "...que j'ouvre la Vérité," moves to mode 3:1 with the cadential notes D-A♭. Supporting harmonies in woodwinds and trumpet include pitches of the triad of A♭-major that is derived from mode 3:1 (Tableau 3, p. 113). Triadic cadences in all the phrases that embody truth in *Saint François* also allow   moments of repose in the rainbow colors of the modes.

In Tableau 4, the angel-traveller begins to reveal the meaning of truth. With his first phrases, the E♭ triad suggested in the third tableau affirms the cadences. In his rebuke to Frère Élie for his impatience and officiousness toward the angel-in-disguise, the melodic tones on the words "...de la Vérité," E-F-G-A♭, move from mode 2:2 to mode 3:1. At the word "Vérité," the supporting harmonies resolve to the second inversion of an A♭-major triad (Tableau 4, p. 88). In the angel's completed statement on justice and the holiness of truth, the cadence on the words "la sainteté de la Vérité," E-G-B♭-C♯-A-B♭-G, remains in mode 2:1 (Tableau 4, pp. 96, 147–148). The cadential phrase is again supported by the E♭ triad derived from that mode, a triad designated as red in previous Messiaen sources. As Griffiths suggested, the red of the E♭ triad that accompanies "la sainteté de la Vérité" complements the angel's celestial blue A-major triad.[43]

Continuing the musical Theme of Truth, Tableau 5 brings the angel-musician's complete paraphrase of Saint Thomas's text. Themes in timbres and registers on the ethereal plane precede and follow the angel's theme: Saint François's motif of joy and the duet for two piccolos of the angel's companion bird, the New Caledonian *gerygone*. In this full statement, the angel's melody and harmonies do not depart from the tones of mode 2:1. For "Dieu nous éblouit par excès de Vérité," the accompanying timbres begin with vibraphone and flutes in thirds, followed by clarinet triads, a horn triad, and full string chords. From the beginning of the vibraphone introduction, pitches of the E♭ triad solidify and purify the passage. As in Tableau 4, the angel's Theme of Truth returns to the red triad of E♭ for its basic cadence, with the E♭ sounded by the cello, horn, and double bass (Tableau 5, pp. 89, 91; see Example 1 on the two preceding pages).

In the conclusion of Tableau 5, the Theme of Truth leads to the angel's viol music that initiates Saint François into celestial joy. For the sublime moment when the melodic phrases of the three Ondes Martenot echo from their widely-spaced locations, the strings sustain the triad of

C (Tableau 5, p. 117). This most heavenly of triads is the one Messiaen designates as "white" in the color catalogue of Tableau 6.

In Tableau 6, where the reference to truth is veiled in Keats's words, Saint François sings "Toute chose de beauté..." on the Ab-C of the Theme of Solemnity that highlights his sermons. In Tableau 7, the chorus represents the voice of Christ: "Je suis la Vérité d'où part tout ce qui est vrai..." [I am the Truth from whom all that is true emanates]. The tones of the choral melody (C-D-Bb-F#-C) are derived from mode 3:1 (Tableau 7, p. 90). A *fortissimo* cluster glissando in strings and wind machine, which elides with a pure C-major cadence in the winds, prepares the unison choral phrase. As the chorus continues with "...la première Parole" [the first Word], the theme changes to the rising chromatic line that suggests approach to God and resurrection (Tableau 7, p. 92). Since the enveloping instrumental timbre is independent of pure mode or primary color, the colors Messiaen intends here must again be rich and swirling. The fantastic timbres lead to a static cadence only when the chorus calls to Saint François before he receives the stigmata. At the climactic call to François, the E-major triad that described the red leaves in Tableau 6 now represents the blood of Christ, as the scene is bathed in red-orange (Tableau 7, p. 114).

Finally, in Tableau 8, the angel returns to prepare Saint François for death. In a reprise of his first appearance, his themes move from the A major to the Eb-major triads, and his musical Theme of Truth is now fulfilled in the Themes of Resurrection and Joy.[44] Saint François calls to God on the pitch e3, recalling the e5 with which the angel had addressed him. The three Ondes Martenot double his pitch, while woodwinds and strings fill in harmonies of the G-major triad from mode 3:1. François's expansion of the Saint Thomas words, "Musique et poésie...," begins on a melodic perfect fifth, with the support of the pure A triad that had first been heard when the angel arrived in Tableau 3. The words "...m'ont conduit vers toi" [have led me toward you] sweep upward in a tone painting of ascension: C#-D-Bb-E (Tableau 8, p. 119). The full orchestra responds with a two-chord "Amen" that reflects on François's Theme of Decision. "Par image, par symbole..." ushers in a descending melodic and harmonic sequence, moving from the A triad back to the G triad, each enriched by the added sixth. "Et par défaut de Vérité" [and for lack of truth] rises again by step to e4, with the three Ondes harmonizing Saint François's ascending line. After the culminating A-major triad, a theme in the chimes symbolizes joy (Tableau 8, pp. 118-123).

"Délivre-moi, enivre-moi..." [deliver me, intoxicate me] brings a repeat of the sequence, and "éblouis-moi pour toujours" [dazzle me forever] ascends once more in a nearly-whole-tone resurrection scale (C♯-D♯-E-F♯-G♯-B♭-C). Finally, "...de ton excès de Vérité" [with your excess of truth] leads another ascent to e4, this time supported by the E triad that is enriched with the added pitches D and F♯ from mode 3:1 (Tableau 8, pp. 134–135). With the angel's A-major triad from mode 2:1 and the culminating E major from mode 3:1, the celestial blue leads to the red-orange of the stigmata.

When the Theme of Truth joins with Themes of Resurrection and Joy, the color of sound shifts to the white C-major triad, the foundation tone of the opera and of the first transposition that is the basis of all modes of limited transposition. Repeating the harmony of the angel's viol music of dazzlement heard in Tableau 5, the C triad now affirms the realization of truth in new life. In a final summation, a brilliant white light washes over the scene, while chorus and full orchestra sustain the extended white C-major triad that points to eternity (Tableau 8, pp. 200–202).

As supporting harmonies for the Theme of Truth, the triads of A, E♭, E, and C carry both mystical and practical meanings. On the one hand, the sustained triads evoke the blue of the angel's call, the red of his message of truth, the red-orange of the stigmata, and the white of eternal life. At the same time, they permit tonal reference points within the symmetrical modes of limited transposition. Triads mark both Saint François's progress on his journey toward truth and the harmonic progression of the tableaux.

MESSIAEN, SAINT THOMAS, AND MUSIC THAT LEADS TOWARD GOD

In *Saint François d'Assise*, Messiaen succeeds in adapting the passage from the *Summa theologiae* to François's journey from human lack of truth to spiritual fulfillment in divine truth. The voice and the viol of the angel, the songs of the birds, and the choral voice of Christ accompanying the stigmata are all musical symbols that lead François toward God. When Saint François approaches death with an interpretation of the Truth Theme: "Musique et poésie m'ont conduit vers Toi: par image, par symbole, et par défaut de Vérité," Messiaen places his own credo concerning the power of music to draw men toward God in the exultant words of the saint. As he extends Saint Thomas's notion of excessive truth to *éblouissement* and the phantasm of poetry to *musique*, Messiaen applies the passage to his own musical language.

In Messiaen's faith, in his musical language, and in his composition, he expresses the dazzlement of excessive truth both through studied
technique and fantastic images. Messiaen's complete confidence in the
Catholic faith grows in part from his extensive reading of Catholic
literature, including the scholarly writings of Saint Thomas Aquinas.
Just as Messiaen believes implicitly in the doctrines of the church, he
embraces its wonders and miracles, the "true fairy tales." The miracles
of the leper's healing, the angel's music, and the receiving of the stigmata illustrate these wonders. Whether or not Messiaen's listeners share
his beliefs, they may comprehend his combination of childlike acceptance and mature knowledge. *Saint François d'Assise* is infused with
Messiaen's abundant faith, expressed with imagination and genius.

Messiaen's dazzling sounds expand musical language through the
exotic timbres of Ondes Martenot and wooden mallet percussion and
through complex layers of bird-song. By contrast, the music for the
Theme of Truth comprises even rhythms, subdued tone color, and
stable triads from the modes of limited transposition. The modal combinations and the pure triads that evoke sound-color dazzled Messiaen
with a reflection of the truth of God, although the rainbows and spirals
that he could visualize from the sounds of modes remain inaccessible to
the ordinary listener.

Messiaen's composition in sound-color demonstrates Saint
Thomas's contrast between excessive truth and imperfect human
reason. In preserving his personal vision, Messiaen composed in
privacy, and he left no working sketches to reveal the process of his
thought. For both the inspiration and the materials of his music, he
reached into realms of the ethereal. At the same time, the composer,
meticulous in every detail of his work, set up notebooks of sounds and
their colors. While composing, he referred to his notebooks to verify
the consistency of the colors he imagined.[45] He labelled specific sound-
colors in his scores, and he offered spoken and written explanations of
his methods. A dedicated teacher, Messiaen clarified aspects of his
musical language for several generations of student composers.

In that contrast between private imagination and public explanation
lies the sense of Saint Thomas's meaning. The human mind is not capable of understanding everything. One can perceive beauty as it is stated
in words and music, and the experience may indeed draw each listener
closer to God. Nonetheless, musical and spiritual dazzlement exist in a
realm beyond comprehension. The *merveilleux*, in a sound-color produced by Messiaen's own system of harmony, permits a vision that
transcends human thought and verbal communication.

"God dazzles us with excess of Truth. Music draws us to God for lack of Truth." For Saint Thomas Aquinas, the passage expresses his belief that phantasms can lead from the limitation of human reason toward the perfect truth of God. For Saint Francis, his own poetry and music leads to the higher revelation of the angel, and finally to sanctification and knowledge. For Olivier Messiaen, the passage states the meaning of his own musical language of bird-song and sound-color.

NOTES

[1] Olivier Messiaen, *Saint François d'Assise*, orchestral score, 8 volumes (Paris: Leduc, 1985-1992), Tableau 5, pp. 89-91 (all translations mine, unless otherwise indicated).

[2] Claude Samuel and Olivier Messiaen, *Musique et couleurs: nouveaux entretiens avec Claude Samuel* (Paris: Belfond, 1986), p. 237.

[3] Messiaen and Jean-Christoph Marti, "Entretiens avec Olivier Messiaen: propos receuillis par Jean-Christoph Marti en janvier 1992," *Saint François d'Assise* Program Book, Salzburg Festival (1992): 16.

[4] Messiaen, "Ariane et Barbe-Bleue," *La revue musicale* 166 (May/June 1936): 79-80.

[5] Messiaen, "Ariane et Barbe-Bleue," p. 83.

[6] Messiaen, ibid.

[7] Messiaen, *Technique de mon langage musical,* vol. 1 (Paris: Leduc, 1944), pp. 4-5.

[8] Samuel and Messiaen, *Entretiens avec Olivier Messiaen* (Paris: Belfond, 1967), p. 11.

[9] Messiaen, in Brigitte Massin, *Olivier Messiaen: une poétique du merveilleux* (Aix-en-Provence: Alinea, 1989), p. 15.

[10] Thomas Aquinas, *Summa theologiae* I-II, q 101, a 2, ad 2, ed. Petri Carmello (Rome: Marietti, 1952), p. 469 (trans. Karl-Werner Gümpel).

[11] Anthony Kenny, *Aquinas on Mind* (London: Routledge, 1993), 37; *Summa theologiae* I-I, q 74, a 6, 7.

[12] Thomas Aquinas, *Summa theologiae* II-II, q 81, a 7, resp., Latin text and English translation by Kevin D. O'Rourke, O.P., vol. 39 (New York: Blackfriars, 1964), pp. 28, 29.

[13] Etienne Gilson, *Le Thomisme: introduction à la philosophie de Saint Thomas d'Aquin,* sixth edition, *Etudes de philosophie médiévale* I (Paris: Librairie Philosophique J. Vrin, 1965), pp. 279-280.

[14] Samuel and Messiaen, *Musique et couleurs*, p. 231.

[15] Yvonne Loriod Messiaen, letter to the author, August 25, 1993.

[16] Thomas Aquinas, trans. Louis-Antoine, In *Lire François d'Assise* (Paris: Éditions Franciscaines, 1967), p. 73.

[17] Louis-Antoine, pp. 76-77.

[18]Louis-Antoine, p. 73.

[19]Samuel and Messiaen, *Musique et couleurs*, p. 256.

[20]The name "Carceri" means prisons, referring to the grottos that served as places of meditation for the friars.

[21]Saint Francis had restored this church at the beginning of his religious life, and it was here that he had founded the Franciscan Order.

[22]Gilson, pp. 219-220; *Summa theologiae* I, q 54.

[23]Samuel and Messiaen, *Musique et couleurs*, p. 262. When discussing this tableau with Samuel, Messiaen alluded to the *Ode on a Grecian Urn*, in which Keats equated beauty with truth.

[24]Messiaen, *Saint François d'Assise*, Tableau 8, pp. 118-124, 134-137.

[25]Messiaen had not used the Ondes Martenot, a monophonic electronic keyboard invented in 1928, since the *Turangalila-Symphonie* (1949). The instrument has the capacity for a guttural bass or tremulando treble melody, special staccato effects, and a glissando produced by pulling the ribbon controller. In the opera, Messiaen called for the 1975 model, capable of an expanded range of unique timbres.

[26]Messiaen had called for this trio of wooden mallet percussion in *Couleurs de la Cité Céleste* (1966). The xylophone has a four-octave range upward from c5, the xylorimba a five-octave range upward from c4, and the marimba a four-octave range upward from c3.

[27]Messiaen, *Technique*, pp. 51-56.

[28]Samuel and Messiaen, *Musique et couleurs*, p. 256.

[29]Messiaen, *Conférence de Notre Dame*, prononcée à Notre-Dame de Paris le 4 décembre 1977 (Paris: Leduc, 1978); Messiaen and Samuel, *Entretiens*, pp. 37-38. Messiaen frequently compared his colored visions of musical sound to the synesthesia of the painter Blanc-Gatti. For the painter, a physical malady of the optic and auditory nerves brought about the confusion of images, but Messiaen's colored harmonies arose consistently in his imagination.

[30]Messiaen, *Conférence de Notre Dame*, prononcée à Notre-Dame de Paris le 4 décembre 1977 (Paris: Leduc, 1978), pp. 11-12.

[31]Messiaen, *ibid.*, p. 15; John 17:3.

[32]Messiaen, *Saint François*, Tableau 4.

[33]Messiaen, in Almut Rößler, *Beiträge zur geistigen Welt Olivier Messiaens* (Duisberg: Gilles and Francke, 1984); trans. as *Contributions to the Spiritual World of Olivier Messiaen* (1986), p. 125. In the staging of Georges Tsypin for the 1992 Salzburg Festival production, a massive, tilted grid of colored neon tubes hovered over the stage. Although the colors shifted continuously, they were often harsh, distracting, and far short of realizing Messiaen's description of rainbows and spirals.

[34]Messiaen and Samuel, *Entretiens*, p. 42.

[35]Harry Halbreich, *Olivier Messiaen* (Paris: Librairie Arthème Fayard, Fondation SACEM, 1980), pp. 139-140; Jonathan Bernard, "Messiaen's Synesthesia: The Correspondence between Color and Sound Structure in His Music," *Musical Perception* 4:1 (Fall 1986): 47. Halbreich expanded Messiaen's list in his monograph, and Bernard corroborated Halbreich's list with specific examples from several Messiaen works.

[36]Messiaen, *Couleurs de la Cité Céleste* (Paris: Leduc, 1966), p. 57.

[37]Messiaen, *Traité de rythme, couleur, et d'ornithologie*, 7 volumes (Paris: Leduc, 1994-).

[38]Yvonne Loriod Messiaen, letter to the author, February 10, 1993.

[39]Messiaen, *Sept Haïkaï* V, "Miyajima et le torii dans la mer," (Paris: Leduc 1963), p. 58.

[40]Paul Griffiths, *Olivier Messiaen and the Music of Time* (Ithaca: Cornell University Press, 1985), p. 205. Griffiths finds that the combination of these two triads with the added sixth of each (A-C♯-E-F♯, E♭-G-B♭-C) make up the eight pitches of the violet-tinted mode 2, the mixture of blue and red.

[41]Tableau 6, pp. 136-143; Camille Crunelle Hill, The Synthesis of Messiaen's Musical Language in His Opera *Saint François d'Assise* (Ph.D. diss., University of Kentucky, jointly with the University of Louisville, 1996), pp. 226-227. During the composition of *Saint François*, Messiaen visited New Caledonia, where he observed the lustrous colors and transcribed bird-songs of the island.

[42]Francine Guiberteau, "Le *Saint François d'Assise* de Olivier Messiaen: événement et avènement," *Analyse musicale* 1 (November 1985): 66.

[43]See also Zsolt Gárdonyi, "Phänomene harmoniegeschichtlicher Kontinuität in Olivier Messiaens Oper *Saint François d'Assise*," *Melos* 47, no. 3 (1985): 58-60.

[44]Harry Halbreich, "Introduction: Analyse," *Saint François d'Assise* Program Book, Salzburg Festival (1992): 98.

[45]Yvonne Loriod Messiaen, letter to the author, February 10, 1993.

Messiaen's *Saint François d'Assise* and Franciscan Spirituality

Nils Holger Petersen

INTRODUCTION

Messiaen wrote both the words and music for his only opera, *Saint François d'Assise, Opéra en 3 Actes et 8 Tableaux*, between 1975 and 1979; he completed the orchestration for the first performance at the Paris Opera in 1983.[1] As his main sources for the life of Saint Francis, Messiaen mentions two fourteenth-century (Italian) pious works, the *'Fioretti di San Francesco' (The Little Flowers of Saint Francis)* and the *Considerations of the Holy Stigmata.*[2] Furthermore, he draws on thirteenth-century biographical writings: the two *vitae* composed by Thomas of Celano (1228 and 1244 respectively), as well as Bonaventura's later work (1260). Finally, he quotes extensively from Saint Francis's own *Canticle of Brother Sun*, from certain Biblical texts, and —towards the end of the opera—from the man who is considered the most influential of all medieval theologians, the thirteenth-century Dominican theologian, Thomas Aquinas.[3]

The aim of this article is not to give a general introduction to the opera, but rather to discuss the intimate relationship between this twentieth-century music dramatic work and medieval spiritual traditions that are connected with the Franciscan movement of the early thirteenth century. It is necessary first to give a short presentation of aspects of the historical background for the rise of this momentous development in the history of Western culture.

SAINT FRANCIS OF ASSISI AND THE CONFRATERNAL SINGING OF *LAUDE*

Already during Francis's own life time (1181–1226) a popular movement centered around his figure, and his ideals grew to have an enormous impact. What was to become the Franciscan Order—the *fratres minores* or 'little brothers,' recognized by Pope Innocent III during Francis's visit to Rome in 1209—started out as a loosely organized fraternity of people who followed Francis and were eager to emulate his renunciation of all material and worldly aspirations. Large numbers of lay people took up fundamental and, in modern terms, existential or religious questions about the meaning of their goals and lives, becoming in themselves a living question, if not a threat, to the ecclesiastical hierarchy. Saint Francis himself, however, seems to have remained loyal to the church authorities all through his life.[4]

From the very early stages of the popular movement around Saint Francis, one of the important means for expressing the new ideals of living in accordance with the teachings of Christ, in poverty and fraternal love—besides the emphasis on preaching the gospel in the vernacular to ordinary people—was the singing of a new genre of vernacular spiritual song, called by contemporaries the *lauda*, Italian for "song of praise." The name was probably derived from the Latin *laudes matutinae*, morning praise, the old designation for the morning prayer of the monastic liturgy of the hours. The music was cast in a ballad-like form, with the text focusing primarily on Christ's suffering and on the Virgin Mary. The singing of such songs of praise formed the center of activity in so-called *laudesi*, lay confraternities first formed in Florence, Siena, and Bologna with the main purpose of carrying out spiritual vernacular ceremonies to supplement the traditional, authorized Latin liturgy.

For centuries, since the important liturgical reforms under Charlemagne around 800, the official Latin liturgy of the medieval church had increasingly been professionalized. As a result, the laity had become confined to the role of mere spectators at ceremonies in which the clergy representatively carried out all congregational activities, including the singing. It is worth remembering in this context that the theological idea of *transubstantiation* (the miraculous transformation of bread and wine into the body and blood of Christ), which had been discussed for centuries, was made a church dogma at the Fourth Lateran Council in Rome in 1215.[5] This dogma corroborated the dominant role of the clergy, excluding lay members of the community more and more even from participation in the communion.

Seen in this perspective it is not surprising that the beginning of the thirteenth century saw the emergence of a pronounced interest in creating possibilities for active liturgical (or quasi-liturgical) participation for the increasing numbers of religiously and politically conscious laity. It is fundamental to the understanding of the new musico-literary and spiritual phenomena to see them in their social context.

The above-mentioned developments towards vernacular rituals were closely linked to movements governed by ideals of poverty and the attempt to break away from a worldly or materially oriented life. At the same time, the need for the new forms of spirituality was mostly found within the new class of well-educated men (and even women) belonging to the urban society, which was increasingly shaped by mercantile activities. For this new, active and responsible yet worldly type of person, it was apparently of profound concern to be able to engage directly in the establishment of ultimate connections, the ones necessary for salvation. These were up to this time, and remained so within the official liturgy, the exclusive domain of members of the clergy or of recognized monastic orders. Thus the poverty movements and the mercantile world in many ways depended upon each other.[6]

The rise of *lauda* singing and the religious lay confraternities were not, strictly speaking, Franciscan phenomena. They were part of complicated developments of thought, practice, and economy happening in society, in the church, and in the monastic orders. Economic improvements made it possible for lay persons to achieve influence to a hitherto unseen degree. This provided, among other things, new possibilities for at least the upper parts of the secular society to take interest in spiritual matters, which in turn meant that ideals and forms of worship that formerly exclusively belonged to the monasteries permeated into the secular world to a higher degree.[7]

Conversely, the so-called Gregorian reform of the eleventh century (named after the controversial Gregory VII, pope from 1073 to 1085) strongly ideologized the idea of the sacred authority of the papacy and the priesthood. This particular reform was closely linked with new developments in the monastic world, especially with the rise of the monastic 'imperium' of Cluny. Through its liturgy and its sacred splendor the order at Cluny, founded in 909, took to an extreme the age-old Benedictine ideals of the *opus dei*, the (almost) never-ceasing praise of God, as the raison d'être of the monastery.

All these lines of development were part of an overall tendency to upgrade the sanctity of life, whatever circumstance was focused upon. This was also the case in the influential heretical movement of the Cathars, which flourished in the twelfth century, as well as in the conscious attempts of various popular movements at imitating the 'original' apostolic life. These attempts were in their intentions not at all heretical, but soon found themselves in almost unavoidable conflicts with church authorities, often over the right to preach in the vernacular or over necessarily unauthorized translations into the vernacular of parts of the Bible. The Waldenses constituted another important example; this group was named after their founder, Waldes, a rich merchant whose life and ideas in some ways can be said to have anticipated those of Francis of Assisi. This is also true for another movement of the late twelfth century, the *Humiliati*, the humble, whose ideals of modesty foreshadowed those of the Franciscan Brothers. Both of these latter groups were condemned by Pope Lucius III in 1184, but again reconciled with the church under the following, more farsighted Pope, Innocent III (in 1201).

Two other crucial phenomena of the time must be mentioned. Around 1100, new monastic settlements, most important among them those of the Cistercians, were launched. Their goal was the pursuit of holiness in terms of seeking the pure and elementary, in a reaction against the stifling ritualization within the traditional monastic movements. The most famous and influential Cistercian abbot, Bernard of Clairvaux (1090–1153), was probably the single most important contributor to the fervent spirituality that also lies at the heart of the spiritual developments in the centuries following him.

Even the rise of the universities in the same period can be seen, albeit only to some extent, in this context, for the greatly increased administrative and political significance of the papacy created a need for the institution of legal education. Moreover, the lack of a well-educated clergy was exposed both through the Gregorian and the popular spiritual ideals—which were, of course, in some respects obvious opposites.

In this highly complex politico-religious scenario, which included deep political conflicts (notably between the Emperor and the Pope) and family rivalries, the *laudesi* confraternities—fraternities explicitly devoted to the singing of *laude*—arose soon after the revival of 1260, described below.[8]

The singing of *laude* was anticipated in the earliest-known passion drama, a twelfth-century text from Montecassino, which towards the end contains a so-called *planctus Mariae*, i.e. a complaint of Maria at the Cross. Such songs became extremely widespread in the later Middle Ages, in Latin, in the vernacular, or in mixed language, and formed the central scenes of more or less overtly dramatic passion ceremonies. The fragmented vernacular *planctus* text of the otherwise Latin Montecassino passion play seems to be the earliest preserved part of such a *planctus*; unfortunately the music has not been preserved.[9]

The singing of *laude* constituted an important part of the spiritual exercises of the early Franciscan movement and similarly of the other so-called mendicant orders, notably the Dominicans. The figure of Saint Francis in particular lent itself to being associated with *lauda* singing, as he had composed at least one well-known song of praise in the vernacular, the famous *Canticle of Brother Sun*. This, however, is the only vernacular text that can safely be attributed to Francis himself, and might be considered a kind of first *lauda*. The song is mentioned as early as in the first biography of Thomas of Celano, i.e. in 1228, where it is recorded that Saint Francis on his death bed asked two of his brothers to sing the *Canticle of Brother Sun* aloud. Unfortunately, no musical notation was written into the staves included in the oldest extant manuscript.[10]

In the thirteenth century, religious revivals that originated under the inspiration of the poverty and penitential movements resulted in large processions of a politico-religious nature. In northern Italy, these spread through both the cities and the countryside, as was the case for example in 1233, the 'year of the Alleluia'. The most significant event for the development of the North Italian spiritual confraternal ceremonial, however, occurred in 1260 when the hermit Raniero Fasani preached penitence in Perugia. This resulted in momentous processions with singing as well as flagellation. The exact nature of what was sung in the processions is not, unfortunately, easy to establish.[11]

The events in 1260 were witnessed and described, among others, by the contemporary Franciscan chronicler Salimbene de Parma (1221–1288/89), who states: "Men walked in the way of salvation and composed godly songs of praise in honor of the Lord and the Blessed Virgin Mary. And these they sang as they went and scourged themselves."[12]

The revival of 1260 has often been understood as a consequence of the prophecies of the long-deceased abbot, Joachim of Fiore (1135–1202), a Cistercian who eventually founded his own order. In his writings he had divided history into three periods: the periods of the Father, of the Son, and of the Spirit. The last period, according to calculations based on the Book of Revelations, was supposed to commence in 1260. Such thinking would have had great impact in connection with the strongly-felt incompatibilities between the papacy and popular piety. Recently, however, the reality of this connection has been queried. In any case, Joachimism—which was condemned by the papacy in the wake of the dramatic events in 1260—is relevant as a sign of the spiritual mood of the time and certainly must have influenced relevant spiritual thinking of the time.[13]

The penitential and flagellant activities of 1260 spread fast all over northern Italy, and a number of so-called flagellant confraternities, often referred to as *disciplinati,* were founded, some of them possibly through the transformation of *laudesi* confraternities.[14] Although the singing of *laude* may well have been practiced in many individual ways, the known repertory of *lauda* songs is preserved in manuscripts belonging to the related but different *laudesi* and *disciplinati* confraternities. The singing of *laude* in both cases seems to have been incorporated into ritual schedules where the songs were prescribed at particular times during the ceremonies and for particular days during the year, just as liturgical songs would be assigned to their proper places in the liturgical documents of the Middle Ages.[15]

During the fourteenth century a professionalization and artistic development occurred in the repertory of the *laudesi* just as in the 'official' liturgy. In some cases, the use of musical instruments and polyphony were introduced (the latter mainly in the fifteenth century). Where songs remained monophonic, the degree of embellishment increased considerably, from basically syllabic or at least only slightly ornate melodies to a consciously artistic, very melismatic musical style of the *laude*. This can be observed in the two main sources for such songs, manuscripts containing *laude* from, respectively, Cortona in the thirteenth and Florence in the fourteenth century.[16]

Moreover, vernacular dramatic ceremonies became part of the spiritual exercises in the confraternities, sometimes in the form of dramatic *laude* that gradually evolved into fully staged music-dramatic vernacular representations, deriving from the dialogical texts in some *laude*, and sometimes in terms of an incorporation of the traditional, *laude* into a staging of spoken *sacre rappresentazione.* [17]

MESSIAEN'S *SAINT FRANÇOIS* AND CONFRATERNAL SPIRITUALITY

Before going into details both of confraternal ceremonies and of Messiaen's opera, I will make some general observations concerning the way Messiaen has treated his material in agreement with some basic spiritual attitudes found in the early mendicant confraternal context.

Messiaen has stated that he chose the subject of Saint Francis because he wanted to write a religious work which also contained the miraculous—and which had to allow the inclusion of bird song as well. He had never felt it possible to make a stage representation of the Passion, but Saint Francis seemed to him an image of Christ, so that in writing the Franciscan scenes he at least approached the Passion.[18] Francis's preaching to the birds, related for instance in chapter 21 of Thomas of Celano's first *Vita Sancti Francisci*, was naturally used in the opera, where it is incorporated into the sixth scene. In the present context, however, it is of more importance to note that in the interview with Brigitte Massin referred to above, Messiaen explicitly mentions the stigmata of Saint Francis. According to the early biographies, the saint had received these as a particular grace two years before his death, and the composer chose them as the subject of the seventh scene in his opera. Other features that made Messiaen perceive Saint Francis as Christ-like are the characteristics of his life style: his poverty, his chastity, and his humility.

The explicit linking of Saint Francis to the Passion of Christ is in itself a special trait of the cult of Saint Francis. In a certain sense such a link can, of course, be found for all saints, especially martyrs. In the case of Saint Francis, who was not a martyr, the connection was seen on the basis of reading his stigmata as a substitution for a martyrdom that would intimately replicate Christ's own death on the Cross.

The earliest account of the stigmata (in Thomas of Celano's first *Vita Sancti Francisci*) makes it clear that they marked his body, in the five characteristic places, "as though he had hung upon the Cross with the Son of God".[19] After Saint Francis's death, when the wounds, which until then had only been witnessed by two of the brothers, were seen by many brothers, they changed their sorrow into joy. There follows a description of Saint Francis's body: "For in truth there appeared in him a true image of the cross and of the passion of the lamb without blemish who washed away the sins of the world, for he seemed as though he had been recently taken down from the cross, his hands and feet were pierced as though by nails and his side wounded as though by a lance."[20]

Early Franciscan writers seem to understand the four then-known biographies of Saint Francis as his gospels in accordance with these narrative traditions about the life of Francis, thus furthering the idea of a conformity between Christ and Saint Francis.[21]

Messiaen's intentions in choosing the subject matter for the opera can be further elucidated through a discussion of Franciscan medieval piety.

Blake Wilson, who writes about the urban context of the early mendicant spirituality, stresses how the religious societies of lay people were encouraged by the friars and—in terms of religious content and devotional practice—governed by the exact same ideals as the friars. In terms of administrative structure, however, they were closely modeled on the contemporary guilds.[22] He refines this observation into an understanding of the important new relationship between the secular and the spiritual world at work here.

The sacred was made secular in the sense that the vernacular devotions of the confraternities, as well as the administrative functions just mentioned, were conducted in a hitherto unprecedented agreement with the everyday world of the urban merchant population that constituted the majority of their members.[23] More surprising is the opposite side of this relationship, as described by Wilson. Not only was the sacred "made secular" in this sense, but the secular was similarly made sacred. The friars took up the legal and everyday language of the urban society, using it metaphorically in their sermons. Similar language is also found in certain *laude* texts.[24]

This could be understood as a secularization of the sermon just as well as a sacralization of the everyday language, if not for the fact that the friars actually ascribed a dignity and value, hitherto unheard of, to all of creation. This is less a matter of dogmatic statement than of human feeling and expression as it comes down to us mainly in the preserved works of art, poetry, and music. Creation, of course, had always been considered part of God's fundamentally good work in non-heretical Christianity as well (as is shown, for instance, in Saint Augustine's deliberations about his own Manichean past at the end of the fourth century).

Just as an interest in the humanity of Christ becomes discernible in contemporary religious art, and just as the dramatic ceremonies in the Latin liturgy similarly supplement the long tradition for resurrection plays at Easter with representations of the Passion and of the weeping Mary at her Son's Cross (both major themes for the new genre of the *lauda*, as well as already mentioned), so the Franciscans brought with them also a new interest in ordinary people as well as in following the simple and brotherly love of Christ.

This interest went far beyond the sacred liturgical space. In a sense it sanctified the secular realm. Actual relations between a person and his 'brothers and sisters' became the most important ideal, an attitude that referred back to the apostolic age. As Blake Wilson makes it clear— quoting Honorius of Autun—the mendicant movements in this respect also took up recent theological thoughts from the late twelfth century concerning the divinity present in all of creation.[25] Furthermore, the use of devotional pictures, which were owned by the *laudesi* confraternities and in front of (and directed towards) which many *laude* were sung, is indicative of this basic idea that the sacred could be manifested in material things.[26]

How deeply such ideas were embedded in the faith and life of Saint Francis is attested to in his already-mentioned *Canticle of Brother Sun*. If we leave aside its general praising of God in the beginning and its last stanzas on forgiveness, peace, and death (later added by Francis himself), this seemingly simple song praising the Lord for his creation divides creation into the following main components, each the object of individual praise: Brother Sun, Sister Moon with the Stars, Brother Wind, Brother Water, Brother Fire, and "Sister, our Mother the Earth."

In his discussions of the *Canticle* text Éloi Leclerc remarks that Francis did not conform to the traditional order of the four elements: Earth, Water, Air, and Fire. Drawing upon, among others, the historian of religion, Mircea Eliade, he reads the organizational pattern as one of opposite, complementary pairs which create a fundamentally symbolic description of the universe, with, for instance, the pair Wind (Spirit)/ Water associating to spiritual and earthly rebirth (John 3,5–8).[27]

Commenting on the fact that Christ is not mentioned in the text of the canticle, Leclerc proposes to read the canticle as a whole, including the parts written last, as an expression of the deep integration of the mystery of Christ into the world as Francis perceived it—an expression in agreement with the traditional theological concepts of the Incarnation and the Passion and humiliation of the Son of God.[28] Thus also the *Canticle* seems to promote the sanctification of the everyday world.

It is interesting to read certain statements by Messiaen concerning his opera in the light of such Franciscan traditions. Whereas the human orientation in the spiritual movements of the twelfth and thirteenth centuries later became extremely influential in Protestant, Catholic, and humanistic thinking, and thus has established itself as a commonplace for the modern Western world, the opposite idea of the sanctification of the secular is far from widespread in the twentieth century, even among religious people.

It is a natural question for a modern audience to ask why one would want to create a religious opera, particularly considering the history of opera. Generally, and certainly in the classical period of *opera seria*, composers in this genre did not take up biblical or overtly religious themes, presumably in order not to confuse the theatrical with the religious. When biblical themes began to emerge around 1800, as in Étienne Méhul's *Joseph* (1807) and Rossini's *Mosé in Egitto* (Moses in Egypt, 1818), it was the narrative—just as in the oratorios of Handel—on which librettists and composers focused.

Messiaen expressed the opposite ideals in his comments on his opera. He avoided all the parts of Saint Francis's life that would have given opportunity to the most obviously dramatic action, such as the confrontations between Francis and his father after Francis's conversion, and also the most outwardly colorful events from Francis's later life. The point for Messiaen was the inner development of the saint, his struggle with his own mind as it is expressed, for instance, through the repeated appearance of the figure of the leper.[29]

In his interview with Brigitte Massin Messiaen gives a number of explanations for omitting otherwise important and dramatically relevant parts of the transmitted narratives about Saint Francis. One of his reasons is his dislike for psychoanalytical approaches and purely pragmatic staging arguments.[30] More significantly, the fundamental (and also explicitly stated) reason for his dispositions is clearly the wish to portray the inner religious battle in the life of Saint Francis.

In its theme the opera harks back to much earlier traditions, as for instance the twelfth-century Latin music-dramatic ceremony by Hildegard von Bingen, the *Ordo Virtutum,* which similarly describes a soul's inner drama. One difference in terms of genre, however, is obvious. Whereas Hildegard's *Ordo* was doubtlessly planned for performance in Hildegard's convent church, Messiaen uses the totally secular space of an opera theater for his sacred drama.

It is noteworthy how Messiaen, in his directions concerning costumes, refers to particular pictorial traditions connected with mendicant spirituality. He mentions Cimabue (active at least between 1272 and 1302) and Giotto (c. 1266–1337), two painters who were connected with important frescoes in the Basilica of Saint Francis in Assisi. (This basilica was built already at the time of his canonization to house the earthly remains of Francis. It became a focal point for the conflicts between Franciscan fractions, some of whom considered the fraternity's ideal of poverty violated by the splendor of the church). The frescoes of Cimabue and Giotto are thought to be among the earliest pictorial sources of the life of Saint Francis. However, the fact that Messiaen also points to the Dominican Fra Angelico (1400–1455), whose art was historically remote but devotionally essential to the mendicant spirituality, gives a clear indication of the composer's religious intentions behind the staging of his opera.[31]

Messiaen's attitude to his theatrical work doubtless constitutes a sacralization of the secular. Just as all of Messiaen's music constitutes a praising of God, this particular work is in itself both a praise and a sermon. Messiaen, like the mendicant friars, approaches one of the places where one can meet the influential urban elite, building a devotional service through his musical and spiritual universe in the opera house.

FROM LITURGY AND PIOUS CEREMONIAL TO OPERA

In the article "L'opéra avant l'opéra," published in *Revue de Paris* (February 1904) and later republished in *Musiciens d'autrefois*, the famous French author and music connoisseur, Romain Rolland (1866–1944) criticized the established idea that opera was created by a number of Florentine musicians and poets towards the end of the sixteenth century.[32] He drew the readers' attention to the music-dramatic forms anticipating opera, in particular to the vernacular *sacre rappresentazioni* of fifteenth-century northern Italy. Rolland's remarks should come as no surprise today when scholarship has been treating both these and other medieval music-dramatic genres extensively. However, the well-known fact that music-dramatic forms preceded the opera by centuries, particularly in Latin and vernacular religious plays or ceremonies, has not yet been fruitfully applied to a cultural interpretation of the operatic genre.[33]

A point of departure for a discussion of this perspective is the fact that the basic Western music culture, a culture of musical composition or of music writing, fundamentally can be traced back to the above-mentioned liturgical reforms of Charlemagne and his father, Pepin III, in the second half of the eighth century. The beginnings of Western musical composition are marked by the sacred distance of the medieval liturgy as well as by an emerging interest in making music theologically or liturgically true, intentions that gradually brought with them attitudes much closer to the artistic considerations of later times.

The beginnings of the so-called liturgical drama can be described as ceremonial re-enactments of biblical episodes which were sung, as was all of the liturgy. To talk about drama is anachronistic in the sense that nothing in the early manuscripts gives us reason to think of these stylized and brief dialogues as transcending mere liturgical practice and involving theatrical elements. These ceremonies were conceived with ritual intentions and at the same time artistically crafted, which was also true of the music of the Carolingian liturgy.[34]

However, the history of the liturgical drama is also part of the history of the European medieval and modern (music) drama. Just as music through many centuries developed its liturgical and artistic features more or less simultaneously, so also did the Latin music drama. In the later Middle Ages, certainly since the twelfth century, compositions began to include more or less devotional vernacular plays; these were developed along lines similar to those described above. Like some of the larger Latin music plays of these centuries, these were not in any strict sense part of the liturgy. Although they were not normally set to music, they carry some marks of their liturgical roots, as witnessed, for instance, by the interpolations of liturgical songs in the English so-called cycle plays.[35]

The earliest recorded music-dramatic activity within the Latin liturgy consisted of representations of the biblical accounts of Christ's Resurrection. These dialogues—later referred to as *Quem quaeritis* dialogues (after the beginning line, "whom do you seek...")—portrayed conversations between the women at the grave of Jesus and one or more angels on Easter morning, as found in liturgical manuscripts early in the tenth century. The biblical enactment took its point of departure from the ritual of prayers, praisings, announcements, and exhortations, thus enabling the congregation to experience the historical myth at the basis of the Christian religion. Through this it aimed at creating a new foundation for the ritual celebration, which could connect the lives of the congregation with the efficacious mythico-historical events upon which it drew. In this way, historical or narrative linear time can be said to have been combined with a different temporal concept (sometimes described as absolute or punctual) that is connected with the transcendent aspect fundamental to a religious ritual, with its basic assumption of a divine presence here and now.[36]

The two aspects of the liturgy that came into play here depended on each other: the ritual would have become devoid of meaning if it lost its historical basis, while the liturgical function of the narrative consisted in its pointing towards the celebration or praising and towards the divine presence in the very moment.

Although such liturgical aspects obviously were no longer present in plays outside the liturgy, there seems to have been, during the following centuries, an almost universal connection between narration and some kind of celebratory practice, both in all Latin music drama and in the vernacular and spoken medieval dramas or ceremonies mentioned above. In fact, even the European music dramas in the much later secular context of the opera seem to carry within them such a division between the narrative and the celebratory.[37]

As I have tried to show, the emphasis on preaching the gospel in the vernacular to ordinary people, and on lay piety in the confraternities associated with the new mendicant movements of the thirteenth century, affected the medieval and post-medieval culture in ways that can hardly be overrated. Yet it must be noted that there were important continuities between the much more hierarchical earlier medieval forms of liturgical piety and the new popular spirituality.[38] In a sense what happened was that certain ideas and structures from the Latin high culture of the church and the monastic world were transformed so as to make them function in a society in which the first signs of the later characteristic European city culture were emerging.

Cyrilla Barr has described a number of devotional ceremonies from the early *disciplinati* (flagellant) confraternities with the scourging placed between traditional Latin liturgical items and the singing of *laude* as well as the development of the dramatic *lauda* itself. Her examples clearly show a continuity between, on the one hand, the Latin liturgical ceremonies and the liturgical dramas and, on the other hand, these more or less vernacular devotions: processions, various narrative or linear structures interrupted by and at last ending with the singing of exhortational or celebrational songs. (An example of such a devotion is the *mandatum* ceremony, the ritual of feet washing based on the account of Jesus washing the feet of the disciples as told in John 13, 1–17, whether or not such a representational ceremony should be called dramatic).[39]

The way of dealing with religious narrative in an edifying context, particularly the juxtaposition of the two basic liturgical representations of time, was not only preserved from earlier eras and carried over to the new evangelical lay movements of the high and late Middle Ages. What is more, it had a pronounced influence on musico-dramatic devotional forms in the period of the Counter-reformation. In this context the *laude,* and the devotional services in which they were mainly sung, became an inspirational force behind the edificational endeavours that led to the establishment of the Roman confraternity *Congregazione dell'Oratorio* founded by Filippo Neri (1515–95) at the *Oratorio di S. Maria in Vallicella.* The musical assemblies here led to the further development of a spiritual equivalent to the opera, the oratorio which in turn gave rise also to the Protestant oratorio (and Passion oratorio) traditions.[40] Using the so-called *stile rappresentativo*, the musical style developed together with the new genre of the music drama in Florence towards the end of the sixteenth century, the dialogues and later the Roman oratories presented mainly biblical narratives. These were incorporated into devotional services comprising praises, prayers, and sermons, a setting the confraternities of the thirteenth century had first introduced.

In imperial Vienna and in Salzburg during the Baroque period, the *oratorio* was combined with liturgical Passion traditions to form a new genre, the *sepolcro*. In the initial stages, such oratorios were theatrically performed in a church, in front of the holy sepulchre (the sepulchre of Christ). This genre must be seen in the light of medieval liturgico-dramatic traditions concerning the Passion, as for instance the burial of the host or of a cross. Another example for this tradition was called the *improperia*. This was a liturgical representation of Jesus reproaching the congregation for his Crucifixion. In the medieval church it was typically carried out on Good Friday. Also part of this group were Passion recitations and Passion dramas. Many composers in seventeenth-century Vienna wrote *sepolcri*, among them Antonio Draghi (1635–1700).[41] In the eighteenth century such performances were no longer theatrical as a rule.

In the cathedral of Salzburg, a *Grabtheater* (sepulchral stage) had been built, presumably by the prince archbishop von Schrattenbach (1753–71), for ceremonies at the holy sepulchre. With the arrival of enlightenment ideas such lavish ritual was no longer tolerated and the *Grabtheater* was removed by the prince archbishop von Colloredo in 1782. Before this, however, in 1767, the young Wolfgang Amadeus Mozart had written his short music-dramatic Good Friday devotion, *Grabmusik* (Sepulchre Music) K. 42, in the German *sepolcro* tradition.[42]

The Latin music drama had not disappeared when new genres of music (or spoken) drama entered the stage. Up to the Reformation in the early decades of the sixteenth century and the Council of Trent (1545–63), the short liturgical *Quem quaeritis* plays were very common, and in spite of a clear decline in the practice after the middle of the sixteenth century, such liturgical music dramas were still written —and no doubt performed—even as late as the end of the eighteenth century.[43]

A continuity from the liturgical drama to the genre of opera may seem less surprising when we notice that influential individuals bridged this gap in their person. The famous Florentine sponsor of the arts, Jacopo Corsi (1560–1602), patron of the musico-literary academy where the opera was created, in the very same period was a member of the religious confraternity *Compagnia dell'Arcangelo Raffaello*, which among other activities also performed sacred music dramas.[44]

In terms of celebratory items included in operatic narratives, some very few examples must suffice: the praise of the *musica* in the prologue of Monteverdi's *Orfeo* (1607), the forgiveness and its praise at the end of Mozart's *Le Nozze di Figaro*, and, in a more complex way, the interweaving of narrative and absolute time in the judgment scene of *Don Giovanni*.[45] The finales of both acts in Mozart's *Die Zauberflöte* also provide such examples, as do the finale of Beethoven's *Fidelio* and that of Weber's *Der Freischütz* with the exhortations of the hermit. It was only with through-composed operas that the genre took a decisive step away from such traditions, although the scheme celebration/action is fundamental in operas such as Wagner's *Tannhäuser* (1848) and *Parsifal* (1882)—and in many more.

Medieval liturgical music-dramatic traditions were thus preserved or transformed to some extent into the music dramatic traditions of modern Europe, often retaining the above-mentioned play between celebration and narration.

In this century, composers for whom the modern distance to the old musico-religious dramatic traditions may have opened a new interest in the original genre have again begun to draw upon the original medieval genres. These include particularly Benjamin Britten and Peter Maxwell Davies. Britten's *Noye's Fludde* (1957) is based on the third play of the *Chester Mystery Cycle* of the late sixteenth century.[46] While Davies's *The Martyrdom of Saint Magnus* (1976) draws most immediately on the novel *Magnus* (1973) by the Orkney writer George Mackay Brown,[47] it ultimately goes back to an account in the *Orkneyinga Saga*[48] about the death of the local saint Magnus, in 1116. Davies's music drama is a veneration of Magnus's saintly, pacifistic attitude.

THE SECOND TABLEAU OF MESSIAEN'S *SAINT FRANÇOIS D'ASSISE*

In the final section of this chapter I will discuss one scene from Messiaen's opera in the context of the account given of the continuity of the Latin medieval liturgy, the Franciscan pious vernacular *lauda* singing, and modern opera.

The second tableau or scene is explicitly called *Les laudes* (The Praises, alluding to the morning prayer of the Office).[49] Saint François is singing the Office of Matins together with the brothers Sylvestris, Rufinus, and Bernardus and a choir of other brothers. After an orchestral introduction the curtain is raised and the end of the prayers heard. The text quotes those stanzas from the *Canticle of Brother Sun* that deal with the four elements, Brother Wind, Brother Water, Brother Fire, and Sister, our Mother the Earth.

Saint François:

> *Loué sois-tu, mon Seigneur, pour frère Vent, pour l'air et les nuages, le ciel pur, le ciel pur et tous les temps! Loué sois-tu, Seigneur!*

Praised be you, my Lord, for Brother Wind, For the air and the clouds, the clear sky, the clear sky and all weather! Praised be you, Lord!

The three Brothers:

> *Vous êtes digne, Seigneur notre Dieu...*

You are worthy, O Lord our God...

First and second basses of the Choir take over: (they all, both the three brothers and the choir, sing in unison on one note: a C♯):

de recevoir louange et gloire, honneur et bénédiction.[50]	to receive praise and glory, honour and blessing.

The three Brothers:

Digne est l'Agneau, l'Agneau immolé...	Worthy is the Lamb, the Lamb who was slain ...

First and second basses of the Choir (in unison on C♯):

de recevoir force et divinité, sagesse et puissance, honneur, gloire, et bénédiction.[51]	to receive strength and adoration, wisdom and might, honor and glory and blessing.

Saint François:

Loué sois-tu, mon Seigneur, pour sœur Eau, elle est très utile et humble, précieuse et chaste!	Praised be you, my Lord, for Sister Water, she is very useful and humble, precious and chaste!
Loué sois-tu, mon Seigneur, pour frère Feu, pour frère Feu par qui tu éclaires la nuit! il est beau, joyeux, robuste et fort!	Praised be you, my Lord, for Brother Fire, for Brother Fire through whom you light up the night! He is very beautiful, joyful, sturdy and strong!
Loué sois-tu, Seigneur!	Praised be you, Lord!

The three brothers:

Bénissez le Seigneur toutes les œuvres du Seigneur.[52]	Bless the Lord, all you works of the Lord.

First and second basses of the Choir (in unison on C♯):

Qu'il soit loué par le ciel et la terre, et toute créature du ciel et de la terre.[53]	That He may be praised by Heaven and Earth, and by all creatures of Heaven and Earth.

The three brothers:

Bénissons le Père, le Fils, et le Saint Esprit.	Let us praise the Father, the Son, and the Holy Spirit.

First and second basses of the Choir (in unison on C♯):

Louons le, et surexaltons le à jamais, maintenant et dans les siècles de siècles!	Let us praise him and highly exalt him forever, now and in eternity!

Saint François:

> *Loué sois-tu, mon Seigneur,*
> *pour sœur notre mère la*
> *Terre, qui nous soutient et*
> *nous nourrit, et produit tous*
> *les fruits, et les fleurs, les*
> *fleurs aux mille couleurs, le*
> *fleurs et l'herbe!*
> *Loué sois tu, loué sois tu,*
> *Seigneur!*

Praised be you, my Lord, for
Sister our Mother the Earth
who sustains us and feeds us
and produces all the fruits, the
flowers of thousands of
colours, the flowers and the
herbs!
Praised be you, praised be
you, Lord!

Choir:

> *Saint! Saint! Saint! le*
> *Seigneur Dieu! qui est, et qui*
> *était, et qui vient!*[54]

Holy, Holy, Holy, the Lord
God! Who is and was and is
to come!

(The three brothers and the choir leave the stage slowly while the choir sings):

> *Loué soit Dieu! Loué soit*
> *Dieu! et loué soit Dieu!*

Praised be God! Praised be
God! And praised be God!

Saint François:

> *O Toi! Toi qui as fait le*
> *Temps! le Temps et l'Espace,*
> *la lumière et la couleur, le*
> *papillon parfumé, la goutte*
> *d'eau claire, et la chanson du*
> *vent qui change de ton dans*
> *chaque arbre!*
> *Tu as permis aussi l'existence*
> *de la laideur: que le crapaud*
> *pustuleux, le champignon*
> *empoisonneur, voisinent, voi-*
> *sinent avec la libellule et*
> *l'oiseau bleu...*
> *Tu sais combien j'ai peur,*
> *combien j'ai horreur des lé-*
> *preux, de leur face rongée, de*
> *leur odeur horrible et fade!*
> *Seigneur! Seigneur! fais moi*
> *rencontrer un lépreux... rends*
> *moi capable de l'aimer...*[55]

O You! You who have
created Time! Time and
Space, Light and Colour, the
fragrant butterfly, the taste of
clear water, and the song of
the wind changing its tone in
every tree!
You have even permitted the
existence of the ugly: that the
pustulous toad, the poisonous
fungus live side by side with
the dragon fly and the blue
bird...
You know how much I fear,
how much I feel horror of the
lepers, of their corroded faces,
their horrible and insipid
smell! Lord! Lord! Let me
meet a leper... make me
capable of loving him...

The *Canticle of Brother Sun* in this scene has become part of a responsorial song in which the parts of the choir almost function as in a medieval responsory. A small group of lead singers (in the Middle Ages called the *paraphonistae*), here the three brothers, is answered by the full choir (the *schola*). In this responsorial song Saint François sings his own words reflecting a more independent praise than the others' Biblical paraphrases.

This second scene of the drama is fundamentally celebratory in its mood and refrains from any real action. The meditative and celebratory approach is to a large extent characteristic of the whole work, as already mentioned. A certain kind of dramatic development does happen, however, as the responsorial prayer ends when the brothers leave the stage. François, staying alone on the stage, sings the 'free' words of Messiaen to express his inner conflict, the fear of the lepers (and of ugliness in general), and his prayer that he may be able to love even this part of reality.

The *Saint! Saint! Saint!* (Holy!, Holy!, Holy!) that the full choir sings in dissonant chords ends the responsorial singing of the morning prayer. François's melody for the stanzas of the *Canticle of Brother Sun* is partly based on a diminished seventh and partly chromatic, whereas the biblical responses by the three brothers (all basses) and the basses of the choir simply consist of the recitation note, C♯.[56]

An interlude of bells, xylophone, xylorimba, and marimba follows, after which the choir ends the "formal" Matins with the triple *Loué soit Dieu!* (Praised be God!) as it leaves the stage, together with the brothers. A new orchestral liveliness, beginning in the deep strings, leads into François's exclamation, initially dominated by an upward major third (A♭-C) with the "bell music" repeated in between.[57] Both François's melody and the orchestra become increasingly agitated, until the saint's melody suddenly calms down at the text: *Tu as permis...* (You have permitted...). His vocal gesture is now basically limited to a recitation on F♯, interrupted by occasional dissonant tritone intervals and other musical exclamations, and accompanied by unabatedly strong orchestral eruptions.[58]

When François admits his fear of the lepers with their terrible look and smell, his basic recitation tone is C, with F♯ as a kind of "tenor", but his singing gradually changes into a flowing melodic expression.[59] The following orchestral interlude depicts the inner battle of Saint François, leading to his exclamation *Seigneur!* (Lord)—again on the leitmotivic major-third interval A♭-C.[60] His subsequent prayer begins as a recitation on F♯, now with C as the secondary tonal center.[61] After further eruptions in the orchestra a very expressive melody unfolds, which concludes the prayer, *rends moi capable de l'aimer...* (make me capable of loving him...).[62] The "bell music" returns and is violently interrupted by the final chords of the full orchestra.

This description aimed to give a sense how Messiaen has managed to let the static celebration gradually move into a different—although not opposed—mood, where the recitation of the Office is never far away, but where the personal conflicts of man are not remote either, even for the saintly François. The play between celebration and action here becomes a play between celebration and the action of an inner battle in which the protagonist François in the end dares to expose the conflict so that he can ask for help—in the celebratory mood, but also in an honest presentation of his feelings.

Messiaen does not literally quote the medieval liturgy or medieval singing at all. Yet, by means of the vocal gestures he chose for his opera he hints at the fundamental differences between recitation and melodic singing, and thus implicitly touches upon essential characteristics of the medieval liturgy. From the point of view of overall compositional technique, style, or musical expression there certainly is an enormous distance, but through the described kind of liturgical typology the Middle Ages are evoked nonetheless.

Without any strict musical medievalism, then, the structural features of the medieval liturgy are present in some way. Furthermore, the distinction between the linear unfolding of François's feelings and the Biblical and liturgical praises evokes the kind of spirituality discussed above, one that is connected to the Gothic age and mendicant piety. What is witnessed in the scene is in the end a personal, not a liturgical prayer voiced by François. Even in the part of the scene where we should still be in the morning prayer, his own words, from the *Canticle of Brother Sun*, are appropriately used to lead him into the secret recesses of his heart, to a place where he is still not able to praise God through all of creation.

The demand on his personal feelings, subjectively felt by the protagonist François, is far removed from the collective mood of the Latin liturgy. It does, however, accord well with the new individual piety of the thirteenth century, which departed from the collective traditional liturgical praising while retaining it as its basic ideal and goal.[63]

NOTES

[1]For general and biographical information about the composition of Messiaen's only opera see Paul Griffiths, *Olivier Messiaen and the Music of Time* (Ithaca, New York: Cornell University Press, 1985), pp. 235-243, Aloyse Michaely, *Die Musik Olivier Messiaens. Untersuchungen zum Gesamtschaffen* (Hamburg: Verlag der Musikalienhandlung Karl Dieter Wagner, 1987), pp. 679-680 (and p. 507), Theo Hirsbrunner, *Olivier Messiaen. Leben und Werk* (Laaber: Laaber-Verlag, 1988), pp. 192-200, and Brigitte Massin, *Olivier Messiaen: une poétique du merveilleux* (Aix-en-Provence: Éditions Alinéa, 1989), pp. 187-201.

[2]*The Little Flowers of Saint Francis. First Complete Edition, and Entirely New Version, With Twenty Additional Chapters.... Considerations on the Holy Stigmata, Life and Sayings of Brother Giles, Life of Brother Juniper.* A modern English translation from the Latin and the Italian with introduction, notes and biographical sketches by Raphael Brown [pseud.] (Garden City, NY: Image Books, 1958).

[3]I refer to Théophile Desbonnets and Damien Vorreux O.F.M., eds., *Saint François d'Assise. Documents écrits et premières biographies* (Paris: Éditions Franciscaines, 1968), containing French translations of the works of Saint Francis himself as well as the early Franciscan writings with introductions. The two works which Messiaen mentioned as his most important sources are found edited by Alexandre Masseron on pp. 1157-1384 (introduction pp. 1159-74, *Les Fioretti* pp. 1175-1324, and *Les considérations* pp. 1325-1384). Other material of high importance is found in the *Writings of Leo, Rufino and Angelo Companions of Saint Francis*, the early traditions behind the more well-known *Legend of the Three Companions*. See Rosalind B. Brooke, *Scripta Leonis, Rufini et Angeli Sociorum S. Francisci* (Oxford: Clarendon Press, New Corrected Edition, 1990) with a very clarifying introduction on the early Franciscan writings. Concerning Messiaen's use of the fourteenth-century works, see Massin, *op. cit.*, pp. 189-190, 195-197, and 200, Hirsbrunner, *op. cit.*, pp. 193 and 196-197, and Michaely, *op. cit.*, pp. 396, 507, 759.

[4]The account given here of the beginnings of the Franciscan movement only gives the most necessary information in particular focusing upon relevance to the following discussion of the forms of pious ceremonies. Although there exists information about the biography of Francis and the movement from very early times (see above at note 3), it has seemed very hard, indeed, to arrive at a general concensus about important questions, due to the particular historical circumstances within the Franciscan Order connected with the genesis (and the suppression) of much of the early material.

I refer in particular to the following fairly recent treatments of Saint Francis and the beginnings of the Franciscan movement: C.H. Lawrence, *The Friars. The Impact of the Early Mendicant Movement on Western Society* (London and New York: Longman, 1994) particularly pp. 26-64, and Adriaan H. Bredero, "The Beginnings of the Franciscan Movement and the Canonization of Its Founder," in Adriaan H. Bredero, *Christendom and Christianity in the Middle Ages* (Grand Rapids, MI: William B. Eerdmans Publishing Company, 1994), pp. 246-273. Note for instance the interesting discussion around the unusually rapid canonization of Francis in 1228 by Gregory IX and the possibility that this at least partly was due to a papal effort to keep the Franciscan movement within the church. In this context it is also important to note that the first biography of Thomas of Celano was commissioned by Gregory IX (at the same time), *ibid.*, pp. 260-65.

[5]For a broad discussion of this debate and the connections between the liturgico-theological decisions of the early thirteenth century, see Miri Rubin, *Corpus Christi. The*

Eucharist in Late Medieval Culture (Cambridge: Cambridge University Press, 1991). She treats the important contributions to the cultural and dramatic history of Europe which were the result of the creation of a feast for the consecrated 'host', the *Corpus Christi* feast, with its processional and dramatic activities, among them the famous cycle plays from the fourteenth and the following centuries.

[6]See Blake Wilson, *Music and Merchants. The Laudesi Companies of Republican Florence* (Oxford: Clarendon Press, 1992), esp. pp. 5-13. Among other things he writes: "... a closer look at lay company activities reveals what they considered to be one of the most effective means of persuasion—song. The lauda of the laudesi companies was deemed strong spiritual currency, for as sung prayer it passed swiftly up the ladder of carefully cultivated sacred connections, from deceased members, through the saints small and great, to Mary and Jesus to join the eternal *canto celestiale.*" *Ibid.,* p. 7.

[7]Preserved prayers composed by Saint Anselm (1033-1109), Archbishop of Canterbury, were created for private spiritual use in monasteries but also outside the monastic world. See Benedicta Ward, *The Prayers and Meditations of Saint Anselm* (Harmondsworth, Middlesex: Penguin Books, 1973), Introduction, pp. 35-43, and the translated edition of the letter to the Countess Mathilda, *ibid,* p. 90.

[8]The dating of the earliest *laudesi* confraternities has been debated among scholars. According to Blake Wilson no *laudesi* company can be dated earlier than the 1260s (Wilson, *Music and Merchants,* 1992, p. 29). See more generally the thorough discussion of the rise of the early confraternities pp. 28-45. Similarly, Giulio Cattin, *Music of the Middle Ages I*—translated from the Italian by Steven Botterill—(Cambridge: Cambridge University Press, 1987), p. 183, as Wilson referring to the pioneering work of G.-G. Meersseman (in Italian) in the 1960s and 1970s.

Sandro Sticca, in contrast, claims that the earliest record of a *laudesi* confraternity is known from Florence as early as 1183. Sandro Sticca, "Italy: liturgy and christocentric spirituality" in Eckehard Simon ed., *The Theatre of Medieval Europe. New Research in Early Drama* (Cambridge: Cambridge University Press, 1991), pp. 169-188, see p. 169.

Cyrilla Barr, *The Monophonic Lauda and the Lay Religious Confraternities of Tuscany and Umbria in the Late Middle Ages* (Kalamazoo, Michigan: Medieval Institute Publications, 1988) does not give a precise dating, but claims (p. 13) that "there is very substantial evidence of such singing activities from before the *flagellanti* period," and seems to indicate that one of the confraternities founded in Florence by Peter of Verona in 1244 was a *laudesi* society. Compare, however, (also concerning the early datings followed by Sticca) Wilson, *Music and Merchants,* 1992, p. 29, notes 115 and 120.

[9]Sandro Sticca, "Italian Theater of the Middle Ages: From the *Quem Quaeritis* to the *Lauda.*" *Forum italicum* 14 (3), 1980: 275-310, here pp. 294-295 proposing a connection between the early liturgical drama and the genesis of the *lauda*. See also Sandro Sticca, *The Latin Passion Play: Its Origins and Development* (Albany, NY: State University of New York Press, 1970), pp. 61-62 and 77-78 (edition of text) and Robert Edwards, *The Montecassino Passion and the Poetics of Medieval Drama* (Berkeley: University of California Press, 1977), pp. 21 (English translation of text) and 54-55.

[10]An English translation of the two *vitae* by Thomas of Celano with an introduction is found in Placid Hermann, ed., *Saint Francis of Assisi. The First and Second Life of Saint Francis with selections from The Treatise on the Miracles of Blessed Francis* (Chicago: Franciscan Herald Press, 1988 (1963)), see section 109 of the first biography, p. 99.

For the text of this *"lauda"*, see Damien Vorreux, Paul Bayart et al. eds., *Les opuscule de Saint François d'Assise* (Paris: Éditions franciscaines, 1956), pp. 309-314, giving the oldest preserved and seemingly original—Umbrian—text, a French translation and a reconstruction in Tuscan as well as a short introduction. See *ibid.* p. 309. Also Théophile Desbonnets, Jean-François Godet et al., eds., *François d'Assise: Écrits*—texte latin, introduction et traduction—sources chrétiennes 285 (Paris: Les Éditions du Cerf, 1981), pp. 342-345, and introduction, pp. 10-13, and 45-46. According to both editions the oldest manuscript (ms. 338 from the municipal library of Assisi) dates from the thirteenth century (1279 resp. the middle of the century). On Francis as the "inventor" of the *lauda*, see Barr, *op. cit.*, pp. 2-3. On the lack of musical notation in the *Canticle of Brother Sun* in ms 338, see Cattin, *op. cit.*, p. 146.

[11]According to Sticca, *Italy: liturgy and christocentric...*, 1991, pp. 169-170, in 1233 they were singing "early forms of the *laude.*" Cf. Elisabeth Diederichs, *Die Anfänge der mehrstimmigen Lauda* (Tutzing: Hans Schneider, 1986), pp. 25-27. Diederichs makes it clear that there is no clear evidence on the singing in 1233, whereas she considers it likely that *laude* were sung during the processions in 1260. See also the more cautious discussion in Barr, *op. cit.*, pp. 32-33, on the processions of the *gran devozione* of 1260, and Cattin, *op. cit.*, pp. 182-183, who gives an English translation of parts of the chronicle of Salimbene (see below at note 12) relating the events of 1233.

[12]Quoted from Barr, *op. cit.*, p. 32.

[13]Barr, *op. cit.,* pp. 2-6.

[14]Barr, *op. cit.*, p. 16, compare however, note 8 above.

[15]Barr, *op. cit.*, pp. 17-24 resp. 36-59.

[16]Wilson, *op. cit.*, pp. 141-182, Barr, *op. cit.*, pp. 22-24; Cattin, *op. cit.*, 1987, p. 150. See also Diederichs, *op. cit.*, pp. 41-42.

[17]Barr, *op. cit.*, pp. 58-59; Cattin, *op. cit.*, p. 147.

[18]Massin, *op. cit.*, p. 189, also Griffiths, *op. cit.*, pp. 235-236.

[19]Hermann ed., *op. cit.*, p. 81 (First Life, section 90).

[20]Hermann ed., *op. cit.*, pp. 101-102 (First Life, section 112) with clear biblical references: 1. Pet. 1,19; John 1,30; and John 19,34.

[21]Desbonnets et Vorreux eds., *Saint François d'Assise. Documents*, 1968, Avant-propos, pp. 8-9.

[22]Wilson, *op. cit.*, pp. 14-15.

[23]Wilson, *op. cit.*, pp. 16-28.

[24]Wilson, *op. cit.*, pp. 19-28.

[25]Wilson, *op. cit.*, p. 17.

[26]Wilson, *op. cit.*, pp. 48 and 183.

[27]Éloi Leclerc, *Le cantique des créatures ou les symboles de l'union. Une analyse de Saint François d'Assise* (Paris: Le Signe/Fayard, 1970), pp. 37-41.

[28]*Ibid.*, pp. 44-54. See especially p. 53, where Leclerc concludes that the *canticle* is a song of the soul having united in Christ the finite and the eternal, the depths of the Earth and the infinity of the Heavens. This becomes the key to Leclerc's following more detailed reading of the poem.

[29]Massin, *op. cit.*, pp. 190-191. Concerning the leper see below, note 53.

[30]*Ibid.*

[31]See Messiaen's instructions concerning Francis in the note on costuming in the score for the second scene (for the bibliographical reference see below note 49) and the instructions concerning the Angel printed in Massin, *op. cit.*, pp. 187-188. Cf. also Griffiths, *op. cit.*, pp. 241-242.

[32]Romain Rolland, "L'opéra avant l'opéra," *Musiciens d'autrefois* (Paris: Librairie Hachette, 7ème édition, 1921), pp. 19-54, see pp. 19-20.

[33]Certainly, such perspectives have entered historical accounts of the opera only to a very limited degree. See for instance the following recent and in most respects highly qualified books: Robert Donington, *The Rise of Opera* (London: Faber and Faber, 1981), Robert Donington, *Opera & Its Symbols. The Unity of Words, Music, & Staging* (New Haven: Yale University Press, 1990), and F.W. Sternfeld, *The Birth of Opera* (Oxford: Clarendon Press, 1993), which at most mention the *sacre rappresentazioni* in passing, and not at all the long-standing tradition for sung music drama in the Latin liturgy.

[34]For a general introduction to such ceremonies see Susan Rankin, "Liturgical Drama." *The New Oxford History of Music*, volume II: *The Early Middle Ages to 1300*, Richard Crocker and David Hiley, eds. (Oxford: Oxford University Press, 1990), pp. 310-356.

[35]See Richard Rastall, "Music in the Cycle," *The Chester Mystery Cycle. Essays and Documents*, R.M. Lumiansky and David Mills, eds. (Chapel Hill: The University of North Carolina Press, 1983), p. 111-164.

[36]See my "A Newly Discovered Fragment of a *Visitatio Sepulchri* in Stockholm." *Comparative Drama*, vol. 30, no. 1 (Kalamazoo, MI, 1996), pp. 32-40, and my two forthcoming papers: "The Musical and Liturgical Composition of *Visitatio Sepulchri* Offices." *Cantus Planus. Papers Read at the 7th Meeting in Sopron, Hungary, Sept. 1995*, Laszlo Dobszay and David Hiley, eds., in print, and "Les textes polyvalents du *Quem quaeritis* à Winchester au dixième siècle." *Le Drame liturgique médiéval*, Marie-Noël Colette, ed., in print.

[37]See my forthcoming paper: "Biblisch-mythische, mittelalterliche liturgisch-musikalische und literarische Traditionen in der Oper *The Martyrdom of Saint Magnus* (1976) von Peter Maxwell Davies." *Kontext 4. Religion und Literatur. Aspekte eines Vergleichs*, Peter Tschuggnall ed. (Salzburg: Verlag Ursula Müller-Speiser, in print).

[38]In addition to the publications already cited, see also Kathleen C. Falvey, "The Italian Saint Play: The Example of Perugia," *The Saint Play in Medieval Europe*, Clifford Davidson, ed. (Kalamazoo, MI: Medieval Institute Publications, 1986), pp. 181-204, see esp. p. 185.

[39]Cyrilla Barr, "From *Devozione* to *Rappresentazione*: Dramatic Elements in the Holy Week *Laude* of Assisi," *Crossing the Boundaries*, Eisenbichler, ed. 1991, p. 11-32, see pp. 14-18, referring to fourteenth-century manuscripts. Barr, in *The Monophonic Lauda*, 1988, pp. 131-150, also gives examples of vernacular *mandato* celebrations clearly modelled on the Latin liturgical practices. Cyrilla Barr writes: "... such popular offices as these are undeniably tributary branches from the same matrix that produced the dramatic representations" (p. 150). See furthermore the descriptions in Wilson, *op. cit.*, pp. 45-73, among other things mentioning how *lauda* singing was incorporated into the Mass in the church with which the confraternity was associated in the so-called *offerta* processions of the *laudesi* societies on a designated Sunday every month. Here the singing of *laude* was incorporated into what "constituted a kind of lay Offertory procession" (p. 58; the Offertory procession during a Mass is the traditional—and in the Middle Ages clerical—procession bringing the elements for the communion to the Altar). Otherwise *laudesi* ceremonies usually took place every evening in front of a devotional picture at the Altar of the patron saint or one of the patron saints of the confraternity and on a

number of special occasions connected with the annual saints' calendar and with funerals.

[40]See Howard E. Smither, *A History of the Oratorio*, (Chapel Hill: The University of North Carolina Press, 1977-1987), particularly volume I, *The Oratorio in the Baroque Era*, pp. 3-145. The use of the term *oratorio* for the narrative musical works of the Roman oratories was established towards the middle of the seventeenth century.

[41]Smither, *op. cit.*, vol. I, pp. 366-382. See also Howard E. Smither, vol. III, *The Oratorio in the Classical Era*, pp. 35 and 340-347.

[42]Concerning Mozart's Grabmusik, see Franz Giegling, ed. *W.A. Mozart: Grabmusik KV 42*, Neue Mozart Ausgabe, Geistliche Gesangswerke, Werkgruppe 4, Band 4. Partitur, BA 4507 (Kassel: Bärenreiter, 1957). See especially, "Zum Vorliegendem Band," pp. VII-IX. Mozart also wrote a few other educational-devotional music dramas in the Jesuit tradition of school music dramas around the same time.

[43]See the documents published in Walther Lipphardt, ed., *Lateinische Osterfeiern und Spiele I-IX* (Berlin: De Gruyter, 1975-90). (Note that more documents have been found since the publication of these volumes). Concerning examples of liturgical drama in the sixteenth to eighteenth centuries see also my article: "Il Doge and the Liturgical Drama in Late Medieval Venice," *The Early Drama, Art, and Music Review* vol. 18, no. 1 (Kalamazoo, Michigan, 1995) pp. 8-24.

[44]Edmond Strainchamps, "Music in a Florentine Confraternity: The Memorial Madrigals for Jacopo Corsi in the Company of the Archangel Raphael." *Crossing the Boundaries. Christian Piety and the Arts in Italian Medieval and Renaissance Confraternities*, Konrad Eisenbichler, ed. (Kalamazoo, MI: Medieval Institute Publications, 1991), pp. 161-178. See esp. pp. 162-163.

[45]See my forthcoming study: "Søren Kierkegaard's Aestheticist and Mozart's Don Giovanni." *Interarts Studies—New Perspectives*, Ulla-Britta Lagerroth, Hans Lund, and Erik Hedling, eds. (Amsterdam: Editions Rodopi B.V, 1997), in print.

[46]Benjamin Britten, *Noye's Fludde. The Chester Miracle Play Set to Music, Op. 59* (London: Hawkes & Son, 1958).

[47]Peter Maxwell Davies, *The Martyrdom of Saint Magnus. A Chamber Opera in Nine Scenes* (London: Boosey & Hawkes, 1977). See also above note 37.

[48]The Saga of the Orkney Islands dates from the end of the twelfthth century, and refers to events happening on the remote Egilsay in the Orkney Islands north of Scotland.

[49]To my knowledge only four of the eight *tableaux* have appeared in print up to now. I refer to tableau 2: Olivier Messiaen, *Saint François d'Assise (Scènes Franciscaines). Opéra en 3 Actes et 8 Tableaux, Acte I—2e Tableau Les Laudes* (Paris: Éditions Alphonse Leduc, 1983/1991). (The other tableaux in print are nos. 4, 5, and 7—printed in resp. 1992, 1992 and 1983/1990).

[50]Paraphrasing *The Revelation to John*, 4,11. For all Biblical texts I refer to the New Revised Standard Version of *The Holy Bible* (Glasgow: Collin Publishers, 1989). I am grateful to the late Père Grégoire, O.P., Copenhagen, for his help in identifying the more or less direct quotes and paraphrases from the French Bible (both canonical and apocryphal) in Messiaen's verbal text.

[51]Cf. *Revelation* 5:12.

[52]*The Prayer of Azariah and the Song of the Three Jews*, 1,35 (Cf. *Psalm* 103,22) i.e., the apocryphal additions to *The Book of Daniel* (in French the "Daniel grec") from the canticle of the three young men in the furnace. The canticle of the three young men in the

furnace constitutes one of the so-called lesser canticles, sung in the medieval office of Lauds on Sundays and feast days. See John Harper, *The Forms and Orders of Western Liturgy From the Tenth to the Eighteenth Century* (Oxford: Clarendon Press, 1991), p. 257. Note that the designations of these additions can be different in different Bible editions. In French as well as in the Latin so-called Vulgate version (the standard Latin Bible text of the Catholic church) the mentioned addition is given as chapter 3 numbering the verses from 24, as it should be inserted at that point in *The Book of Daniel.*

[53]Here and in the following, Messiaen seems to be freely summarizing and paraphrasing *Azariah*, 1:35-68, where individual parts of the creation (sun, moon, stars, winds, fire, the earth, the waters, etc., also including the living creatures) praise God.

[54]*Revelation*, 4,8. Observe the reversal of the order of "is" and "was", as compared to the Biblical text.

[55]Francis's horror of the lepers is attested to by a remark in Thomas of Celano's second biography (chapter 5), see Hermann ed., *op. cit.*, p. 143. Here one finds the following remark:

> *For among all the unhappy spectacles of the world Francis naturally abhorred lepers; but one day he met a leper while he was riding near Assisi...*

Cf. Hirsbrunner, *op. cit.*, p. 196, Michaely, *op. cit.*, p. 679, and Massin, *op. cit.*, pp. 195-196. In the following scene of the opera, *Le baiser au lépreux*, The Kiss for the Leper, Saint François cures a leper with a kiss, an episode told in chapter 25 of the *Fioretti*, where Francis's initial fear of the lepers, however, is not reflected. He also reappears in the last scene of the opera, *La mort et la nouvelle Vie*, The Death and the New Life.

[56]Messiaen, *Saint François d'Assise. Les Laudes*, 1983/1991. The turning point referred to here occurs at cifre 41.

[57]Cifre 55.

[58]Cifre 65-66.

[59]Cifre 67-70.

[60]Cifre 73-74.

[61]Cifre 76.

[62]Cifre 79-80.

[63]I wish to thank Leif Stubbe Teglbjærg and Fran Hopenwasser for valuable help with the English language.

Magic and Enchantment in Olivier Messiaen's *Catalogue d'oiseaux*

Theo Hirsbrunner

Olivier Messiaen drew his strength and the energy to live and compose from three sources: the Roman Catholic faith, the love of nature, and the myth of Tristan and Isolde.[1] These three central ideas complemented each other: without the conviction that nature was God's creation and that love between human beings was God's gift he could not have believed in the omnipotence of the Church to which he remained loyal all his life.

Messiaen built the sounds of nature, the songs of birds, the roar and thunder of water, the proliferation of plants, the shapes of rocks, and the brilliance of light into his music. He explicitly cited Hector Berlioz, Richard Wagner, and Claude Debussy as going back to the same sources and openly declared himself a romantic; according to him, contemporary composers would do well to let themselves be "romanticized" since nineteenth-century composers knew the greatness of nature both in its beautiful and its overwhelming, awe-inspiring guises.[2] Messiaen abhorred big cities, although he was forced by professional necessity to live in Paris. He loved the colorful stained-glass windows of Notre-Dame and Sainte-Chapelle, but also could not forget all the hideousness that had collected in this vast city.[3]

He spent his summers in the country or the mountains, unless he was giving courses or attending performances of his works in America or the Far East. At first he collected birdcalls out of mere curiosity, later he studied the chirping in trees, shrubs, brooks, and rocks with scientific meticulousness and became an internationally renowned ornithologist.[4] He usually noted the melodies by ear, but his wife Yvonne Loriod accompanied him with recording equipment and also photographed the landscape in which they did their research. It was important to have a record of the light, the sunrise, the sunset, and the darkness of the night and thus to provide a context for the many sounds of nature. Colors turned into sounds and sounds into colors. Thus, Messiaen improved on his painter-friend Blanc Gatti's synaesthesia: Gatti painted waves of color streaming out of organ pipes, paintings which hung in Messiaen's music room in Paris.[5] Messiaen did not want to be associated with Henri Michaux, the poet, who also saw colors as sounds and sounds as colors in his mescaline dreams, but in his music he attempted to make us hear what we see.[6] The power given to Messiaen has to be called magic, the power of enchantment. After Debussy, no one else has sung the pantheistic wonders of nature with the same intensity.

I

The *Catalogue d'oiseaux* consists of thirteen pieces symmetrically divided into seven books. The titles of these pieces always refer to the birds that figure most prominently in them, but other birds join in and their names are carefully noted in the score. The result is a concert of many alternating and contrasting voices. In order to give an idea of the enormous length of this work, I will indicate the length of each individual piece:

		minutes
Book 1:		
1)	*Le Chocard des Alpes* — The Alpine Chough	13½
2)	*Le Loriot* — The Golden Oriole	9½
3)	*Le Merle bleu* — The Blue Rock Thrush	13½
Book 2:		
4)	*Le Traquet stapazin* — The Black-Eared Wheatear	16
Book 3:		
5)	*La Chouette hulotte* — The Tawny Owl	8
6)	*L'Alouette Lulu* — The Woodlark	9
Book 4:		
7)	*La Rousserolle effarvatte* — The Reed Warbler	30½
Book 5:		
8)	*L'Alouette calandrelle* — The Short-Toed Lark	5½
9)	*La Bouscarle* — The Cetti's Warbler	11½
Book 6:		
10)	*Le Merle de roche* — The Rock Thrush	19
Book 7:		
11)	*La Buse variable* — The Buzzard	9½
12)	*Le Traquet rieur* — The Black Wheatear	8½
13)	*Le Courlis cendré* — The Curlew	11

A performance of the whole cycle takes approximately 165 minutes. It was first performed by Yvonne Loriod, to whom it is dedicated, at the Salle Gaveau in Paris on 15th April 1959. Such performances are relatively rare. Anatol Ugorsky performed the cycle in several European cities including Basel in autumn 1995. Individual pieces may also be performed out of context—it is a catalogue, after all, where browsing is permitted. But the symmetrical order, the number of pieces in the individual books, points to an overarching plan:

$$3 - 1 - 2 - 1 - 2 - 1 - 3$$

La Rousserolle effarvatte is the central and at the same time the longest piece. Listening from beginning to end, we make a journey through France: *Le Chocard des Alpes* takes place in the high mountains around Grenoble, in the extreme east of France; *Le Courlis cendré* is set in Finistère, a part of Brittany that juts west into the Atlantic. These two points are symbolic: Messiaen claimed to be from Grenoble although he was born in Avignon. As a boy in Grenoble, living with his mother and grandmother while his father fought in the First World War, he made his first important musical experiences.[7] At the other end, Finistère simply means the end of the earth, it is where not just France, but the whole world ends. Listening to the whole cycle, we move from Messiaen's birth as a musician to his anticipated death. At the same time, it takes us through many regions of France in a homage to the country. The south, open towards the Mediterranean, is the most important, while the north is completely absent, probably because the devastation wrought by war and industry would have been foreign to Messiaen's music.

Messiaen is radical in his exclusions. In the commentaries that precede each of the thirteen pieces, human beings are almost completely absent. These commentaries follow the music and describe the events on which it is based. Only once does Messiaen speak about his feelings in the first person: in *La Chouette hulotte.* Cities and villages are mentioned, but they remain remote and do not seem to be inhabited. Only an exotic fairy tale prince and the smile of Leonardo da Vinci's *Mona Lisa* are mentioned in *Le Loriot;* ordinary human beings do not appear. Sometimes the observer's gaze sweeps over terraced vineyards, but no one is at work in them. In *Le Merle de roche,* the rocks with their grotesque shapes remind Messiaen of the painter Max Ernst and his surrealist figures. In *Le Courlis cendré,* the foghorn is heard across the sea; it is the only man-made implement mentioned. On the other hand, a lot of space is devoted to the moods of nature, the color of the sky and the sea. Even the times of the day and the seasons are carefully given.

Not only are there no human beings, but God's name is never mentioned, which is astonishing given that Messiaen is considered a deeply religious artist who wrote all his compositions for the greater glory of God. Even in later years, when he had become very famous and was invited to the United States and Japan, he never missed an opportunity to accompany the service on the organ at the church La Sainte Trinité in Paris. He did not consider himself above this humble duty although he collected honors all over the world. I will return to this problem at the end of this essay and show that God is always present in the creatures of nature and the play of the elements.

But first: Why does Messiaen precede his compositions by commentaries? Would it not have been better to leave the listeners to their own ideas and fantasies? Are not Ludwig van Beethoven's symphonies considered great just because they are purely instrumental and thus evoke more profound emotions than verbal communication? Why those explanations in the *Catalogue d'oiseaux,* which can only circumscribe and hamper the music lover's imagination? These questions are legitimate and cannot simply be disposed of by noting that there are commentaries in all of Messiaen's works. He does not conceal the extramusical relations that his work has. Neither does he make a secret of his compositional techniques, in marked contrast to many of his contemporaries who did not want the sources of their inspiration and their techniques to be revealed. We must assume that for him music was a mere tool with which to sing God's greatness as revealed in nature and human love. That is why he does not use the hustle and bustle of life in the big cities as material and writes, in the *Catalogue d'oiseaux* and many other works, music to which we have to give ourselves up completely if we want to forget time.

Another point should be remembered: Messiaen was an excellent teacher who took pleasure in passing his knowledge on to young people. He was indefatigable: he spent hours and days going through the eight scores for his opera *Saint François d'Assise* with me; he always had time in a world that might have made him vain and self-importantly busy. In the *Catalogue d'oiseaux,* Messiaen invites us to a quiet meditation. We can look at the pictures of the birds on the title pages of the individual books, read the commentaries, which are veritable prose poems, and then lose ourselves in the music which transports us to the magical theater of nature. But do not expect the quick-motion effects of Walt Disney's time exposure films where natural events that take days in reality are compressed into minutes. Once again: Messiaen takes his time and gives us—blissful—time.

II

Now I would like to go through the thirteen movements of the *Catalogue d'oiseaux,* summarize the commentaries, and discuss the music.

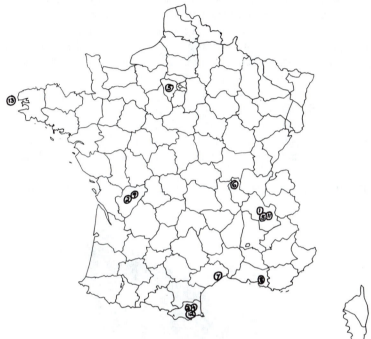

Messiaen's France and Her Birds
(1)   *Le Chocard des Alpes* — The Alpine Chough
(2)   *Le Loriot* — The Golden Oriole
(3)   *Le Merle Bleu* — The Blue Rock Thrush
(4)   *Le Traquet stapazin* — The Black-Eared Wheatear
(5)   *La Chouette hulotte* — The Tawny Owl
(6)   *L'Alouette Lulu* — The Woodlark
(7)   *La Rousserolle effarvatte* — The Reed Warbler
(8)   *L'Alouette calandrelle* — The Short-Toed Lark
(9)   *La Bouscarle* — The Cetti's Warbler
(10)   *Le Merle de roche* — The Rock Thrush
(11)   *La Buse variable* — The Buzzard
(12)   *Le Traquet rieur* — The Black Wheatear
(13)   *Le Courlis cendré* — The Curlew

1. *Le Chocard des Alpes*

We are in the Dauphiné Alps in the extreme east of France—near Italy, to be precise: in the rocks and cliffs of the Meidje, near Grenoble. The Meidje, 3983 meters (13,280 feet) high, was Messiaen's holy mountain; he liked to retire to its foothills to compose his works while facing the glaciers. He would have liked his later work, *Et expecto resurrectionem mortuorum,* to be performed not only in cathedrals, but on the open mountainside, on the slopes of the Meidje. It was here, as I said before, that Messiaen became aware of his vocation to become a composer. In *Le Chocard des Alpes* the grandiose landscape of the Meidje is represented in relentless and massive chords. After a long pause, we hear the cries of the birds—alpine choughs and ravens. Harsh and hideous, they soar over the abysses until the golden eagle rises majestically, carried up into the sky by the winds. The whole grandeur of the mountains is caught in this piece. They are inimical to human beings, but Messiaen is not afraid of them; he carefully gives the names of different rock formations which he climbed himself when he was young.

FIGURE 1: *Le chocard des Alpes* —The Alpine Chough
(Drawings of the thirteen birds were furnished by Siglind Bruhn,
after the watercolors in Auguste Menegaux, *Les Oiseaux de France*
[Paris: Paul Lechevalier & Fils, 1932-39].)

FIGURE 2: *Le loriot* —The Golden Oriole

2. *Le Loriot*

The following piece, featuring the golden oriole, is cheerful and light. We are in the Charente, in the *préfecture* of Angoulême, very near the Atlantic. The oriole, an exotic prince from Africa or Asia, starts to sing at 5:30 in the morning and is soon joined by the wren, the song thrush, the garden warbler, and many others. Their boisterous warbling is only rarely interrupted by a solemn and soothing clarity when the sun with its golden light stands in the south. In French, *Loriot* is pronounced the same way as Loriod; Messiaen's second wife's name was Yvonne Loriod, and she, as I mentioned, first performed the whole cycle and it is dedicated to her. It is safe to assume that in this piece Messiaen wanted to pay homage to his love. The homage is covert, only connoisseurs will notice it, but it is testimony to the happiness she brought into Messiaen's life during his first wife's incurable illness. After years of despair he found peace, was again able to appreciate the beauty of life.

FIGURE 3: *Le merle bleu* —The Blue Rock Thrush

FIGURE 4: *Le traquet stapazin* — The Black-eared Wheatear

3. *Le Merle bleu*

The blue rock-thrush, singing on the shore of the Mediterranean in Roussillon, near the Spanish border, sounds optimistic as well. The cliffs fall in a sheer drop to the water, azure under the sun. The vastness of the horizon encourages tranquil meditation. Waves slap and sparkle against the beach intermittently. The soft song of the blue rock thrush is interrupted by the shrill cries of the herring gull.

4. *Le Traquet stapazin*

Messiaen particularly loved the region of Banyuls in Roussillon because it is home to the black-eared wheatear. Instead of cliffs there are terraced vineyards descending towards the path where this bird sings. Its song sounds capricious like that of the goldfinch, but the herring gull interrupts it with its unmelodious screech. Suddenly the red and gold ball of the sun rises from the sea with sonorous chords across the whole range of the piano. The brighter the sun gets, the more majestic the piano sounds. It is hard to believe that a single instrument is capable of such violence, until the sun sets dark crimson behind the Pyrenees. In the dusk, far away over the black sea, the herring gull is heard again. After a full day in a vibrant landscape the piece ends with the soft song of the spectacled warbler.

FIGURE 5: *La chouette hulotte* —The Tawny Owl

5. *La Chouette hulotte*

The next piece is completely different. The tawny owl and its
relatives, the eagle owl and the long-eared owl, only sing at night in the
woods of Saint Germain en Laye (to the west of Paris) and in Petichet
near Grenoble. Messiaen is eloquent in his description of the fear that
the cries of these birds inspired in him. The night did nothing to soothe
his nerves and is here rendered with inhuman, eerie music.

FIGURE 6: *L'alouette lulu* —The Woodlark

6. *L'Alouette Lulu*

This is also a night piece. But now we are in the Massif Central,
where the Loire has its source, and the dark feels no longer threatening.
The wood lark is softly and melodiously answered by the nightingale;
the calls come from far and near, interrupted by some soothing pianissimo chords. The vastness of the black sky promises safety after the
excitements of the day.

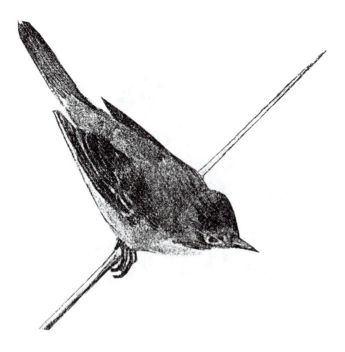

FIGURE 7: *La rousserolle effarvatte* —The Reed Warbler

7. La Rousserolle effarvatte

While in the preceding pieces the impressions of a whole day or a whole night were captured, the piece under discussion now covers a whole day *and* a whole night, from three o'clock in the morning to three o'clock in the morning, and is thus the longest and most important of the cycle, which it bisects. The scene is the *département* of Hérault, west of the Rhone estuary on the Mediterranean. The *préfecture* is Montpellier. On the edge of a pond, whose mysterious sounds we hear, various birds sing in the solemnity of the night which is gradually dispersed by the rising sun. The music is even more mysterious, more subdued than in *Traquet stapazin* and takes its time. Nowhere else in this work is the slowness of natural events as clear as here; no human intervention disturbs the music which at the end returns to its starting point like the cycle of time. The mirror of the pond, the setting for these events, is thus a magical mirror where, held in a trance, we feel things that escape our comprehension.

FIGURE 8: *L'alouette calandrelle* —The Short-toed Lark

FIGURE 9: *La bouscarle* —The Cetti's Warbler

8. *L'Alouette calandrelle*

We are in Provence, on a very hot afternoon in July. The plain of Crau east of the Camargue is scorched by a pitiless sun. There is hardly any vegetation, only pebbles and sand cover the ground. The sound of the crickets is dry and monotonous, interspersed with the calls of birds. Even they are short, terse, as if in response to their environment. This results in a dance-like music of great vivacity, only briefly interrupted by the quail.

9. *La Bouscarle*

This movement is again different. In the Charente, on the banks of a tranquil little stream, the water birds sing in the willows and poplars. Apart from Cetti's warbler, we hear mainly the kingfisher with its magnificent plumage, but the wren and the nightingale also have important parts. The calm of the slowly moving water forms the background to the lively conversation of the birds.

FIGURE 10: *Le merle de roche* —The Rock Thrush

10. *Le Merle de roche*

As so often before in this work, we enter the eerie night. Messiaen does not only present the bright sides of nature, he also knows its abysses and horrors. Here it is mainly the rocks that frighten him and us. They are compared to primeval beings, to stegosaurs, dinosaurs, and human shapes reminiscent of Max Ernst paintings. After the moon-soaked night the sun rises, the rock thrush starts to sing and sings until the evening, when everything is again bathed in pale colors. *Le Merle de roche* is the counterpart to *Le Traquet stapazin*. Both form a book, both are set off from the other movements, both accompany birds through a whole day.

FIGURE 11: *La buse variable* —The Buzzard

11. *La Buse variable*

The cry of the buzzard is fierce and ugly; sometimes it sounds like the meowing of a cat. Other birds join in with sounds that are no less jarring. But when the enormous bird of prey starts to circle over Peti-chet in the *département* of Isère an uneasy calm takes over: monotonously, the notes spread out into ever wider circles, symbolizing the vastness of the sky in which the bird has dwindled to a mere dot.

12. *Le Traquet rieur*

As in *Traquet stapazin* and *Le Merle bleu,* we are in Roussillon; the blue rock thrush from *Le Merle bleu* actually sings again. The sky and the sea are deep blue on this sunny morning in May. The birds and their surroundings radiate laughter and the joy of being alive. Here and there the wind sweeps over the water, making it sparkle.

FIGURE 12: *Le traquet rieur* — The Black Wheatear

13. *Le Courlis cendré*

An island on the most westerly point of the Brittany; if one went further west one would reach America without setting foot on land. The setting is dark, wrapped in fog. Only the lighthouse siren signals the presence of human beings. The cries of the curlew sound faint, melancholy: the last signal of life in this wilderness.

Grandiose as the cycle of *Catalogue d'oiseaux* may have started, it ends subdued and makes one ponder the mystery of a world which is so rich and yet has so many gloomy aspects. I have given the precise surroundings in which the birds sing so that the readers of this essay can follow the journey on a map and get to know a France far from the urban centers. Messiaen does not here talk of art and culture, although they were very important to him. He wanted to show an untouched nature which is more than ever threatened by modern technology. But he never took part in the fight against civilization and its destructive frenzy. He told me he had refused the honorary chairmanship of an association against cruelty to animals. It was only in his art that he could express his love of defenseless creatures. His music, brilliantly performed in the concert hall, gives us an idea of what we would lose if our environment were no longer intact.

FIGURE 13: *Le courlis cendré* —The Curlew

III

For Messiaen, the respect for animals and plants has more than a worldly aspect. Nature in all its beauty is a proof of God's loving kindness towards human beings, however frightening mountains and dark woods may often appear. The text of his opera *Saint François d'Assise* gives us the key to an understanding of our relationship to the world.

It starts in the first act when brother Léon sings: "J'ai peur, j'ai peur, j'ai peur sur la route." [I am afraid, I am afraid, I am afraid on the road.][8] Saint Francis reassures him and proves to him that all the dangers and all the troubles of life are part of God's plan. The fear of the night as expressed in *La Chouette hulotte* of the *Catalogue d'oiseaux* recurs here. In the following operatic tableau it becomes clear that humankind is related to nature, since the wind is its brother, the water its sister.[9] And Saint Francis intones a hymn to time and space, the two factors without which life would be impossible.[10] In later tableaux the family takes on cosmic dimensions: The sun is the brother, the moon the sister of the earth and hence of humankind.[11] Music is meant to bring us nearer to God and to celebrate the unity of all things that have their origin beyond the visible.[12] In the sixth tableau the birds are mentioned:

> *"Frères oiseaux, en tous temps et lieux, louez votre Créateur. Il vous a donné la liberté de voler, présageant par là le don de l'Agilité. Il vous a fait cadeau de l'air, des nuages, du ciel, de frère Soleil et frère Vent pour guider vos voyages."*

> [Birds, my brothers, praise the Creator wherever you are, whenever you can. He has given you the freedom of flight, heralding thus the gift of Agility. He has given you the air, the clouds, the sky, and brother Sun and brother Wind to guide you on your journeys.][13]

Yet at the end of the work Saint Francis takes his leave of the world:

> *"Adieu, créature du Temps! Adieu, créature de l'Espace!"*

> [Adieu, creature of Time! Adieu, creature of Space!][14]

In the *Catalogue d'oiseaux* we have not reached that point yet, it marks the middle, not the conclusion of Messiaen's work. As yet, the world holds him and encloses him with its multifarious appearances. In other works, Messiaen uses bird calls from different continents in order to emphasize the universal character of his music. But here, in the *Catalogue d'oiseaux,* he restricts himself to France, not out of chauvinism, but in order to show how a comparatively small expanse of land can contain all the riches of the world. In thirteen pieces, symmetrically divided into seven books, Messiaen presents a view of his country.

The French like to term their country the hexagon. Yet what appears on the map as a six-sided shape is not arrogant and egotistically closed in on itself. The last piece of the cycle leaves solid ground behind: *Le Courlis cendré* takes us, as I said, to Finistère, to the end of the world. Walking or flying onwards, one enters the uncertain, the unlimited. All orientation in time and space becomes impossible. We are at the threshold to the invisible of which Messiaen would speak mysteriously in his last years. He would leave the beauties of nature and the values evoked in the Tristan and Isolde myth—I mentioned them at the beginning of my essay—behind him. Whether it was only the Catholic faith that accompanied him to the next world has to remain open. Like no other composer of his time Messiaen remained loyal to the Church authorities, but he was also interested in the mystics and far eastern religions which he generously integrated into his universe. He claimed to be better understood in Japan than Beethoven. The synthesis of distant cultures, he believed, made his music accessible to everybody. His music is catholic beyond dogma. The word "catholic," of course, is originally Greek; "kat'holén gén" means "through the whole world." Messiaen perfectly realized this program of the Roman Church in his music. Even if in the *Catalogue d'oiseaux* he indicates times and places almost pedantically, he reaches beyond, into universality.

NOTES

[1]Claude Samuel: *Entretiens avec Olivier Messiaen* (Paris: Belfond, 1967), p. 11 ff.

[2]Samuel, pp. 28, 141.

[3]Samuel, p. 24.

[4]Samuel, p. 110.

[5]Samuel, pp. 30, 36.

[6]Samuel, p. 36.

[7]Samuel, p. 9 ff.

[8]Olivier Messiaen, *Saint François d'Assise*, libretto (Paris: Leduc, 1983), p. 7

[9]Messiaen, p. 13.

[10]Messiaen, p. 14.

[11]Messiaen, p. 31.

[12]Messiaen, p. 32.

[13]Messiaen, p. 40.

[14]Messiaen, p. 51.

PART FOUR

Poetry, Angelic Language, and Contemplations

Messiaen and Surrealism: A Study of His Poetry

Larry W. Peterson

INTRODUCTION

With the exception of one song in *Trois Mélodies* (Le sourire) in which he set a poem written by his mother, Olivier Messiaen wrote himself the poems for his vocal works, for his single opera, and for all but one of his published choral works. His family certainly provided a context supportive to creative writing: his father translated the complete works of Shakespeare into French and his mother, Cécile Sauvage, wrote poetry as did his brother, Alain. Composers who write their own opera libretti are relatively uncommon though several examples come to mind: Richard Wagner, Ruggero Leoncavallo, Paul Hindemith, Gian Carlo Menotti, Thomas Pasatieri, and Arnold Schoenberg. But composers who write their own poetry to set as art songs or as choral works are even more rare. Again, one thinks of Schoenberg who wrote the texts to at least seven of his compositions for choir. Messiaen wrote the texts to three of his four published choral works; the only exception is his oratorio, *La Transfiguration de Notre-Seigneur Jésus-Christ*, for which he selected passages from scripture and the writings of Saint Thomas Aquinas. It is also noteworthy that Messiaen did not discuss his poetry or the poetry of others in his many publications or in any of his notes to accompany the recordings of his vocal compositions.

The purpose of the present study is to explore the relationships of Messiaen's poetry to Surrealist poetry, especially to that written by the "love" poet of Surrealism, Paul Éluard (the *nom de guerre* of Eugène Grindel, 1895–1952). The works by Messiaen that were consulted include the art-song collections—*Trois mélodies* (1930), *Chants de terre et de ciel* (1938), *La mort du nombre* (1930), *Poèmes pour Mi* (1936), *Harawi, chant d'amour et de mort* (1945)—and two choral works: *Trois petites liturgies de la Présence Divine* (1944) and *Cinq rechants* (1949). The two other published choral works, the motet *O Sacrum*

Convivium (1937) and the oratorio *La Transfiguration de Notre-Seigneur Jésus-Christ* (1965–69), use latin texts and are not discussed within this study.

SURREALISM AND POETRY

Surrealism refers to the prominent poetic-artistic activity that centered in Paris between the two world wars. Theories and tenets vital to Surrealism include the Freudian concept of the mind, objective chance and the alienated object, and the Surrealist's approach to the relationship between the artist and his work. Among the subjects that frequently appear in Surrealist poetry, love and humor were favorites. To Messiaen, love is particularly important.

The Freudian concept of the mind is the fundamental principle by which most of the other theories interrelate. The subconscious is the reservoir, as it were, from which the Surrealist artist derives his or her inspiration, adventures, and reality. Surrealism thus discredits reality as it previously had been constituted and even disdains logic and pragmatism. The official definition of Surrealism, written by André Breton, its founder, appears in his First Surrealist Manifesto:

> Pure psychic automatism, by which an attempt is made to express verbally, in writing, or in any other manner, the true functioning of thought. Dictation of thought in absence of control by reason, excluding any aesthetic or moral preoccupation. Surrealism rests on belief in higher reality of certain neglected forms of association, in omnipotence of dream, in disinterested play of thought. It tends to destroy the other psycho-mechanisms and to substitute itself for them in the solution of life's principal problems.[1]

To the Surrealist, a Surreal object is any object alienated from its habitual context, an object whose function is unknown, an object used for purposes different from those usually intended, or an object that realizes the desires of the unconscious. To the Surrealist, coincidence is objective chance and dreams are adventures that reflect the uncontrolled expression of the unconscious. One may best understand the relationship of the Surrealist artist to his work by understanding that the Surrealist artist considers the work to be an expression of the artist's soul, that is, of his inner feelings, experiences, sensations, and desires. Thus, the Surrealist poet places great emphasis on language and imagery through which the reader can discover or touch sensations, dreams, or obscure experiences and thus, the soul.

One of the first creative techniques adopted by Surrealist poets was that of automatic writing, in which the conscious mind is bypassed and, presumably, the unconscious is free to express itself. Automatic texts and speeches made in a state of trance were complimented by accounts of dreams. Automatic writing is characterized by an exterior lack of logic. It proceeds by an interior stream of consciousness that records what comes to mind. The following excerpt from Breton's *Soluble Fish* (1924) illustrates automatism:

> The park, at this time of day, stretched its blonde hands over the magic fountain. A meaningless castle rolled along the surface of the earth. Close to God the register of this château was opened at a drawing of shadows, feathers, irises. The Young Widow's Kiss was the name of the country inn caressed by the speed of the automobile and the drapings of the horizontal glasses. Thus the branches dated the year before never stirred at the approach of the window blinds, when the lights sends the women hurrying to the balcony. The young girl from Ireland, troubled by the jeremiads of the east wind, listened in her breast to the seabird's laughing.[2]

One also identifies Surrealist imagery by its radical juxtaposition of objects—the bringing together of things that are not usually associated, in a way that is highly surprising and sometimes shocking. Paul Éluard, in an essay, "Le miroir de Baudelaire," in *Donner á voir* (1939), explains the relationship of objects alienated from their usual meanings:

> When there is a total fusion between the real image and the hallucination it has provided, no misunderstanding is possible. The similarity between two objects comes as much from the suggestive element contributing to establish it as from the objective relationship existing between them. The poet, the supremely hallucinated man, will establish similitudes to his liking between the most dissimilar objects (literally he leaves his mark on them)....[3]

> (Il faut aussi admettre que lorsqu'il y a confusion totale entre l'image réelle et l'hallucination qu'elle a provoquée, aucune méprise n'est possible. La ressemblance entre deux objets est faite autant de l'élément subjectif qui contribue à l'établir que des rapports objectifs qui existent entre eux. Le poète, halluciné par excellence, établira des ressemblances à son gré entre les objets les plus dissemblables (littéralement il déteint sur eux)....

Éluard's own poetry provides many examples of Surrealist imagery. In *La rose publique*, one finds the following:

> All along the walls furnished with decrepit orchestras
> Darting their leaden ears toward the light
> On guard for a caress mingled with the thunderbolt.[4]

> (Le long des murailles meublées d'orchestres décrepits
> Dardant leurs oreilles de plomb vers le jour
> À l'affût d'une caresse corps avec la foudre.)

In his "Cœur à pic" from *Cours naturel* (1938), Éluard mixes human images with images of nature, for example, 'Towns of people water full' (Villages peuplés eau pleine), 'lamps of bread children of leaves' (lampes de pain enfants de feuilles).[5] In the poem, he also mixes intangible and tangible elements within the same image:

> Windmills of mirrors and of eyes,
> Islands of breasts furrows of words,
> Caressing snow of strength,
> Faded ponds of fatigue.[6]

> (Moulins des miroirs et des yeux,
> Îles des seins sillons des mots
> Neige câline de la force
> Mares fanées de la fatigue.)

One of the most quoted metaphors in Éluard's poetry is the first line of the seventh poem of *L'amour la poésie* (1929): 'The earth is blue like an orange' (La terre est bleue comme une orange).[7] A chief source of inspiration, which among the Surrealist poets is explored most fully by Paul Éluard, is love. We will explore the topic of love when we consider Messiaen's poetry.

André Breton, in the First Surrealist Manifesto, cites several examples of Surrealist imagery written by himself and other poets, including the following:

> On the bridge the dew with the head of a tabby cat lulls itself to sleep. (Breton)

> A little to the left, in my firmament foretold, I see—but it's doubtless but a mist of blood and murder—the gleaming glass of liberty's disturbances. (Louis Aragon)

The color of a woman's stockings is not necessarily in the likeness of her eyes, which led a philosopher who it is pointless to mention, to say: "Cephalopods have more reasons to hate progress than do quadrupeds." (Max Morise)[8]

THE POETRY OF OLIVIER MESSIAEN

From the twenty-eight examples analyzed, I will provide quotations from the following vocal works: two of the three poems of *Poèmes pour Mi*, all three poems of *Trois petites liturgies de la Présence Divine*, and four of the twelve poems of *Harawi, chant d'amour et de mort*. Messiaen's use of images in these poems often shows striking similarities to Surrealist techniques. For instance, one commonly finds radical imagery or examples of alienated objects:

'Sun of blood' (Soleil de sang), in *Trois petites liturgies*, I;

'Bouquet of laughter, gate that speaks and sun that opens' (Bouquet de rire, la porte qui parle et le soleil qui s'ouvre), in *Trois petites liturgies*, III; (© Éditions Durand, Paris)

'Mountain, listen to the solar chaos of dizziness' (Montagne écoute le chaos solaire du vertige), in "Montagnes," *Harawi;*

'The nebulous spirals, hands of my hair' (Les nébuleuses spirales, mains de mes cheveux), in "Katchikatchi les étoiles," *Harawi;* (© Alphonse Leduc, Paris)

'It [the road] smiles, its hands on its eyes' (Elle sourit, la main sur les yeux), in "Paysage," *Poèmes pour Mi.*
(© Alphonse Leduc, Paris; reprinted with permission)

Also, metaphors like 'The mountain springs like a ewe And becomes a great ocean,' (La montagne saute comme un brevis Et devient une grand ocean), in *Trois petites liturgies*, III, and 'Some bloody scraps would follow you in the darkness as a triangular vomit' (Des lambeaux sanglants te suivraient dans les ténèbres Comme une vomissure triangulaire), in "Épouvante," *Poèmes pour Mi,* suggest Surrealist thought. 'Love bird of Star,' (Amour oiseau d'étoile, *Harawi*), quoted in its entirety, illustrates Messiaen's imagery in context and reveals its lack of logical thought progression, a Surrealist characteristic. Similarly, the striking combinations of words such as 'eye which sings,' 'eye of star,' 'shortest way of the shadow to the sky,' 'from the scene my hands sing,' 'silence augmented of the sky,' and 'My hands, your eye, your neck, the sky,' closely resemble the principle of illogical juxtaposition in many Surrealist works.

> Bird of Star,
> Your eye which sings
> Towards the stars.
> Your head upside-down under the sky,
> Your eye of star,
> Chains falling
> Towards the stars,
> Shortest way of the shadow to the sky.
> All the birds of star
> Far from the scene my hands sing
> Star, silence augmented of the sky.
> My hands, your eye, your neck, the sky.[9]

> (Oiseau d'étoile,
> Ton œil qui chante,
> Vers les étoiles,
> Ta tête à l'envers sous le ciel.
> Ton œil d'étoile,
> Chaînes tombantes,
> Vers les étoiles,
> Plus court chemin de l'ombre au ciel.
> Tous les oiseaux des étoiles,
> Loin du tableau mes mains chantent,
> Étoile, silence augmenté du ciel.
> Mes mains, ton œil, ton cou, le ciel.)
>   © Alphonse Leduc, Paris; reprinted with permission.

A portion of the third of the *Trois petites liturgies*, quoted below, illustrates further Surrealist imagery. In particular, the reference to 'orange-blue' is strongly reminiscent of one of Éluard's lines quoted above, 'The earth is blue like an orange.' (La terre est bleue comme une orange; see note 7). Again, we see obvious Surrealist characteristics.

> It is stronger than death, your love.
> Envelop me in your tenderness.
> Yellow-violet, vision,
> White veil, subtlety,
> Orange-blue, strength and joy,
> Celestial arrow, agility,
> Give me the red and the green of your love,
> Flaming leaf of gold, brightness.[10]

(Il est plus fort que la mort, votre Amour.
Mettez votre caresse tout autour.
Violet-jaune, vision,
Voile blanc, subtilité,
Orangé-bleu, force et joie,
Flèche-azur, agilité,
Donnez-moi le rouge et le vert de votre amour,
Feuille flamme or, clarté.)
© Éditionse Durand, Paris; reprinted with permission.

References to love pervade Messiaen's work. The word love is often coupled with a variety of other images, for example, 'breath of love,' 'wing of love,' 'soul, full of love,' 'rainbow of love,' 'desert of love,' 'aureole of love,' 'word of love,' and 'canticle of love.' Messiaen surpasses Breton, Surrealism's founder, and perhaps even Éluard, the love poet of Surrealism, in his use of the word. In fact, in looking at twenty-seven of Messiaen's poems, I find that the word 'love' (amour) appears forty times. The word that comes the next in count is 'heaven' or 'sky' (ciel) with twenty-six, not even a close second. And this count does not include the *Cinq rechants*, a choral work whose text treats the intense love story of Tristan and Isolde. In these five poems, one finds the word 'lovers' six times, 'love' fourteen times, 'love's' twice, and combined words such as 'love-song' and 'love potion.' Also, in the fourth poem, one finds 'love love' in each statement of the refrain: "Oh, love love from light..." (Oha amour amour du clair...).

Messiaen's poetry reveals a kinship to the poetry of Éluard in other respects in addition to his emphasis on the word 'love.' A logical or rational approach does not explain their poems. To Messiaen, love may be sacred or divine as well as secular. And herein lies one important difference between Messiaen and the Surrealists. Most Surrealist poets were definitely opposed to Christianity believing that Christianity proposes that salvation exists outside each human being, whereas Surrealism proposes that each human has within herself the ability to succeed.[11] For example, let us consider the first liturgy of *Trois petites liturgies*, Antiphon of Internal Conversation: God's Presence with Us (Antienne de la conversation intérieure: Dieu présent en nous). It projects the exuberance and excitement of a deeply religious man. Words such as 'rainbow,' 'sun,' 'blood,' 'bird,' 'love,' 'red,' and 'violet' have significant meaning to Messiaen. In this poem, they refer to various aspects of the God-head. They interact to provide an environment of God's presence and divine love:

My Jesus, my silence,
Remain within me.
My Jesus, my realm of silence,
Speak within me.
My Jesus, night of rainbow and of silence,
Pray within me.
Sun of blood, of birds,
My rainbow of love,
Desert of love,
Sing, radiate the aureole of love,
My love,
My love
My God.
This affirmation that sings like a luminous echo.
Red and mauve melody in praise of the Father,
Your hand exceeds the picture of a kiss.
Divine landscape, mirror yourself in the water.

(Mon Jésus, mon silence,
Restez en moi.
Mon Jésus, mon royaume de silence,
Parlez en moi.
Mon Jésus, nuit d'arc-en-ciel et de silence,
Priez en moi.
Soleil de sang, d'oiseaux,
Mon arc-en-ciel d'amour,
Desert d'amour,
Chantez, lancez l'aureole d'amour,
Mon Amour,
Mon Amour,
Mon Dieu.
Ce oui qui chante comme un écho de lumière,
Mélodie rouge et mauve en louange du Père,
D'un baiser votre main dépasse le tableau,
Paysage divin, renverse-toi dans l'eau.)
© Éditionse Durand, Paris; reprinted with permission.

The stream-of-consciousness style pervades the poem. The unusual juxtaposition of objects also suggests Surrealism. In much the same manner, the second poem, "Mountains" (Montagnes) from *Harawi*, reveals impressions and Surrealist states of emotions associated by Messiaen with mountains:

Red-violet, black on black.
The old, useless black ray.
Mountain, listen to the solar chaos of dizziness.
The kneeling stone carries its black masters.
In closely-fitting hoods the fir trees push towards the black.
Gulf thrown everywhere in the dizziness.
Black on black.[12]

(Rouge-violet, noir sur noir.
L'antique inutile rayon noir.
Montagne, écoute le chaos solaire du vertige.
La pierre agenouillée porte ses maîtres noirs.
En capuchons serrés les sapins se hâtent vers le noir.
Gouffre lancé partout dans le vertige.
Noir sur noir.)

© Alphonse Leduc, Paris; reprinted with permission.

CONCLUSION

The Surrealist elements within Messiaen's poetry are clear: radical imagery, lack of rational logic, and the Surrealist concept of the artistic relationship between the artist's work and his soul or inner self. Love as a topic looms large in Messiaen's poetry and relates relatively well to Breton's work, the founder of Surrealism, and certainly to Éluard's poetry. I have selected Éluard because love is such an important subject to both his work and to Messiaen's. Love was not a subject that overly interested some of the other Surrealist poets. Dream and hallucination find no emphasis with Messiaen as they do with Breton, Dali, Miro, and others except for one instance and this unique situation relates to a musical work rather than to a poem. According to Messiaen, *Quatuor pour le fin du temps* was inspired by an hallucination while he was near starvation as a prisoner of war.[13] The quartet's relationship to hallucination remains unique and thus seems unimportant to a consideration of what is his typical approach to writing music or poetry.

A consideration of Messiaen's poetry must recognize certain influences other than Surrealism. For example, one finds traces of romanticism and mysticism. Besides Éluard, Messiaen does recognize the poetic influences of Ernest Hello (1828–1885) and Pierre Reverdy (1889–1960). Hello's major work is *Physionomie de Saints* (1875). Reverdy is considered by some sources to be a Surrealist since his early poetry reveals Surrealist traits. Yet in a conversation with me in May, 1971, Messiaen commented that he personally does not consider Reverdy to be Surrealist. In another conversation with me, Messiaen also

stated that the expressionist painter Wassily Kandinsky was an
important influence in his poetry and referred to Kandinsky's use of
the colors red and green (see note 10). Kandinsky's influence on his
poetry appears to be in Messiaen's choices of colors within his poetry.
Several examples were given above: 'the red and green of your love'
(le rouge et le vert de votre amour, *Trois petites liturgies*, III), and
references to orange-blue and yellow-violet in the same poem. One
also finds references to colors identified by name and standing alone
(rather than modifying a noun) in four poems: "La ville qui dormait,
toi"; "Montagnes"; "L'amour de Piroutcha"; and "Dans le noir" in
Chant d'amour et de mort. However, on balance, the influences most
easily detected within the poetry of Olivier Messiaen remain the
Surrealist ones: the general presentation of words, the imagery, the
artist's soul, and the lack of rational, logical sequences.

NOTES

[1]Richard Seaver and Helen R. Lane, trans., *Manifestoes of Surrealism — André Breton* (Ann Arbor: The University of Michigan Press, 1969), p. 26.

[2]*Ibid.*, p. 51.

[3]Paul Éluard, *Œuvres complétes*, vol. I, p. 955.

[4]*Ibid.*, p. 422.

[5]*Ibid.*, pp. 802-803.

[6]*Ibid.*

[7]*Ibid.*, p. 232.

[8]Seaver and Lane, *op. cit.*, pp. 38-39.

[9]I have translated "Ton" and "Ta" as "your." For a more poetic touch, one can translate "ton" as "thine" and "ta" as "thy" rather than "your" as John Underwood does in the translation printed in the notes to CD UKCD 2084, Unicorn-Kanchana, p. 24.

[10]In an interview in New York City, 9 November 1970, Messiaen commented to me that he loved the interaction of red and green in Wassily Kandinsky's painting. He elaborated that these colors interact by one warming the other, which in turn, cools the first.

[11]J.H. Matthews, *An Introduction to Surrealism* (University Park: The Pennsylvania State University Press, 1965), p. 44.

[12]Olivier Messiaen, *Harawi* (Paris: Alphonse Leduc, 1945).

[13]In a conversation with me (May, 1971) during my period of studies with him in Paris, Messiaen described his conditions while in a Stalag in Görlitz. He was provided only one boiled egg and a glass of water a day. During this period, hallucinations were common. During the hallucination that produced the *Quatuor* he said that he saw flashes of color and saw the Angel of the Apocalypse appear to declare the end of time. His program notes for this work describe the angel in more detail.

Speaking with the Tongues of
Men and of Angels:
Messiaen's 'langage communicable'

Andrew Shenton

> For anyone who speaks in a tongue does not speak to
> men but to God. Indeed, no-one understands him; he utters
> mysteries with his spirit.   (1 Corinthians 14:2)[1]

Messiaen's *Méditations sur le mystère de la Sainte Trinité pour orgue* (hereafter *Méditations*) were completed in 1969, following the monumental orchestral work *La Transfiguration de Notre Seigneur Jésus-Christ* (1963–69). A summation of Messiaen's compositional technique up to this point, the *Méditations* contain a sophisticated semiotic system which includes bird song, modes of limited transposition, *deçi-tâlas*,[2] plainsong, passages from the *Summa theologiæ* by Saint Thomas Aquinas,[3] and text superscriptions from a variety of sources. They reach a new height in Messiaen's idiomatic use of the timbral resources of the organ, and they incorporate an innovative feature, which Messiaen termed the 'langage communicable' (communicable language). This novel musical language, which he explains in the Preface to the score and in conversations with Claude Samuel and others, is comprised of three elements: (1) a musical alphabet, which assigns a rhythmicized pitch to each letter of the Roman alphabet, (2) a system of grammatical cases based on Latin, and (3) a series of leitmotifs. These three categories are combined to transliterate phrases from the *Summa theologiæ* into music. This essay examines the 'langage communicable' linguistically and musically, and places it in the broader semiotic system of the *Méditations*.[4]

The *Méditations* were not commissioned but were written at a time when Messiaen felt confident about tackling a subject as complex as the Trinity. The composer premiered the work himself on March 20, 1972, at the National Shrine of the Immaculate Conception, Washington, D.C. At the European premiere in Düsseldorf in June 1972, he said: "I've been engaged as organist at Sainte Trinité for forty years. I've been waiting forty years for someone to speak about what the Trinity is. But it's spoken about far too little: people don't care to do so. At the age of sixty-four, I believe that I'm now worthy to talk about it."[5] Each of the nine movements reflects on an attribute of the Trinity. The shortest movement (the third) lasts about three minutes, while the longest (the second) lasts about twelve minutes. The complete suite takes around eighty minutes to perform and is one of the most technically challenging pieces Messiaen wrote. The movements are untitled but are prefaced by musical and theological explanatory notes written by the composer.

The Preface to the score, like the Preface to the organ suite *La Nativité du Seigneur* (1935), contains important information about the new techniques Messiaen developed.[6] The following summarizes what he wrote in the Preface to the score of the *Méditations* about how he devised his system:

1) The 'langage' transliterates the *Summa theologiæ* in French, this being Messiaen's native language.
2) The basis of the alphabet is the German musical alphabet (letters a through h).[7]
3) Each letter is represented by a fixed pitch, a fixed duration, and a specific timbre.[8]
4) The rudimentary set of letters is then expanded on the basis of phonetic groups to embrace all twenty-six letters.
5) For the sake of simplicity, all articles, pronouns, adverbs, and prepositions are omitted; only nouns, adjectives, and verbs are used.
6) A system of cases like the declensions in Latin are used by means of three musical formulae: one for genitive, ablative, or locative; one for accusative or dative; and one for the privative (signifying 'the absence of').
7) The verbs 'to be' and 'to have' are expressed by musical formulae that are exactly contrary to one another.
8) God is expressed by means of a theme (*Thème de Dieu*), which occurs in both the forward and the retrograde versions.

The following investigations will begin with a systematic analysis of Messiaen's musico-linguistic system. Having explored the alphabet, the grammatical formulae, and the leitmotifs, the focus will then shift to the question of comprehensibility of the 'langage'. Here, the scope will be widened from the technical to the interpretative, and include some of the extra-musical information supplied by Messiaen in the Preface of his *Méditations*.

EXAMPLE 1: Messiaen's complete alphabet

Messiaen set all twenty-six letters of the modern Roman alphabet, even though the Aquinian texts transliterated in the *Méditations* do not require the letters h, j, k, v, w, y, and z. His 'langage' is based on the written appearance of words, not on their sounds. The fact that his transliteration renders the spelling and not phonetic quality leads to some perplexing details regarding, on the one hand, accent-inflected vowels and, on the other, diphthongs. The French modified letters à, é, è, and ê, while appropriately included in the French translation of the *Summa theologiæ* that Messiaen printed in the score above the music, are merely given the note-equivalent unaccented letters in the music. Diphthongs are equally "spelled out" as chains of separate vowels. (Thus the very different-sounding e, é, and è/ê all appear as "e," while the phonetically identical è/ê and ai/aie are rendered as "e," "a+i" and "a+i+e" respectively). This is noteworthy since, when devising musical representations for the vowels and consonants not included in the rudimentary set a through h, Messiaen proceeded "en groupant les lettres par genres de productions phoniques" (by grouping the letters according to the type of phonic production).[9] A similar mix of spelling-based and phonetically based transliteration can be observed with regard to the letter c. On the one hand, Messiaen does not render either the (spoken) difference between 'hard c' and 'soft c' or the (written) difference between "c" and "ç"; on the other hand, he did include the letter —as 'hard c'—in a category defined by its pronunciation as [k]. This category covers the letters c, q, and k (as in 'cabaret' [kabarɛ]). Example 1 provides the music for the alphabet.

With regard to the production of this musical alphabet, two questions arise: (1) how did Messiaen choose the duration for the letters a to h? and (2) how did he choose the pitch and duration for the remaining letters? To answer these, it is necessary to undertake a phonetic analysis of the alphabet.

In trying to ascertain how Messiaen devised this alphabet we must look more closely at the relationships between the letters and their musical ascriptions. Is there any correlation between the length of the note and the length of the letter in spoken French? The answer to this is quite simply no. The phonetic length of a particular letter depends on its position in a word, on the letters which surround it, and also on what type of sound it is. If Messiaen had been using the length of letters as though they were being recited as part of the alphabet or used in spoken words, he would have made a distinction between an elongated sound such as in vowels and a short sound such as in consonants. In the alphabet of his 'langage', there is no discernible distinction between the note value of these two basic phonetic categories. As was mentioned above, Messiaen did not give diphthongs any special consideration with regard to the phonetic result they produce; however, since he spells them out in consecutive letters, they do differ from simple vowels in length, as they would in a written word.

Is there any connection between the pitch and duration of letters in the same phonetic group? Looking closely at the Preface we can discern certain patterns in the production of letters after the first eight. Messiaen conceives one group for vowels and seven for consonants. Working without the aid of sketch books or other primary source material we can only guess at why Messiaen chose F♯ for the letter i, but it is easy to see that the other two palatals (j and y) are directly related to i in both pitch and duration. A corresponding relationship in descending octaves also regulates the sibilants (s and z) and the 'hard-c' group of consonants (c, k, and q).

In both of these groups, the members are also durationally equivalent. The dentals (d and t) and the linguals (l and n) are represented musically with an octave relationship but without being durationally equivalent in the way of the earlier groups. The labials (b, f, m, p, v), the vowels o and u, and the three letters which do not otherwise fit into Messiaen's system (r, w, x) are harder to explain since they do not seem to be derived by logical extension from a primary rhythmicized pitch.

The greater variety introduced by these additional letters is plausible when one considers that Messiaen no doubt wanted to allow himself a broad range of pitches and durations with which to work. (This may also explain why the dentals and linguals have an octave relationship but are not durationally equivalent.) In any case, in writing about the use of his system Messiaen told Samuel that he reserved the right to modify the alphabet if he thought it made more musical sense.[10] He does this, for example, at [I, 14/5][11] where the word *inengendré* (unbegotten), written using the alphabet, is played for emphasis entirely by the pedals. Here Messiaen has removed the register-specific element of the alphabet, which is given in the Preface and adhered to in all other uses. This pitch specificity is not affected by the multiple pitches heard as the result of the different organ stops drawn for the 'langage'.

In addition to the combination of literal letter-by-letter transcription and phonetically based grouping, Messiaen's alphabet as devised for this work—an organ composition—presents another problem. Subtle variations in the sound of spoken letters are removed in this medium because of the idiosyncrasies of tone production on the organ, which produces each note (and thus each letter) in the same way; no difference in the production of vowels is possible. Each letter of Messiaen's alphabet has the same mode of attack and the same degree of decay, and although this may be controlled to a certain extent by articulation, (especially on a mechanical-action organ where the supply of wind to the pipes is directly controlled by the fingers), its effect is still one of uniformity in production. While this may be seen as an example of the simplification of language to which Messiaen aspired, it actually places additional burden on the significance of each letter.

Taken together, all these difficulties arising from the musical representation of the verbal language may lead to a deeper level of comprehension if we take the limitations to suggest that we should perhaps not be considering the music as too literal an equivalent. This idea is given further weight by the fact that Messiaen did not simply transliterate the French version of the *Summa theologiæ* letter by letter using his musical alphabet, but chose to set part of the texts using a reductive version of Latin grammar.

Messiaen claims in the Preface to have reduced his grammar to nouns, adjectives, and verbs "pour éviter l'accumulation des mots" (in order to avoid the accumulation of words). In actual fact, however, his language does include some of the articles, pronouns, adverbs, and prepositions he claims to have omitted, and he has not reduced the number of words by many (the French translation of Aquinas uses seventy-one words, Messiaen set sixty-two). In any case, in an extended piece such as the *Méditations* where the 'langage' takes up only a small fraction of the entire piece, it seems strange that Messiaen should be concerned about the number of words he set.

The case system Messiaen devised is itself peculiar. In Latin there are seven cases which change the ending of nouns (and pronouns) to indicate relationship with other words and convey meaning.[12] In English only one case is indicated by the word ending and that is the genitive (indicating possession) as in: the *boy's* bike. French, like English, does not use the Latin case system; thus it is interesting that Messiaen decided to develop his 'langage' in this way. Indications for grammatical cases, which in verbal language would be morphological inflections of the words themselves, are musically rendered as separated "formules musicales". This, however, may lead to some confusion and misinterpretation because these motifs have multiple meanings—the meaning is not necessarily clear from the context and could be misread if we did not have Messiaen's indications in the score. For example, the motif by which Messiaen indicates the genitive, ablative, and locative actually stands, in Aquinas's text chosen for the *Méditations*, for six different forms of the three French prepositions *de, par,* and *en*: in the genitive usage it represents *de* or *du*, in the ablative *du*, *d'un*, or *par*, and in the locative *en*.

Messiaen's leitmotifs in the *Méditations* constitute a complex system which, like their predecessors in Wagner, uses musical figures to represent a being or an idea. Messiaen expands the concept to include leitmotifs that are part of the 'langage'. In addition, there are a considerable number of musical motifs to be found throughout Messiaen's compositions that constitute an elaborate system of leitmotifs by association. The three broad categories of leitmotifs used by Messiaen can be identified thus:

a) Representational leitmotifs:
   Musical figures used for the first time in the *Méditations* which represent a being (e. g., the *Thème de Dieu*), or an attribute (e. g., "*Dieu est immense*").
b) 'Langage' leitmotifs:
   Musical figures that are part of the 'langage communicable' (e. g., the musical formula which represents the genitive, ablative, or locative cases).
c) Associated leitmotifs:
   Musical figures used in the *Méditations* that are also found in other pieces by Messiaen, and which by association have come to represent an extramusical idea (e. g., "*Le Souffle de L'Esprit*").

The following paragraphs present a brief discussion of each of these categories.

a) Representational leitmotifs

The *Méditations* include fifteen different leitmotifs that represent a being or attribute. They are all identified by an appellation in the score, and all occur in more than one place. In addition there is one leitmotif that represents neither a being nor specifically an attribute, but a quote: "Je suis Celui qui suis" (I am that I am) occurs three times in *Méditation IX:* [IX, 77/1–3] [IX, 78/8–10] [IX, 87/4–13 (expanded)]. This particular instance is noteworthy because, although a quotation, Messiaen chose to translate the sentence into a specific musical phrase and not to spell it out in his 'langage'. This confirms the restricted and very specific application of the 'langage' which, in the Méditations, Messiaen reserved exclusively for passages from Aquinas. Of these sixteen leitmotifs (the fifteen traditionally defined one and the biblical quotation "Je suis Celui qui suis"), only one is explained in the Preface.

The *Thème de Dieu* has two forms, which Messiaen explained thus:

> ... pour exprimer que Dieu est immense autant qu'éternel, sans commencement ni fin dans l'espace comme dans le temps, j'ai donné deux formes à mon thème: une droite, une rétrograde, comme deux extrêmes qui se regardent et que l'on pourrait reculer indéfiniment ...
>
> *Avant-propos*, 5/22–25

> [... in order to express that God is immense as much as eternal, without beginning or end in space as in time, I have given two forms to my theme: one forward, one retrograde, like two extremes which face each other and that one could move back indefinitely ...
>
> Preface, 5/22–25]

Example 2 gives the leitmotif for the *Thème de Dieu* in its forward and retrograde versions. The leitmotif *Saint Esprit* (see score VII, 62/4) combines the notes of both forms of the *Thème de Dieu* but uses a different rhythmic pattern. Like the mirror form of the *Thème de Dieu*, *Saint Esprit*, too, is rhythmically palindromic.

EXAMPLE 2: *Thème de Dieu*

Thème de Dieu
in forward motion

Thème de Dieu
in retrograde motion

Of the other leitmotifs, two are attributes of God. Both are based on plainsong themes: *"Dieu est Saint"* employs the Alleluia de la Dédicace (Alleluia for the Feast of Dedication), while *"Dieu est simple"* uses the Alleluia de la Touissant (Alleluia for All Saints). The musical phrase signifying *"Le Souffle de l'Esprit"* is a pictorial leitmotif using rapid sixteenth-notes to portray the rushing mighty wind of the Holy Spirit. Messiaen used it in several works composed prior to the *Méditations*. The remaining leitmotifs are musically linked among themselves in an interesting way. For example, the musical symbols for *Père* and *Fils* display the same rhythmic pattern, and, with five slight changes, *Fils* is an intervallic inversion of *Père* (see score I, 10/1 for the leitmotif *Père*, and VII, 61/8 for *Fils*). Example 3 below compares the intervallic structure of the two leitmotifs.

EXAMPLE 3: Interval analysis

| *Père* | M2↘ | M7↘ | P5↗ | M2↘ | M7↘ | M2↘ | m6↗ |
| *Fils* | M2↗ | M7↗ | dim5↘ | aug2↘ | M6↗ | M2↗ | m7↘ |

This is the musical equivalent of what the linguist Ferdinand de Saussure called 'relative motivation' between signs. Saussure is known for his notion of the 'arbitrariness of the sign', the idea that, for example, the word 'cat' in English is arbitrary to the feline creature with which it is associated.[13] He qualifies this further by noting that "some signs are absolutely arbitrary; in others we note, not its complete absence, but the presence of degrees of arbitrariness: the sign may be relatively motivated."[14] What he is suggesting is that there is an 'absolute' and a 'relative' arbitrariness. This can be seen in Messiaen's system. The figure used for *Dieu* seems fairly arbitrary and is not related, as far as we can tell, to a sign in any other system. If we suppose that Messiaen composed this phrase first, then the signs for *Père, Fils,* and *Saint Esprit* can be seen as 'relatively motivated' because of their musical connection to *Dieu*.

Like Wagner, Messiaen develops or modifies some of his leitmotifs. None of the motifs are transposed, but they are, as mentioned earlier, given different registrations which may make them harder to recognize and, thus, to distinguish from one another. For example, *Père* at [I, 10/1] is played on the Positif Clarinette, Quintaton 16, and Cornet, but is heard at [VII, 61/7] on Récit Trompette 8 and Bourdon 16. These are quite different orchestrations of the same theme. Further, in assessing the comprehensibility of the 'langage' some consideration must also be given to the accompaniment of each theme, both in terms of its harmony and its orchestration.[15]

There are three other examples of representational motifs, which, contrary to Messiaen's assertion in the Preface that "La musique... n'exprime rien directement" (music... does not express anything directly), are used to express a specific natural sound. Table 1 lists these themes and their occurrence in the *Méditations*.

TABLE 1: Representational motifs

1) Pizzi (plucked strings):	[IV, 32/9] [IV, 33/1] [IV, 34/5]
2) Gouttes d'eau (drops of water):	[IV, 33/9]
3) Soie déchirée (silk tearing):	[IV, 32/15] [IV, 33/17–18]

b) 'Langage' leitmotifs

There are two groups of musical themes that function as part of the grammatical structure of the 'langage' but are heard as leitmotifs. The first consists of the three formulae which constitute Messiaen's system of cases, the second consists of two formulae which represent the auxiliary verbs *être* (to be), and *avoir* (to have). The verb *aimer* (to love) and its noun *amour*, musically rendered in similar fashion, could be added to this second group. "Love" is not referred to in the Preface, but Messiaen gives the concept a musical motif which he uses four times in *Méditation VII* (twice each for the verb form *aiment* and the noun *amour*).

c) Associated leitmotifs

Comment has often been made about Messiaen's compositional technique of using sections as building blocks and constructing large-scale structures from smaller groups. This technique is evident in the *Méditations*. In addition, Messiaen uses motifs that can be traced back to earlier works, and which have gained extra-musical associations by the context of which they first formed a part. For example, the motif *"Dieu est éternel"* contains a figure that occurs in the third movement of *L'Ascension*, "Transports de joie d'une âme qui désire le ciel" [III, 11/1 and elsewhere]. The figure, which also occurs in an ascending form, is descriptive of an outburst of joy, but acquires a deeper significance by its association with heaven and the eternal. The motif *"Le Souffle de l'Esprit"* is heard outside the *Méditations* in "Sortie (Le vent de l'Esprit)," the fifth movement of the *Messe de la Pentecôte*, where it is labeled *"Le vent"* [V, 22/1–4 and elsewhere]. This motif, like those listed in Table 1, is thus an example of pictorial symbolism, a technique used by J. S. Bach, a composer to whom Messiaen felt a deep inner connection and about whom he often spoke.[16] Messiaen's system of associated leitmotifs is worthy of further exploration and discussion because it may shed light not only on an aspect of his compositional technique, but also on the development of his personal theology as expressed in his music.

One major problem for the leitmotifs, as Messiaen himself noted in the Preface, is the need for them to be known by the listener in advance, "pour en saisir au passage toutes les juxtapositions, superpositions, variations et transformations" (in order to grasp as they appear all the juxtapositions, superimpositions, variations, and transformations). The only way to truly appreciate a performance of the *Méditations* is to come with a detailed prior knowledge of both the music and the extra-musical aspects of the piece. One solution to this problem of familiarity with the leitmotifs would be to play them immediately before a per-formance. If the leitmotifs were regularly isolated in this way, after repeated hearings a listener could develop familiarity with them, and be able to recognize them as they appear. This would also happen as a matter of course after repeated listening if the listener is familiar with the score and is aware when they are due to occur.

What, then, is the function of the leitmotif for Messiaen in the *Méditations*? Like Wagner, Messiaen uses the leitmotif as a communi-cable language. It is a convenient and effective way of expressing extra-musical ideas through music. Because Messiaen's music is primarily devoted to expression of his religious thought, he could use both the 'langage' and the leitmotifs in works which came after the *Méditations*, and he did so in *Des canyons aux étoiles...* (1974), and the *Livre du Saint Sacrement* (1984). The 'langage' occurs in two movements of *Des canyons aux étoiles...* Here Messiaen transliterates the Aramaic words for 'numbered, weighed, divided' ('mene, tekel, parsin') in the third movement ('Ce qui est écrit sur les étoiles...' [III, 63/1 – 64/5] [III, 93/1 – 94/5]), and the Greek words for Holy God, Holy Mighty One, Holy Immortal One in the fifth movement ('Cedar Breaks et le don de crainte': 'Agios o Theos' [V, 112/1 – 113/6], 'Agios ischyros' [V, 121/1 – 122/5], 'Agios athanatos' [V, 135/1 – 136/9]).

In Messiaen's last organ work, the *Livre du Saint Sacrement*, the 'langage' is used to transliterate the following words: *Resurrection* [see VII, 47/1–6] [VII, 51/11–16], *Apocalypse* [XI, 79/3], *Votre Père* [XI, 77/1–2], *Votre Dieu* [XI, 79/1–2], and *La joie* [XVIII, 162/3]. In this work, Messiaen uses *Fils*, *Père*, and *Dieu* in the same form as discussed for the *Méditations*. In addition, the *Livre du Saint Sacrement* contains one new leitmotif expressing a grammatical case: the directional *vers*.[17]

At this point it seems worth looking more closely at the fact that, in the *Méditations*, the 'langage' is solely used to transliterate passages from Aquinas's *Summa theologiæ*. There are three passages, one in each of the first, third, and eighth movements ([I, 10/1 – 12/15], [III, 26/1 – 28/11], [VII, 61/7 – 66/6]).[18] The passages are quoted in Messiaen's program notes for each movement, so the listener is aware that they are embedded somewhere in the music. As part of Messiaen's theological explanation of each piece, they lend an authoritative voice to an otherwise personal reflection on the Trinity.

It is interesting that Messiaen did not choose to transliterate Aquinas in the original Latin but to use a translation in his native French, especially since there are comprehension problems with the 'langage' no matter what the original language was, and texts set using Messiaen's alphabet (as opposed to the formulae or leitmotifs) would sound very different if they were based on Latin or any other language. The musical transliteration from the translated verbal text is further complicated because, by using the cases and leitmotifs in addition to the alphabet, Messiaen did not directly set the French version of Aquinas but modified it further. Table 2 provides the French translation Messiaen gives in the score at the end of the first *Méditation*, for the first passage from the *Summa theologiæ* which he set. Underneath is the text he actually set, with type format signifying how he set it. To indicate how Messiaen parsed the phrase in his 'langage', words that he rendered using his alphabet are given in ordinary type, cases as well as the verbs *avoir* and *être* and the various forms of *amour* are in italics, and leitmotifs are underlined.

TABLE 2: Aquinas translated into the 'langage'

Aquinas:
Par rapport aux Personnes qui procèdent de Lui, le Père se notifie ainsi: paternité et spiration; en tant que 'Principe qui n'a pas de principe', il se notifie ainsi: il n'est pas d'un autre: c'est là précisément la propriété d'innascibilité désignée par le nom d'Inengendré.[19]

Messiaen:
<u>Père</u> *vers les* personnes procédant *du* <u>Père</u> *il a* paternité spiration <u>Père</u> *vers le* principe *sans* principe, *il a ne pas (être) d'un* autre *c'est (avoir)* innascibilité *(être)* inengendré <u>Père</u>

Clearly the text, and therefore the meaning, has been modified first by the translation from Latin into French and second by Messiaen's paraphrase. Translation into the 'langage' adds a third level of alteration which obscures the essential message. Providing the listener with a translation in his or her vernacular from Messiaen's French rather than the original Latin would add a fourth level.

Messiaen's paraphrase is, by normal linguistic standards, neither elegant nor correct. Using some of the language classifications noted by the cognitive scientist Steven Pinker, we can describe Messiaen's 'langage' as an "isolating" language in which he has constructed sentences "by rearranging immutable word-sized units" while retaining a fixed word order.[20] But, because of the simplicity of the 'langage', Messiaen has had to build his sentences from severely limited resources. This explains anomalies such as consecutive use of verbs, and the resultant stilted style.

In addition to the passages from Aquinas there are eleven different superscriptions in the musical score. The questions concerning these additional elements divide themselves into two broad groups. The first group of questions concerns content: What are these texts? Where do they come from? How do they fit in with the *Summa theologiæ* and the Trinitarian theme? How do they fit in with the idea of the meditation? The second group of questions pertains to comprehension: How can the messages intimated in the superscriptions be understood by the listener? Should they, indeed, be comprehended by the listener?

Dealing with the first group we know that the texts come from a variety of sources: the Old and New Testaments, the Mass, the Epistles, and a Litany. Their subject matter is wide-ranging though not specifically Trinitarian. There is no immediate and obvious connection between them until they are read as part of the broad canvas of each *Méditation* described by Messiaen in the score and in conversation. They considerably enlarge the theological scope of the piece as a whole.

The superscriptions are always in parentheses, in italics, and in smaller script than the identifications of the leitmotifs (in the manuscript they are in parentheses but written the same size as the other written indications). This might suggest that they are there primarily for the performer to read while she or he is playing. At the same time, however, these indications clearly mean more than the asides Erik Satie put into his scores for the performer, as Messiaen discusses them in his program notes. Unlike the leitmotifs that can be played before a performance or isolated and learnt in advance, the superscriptions can only be of use to the listener if they are recollected from prior knowledge at the appropriate moments in the music.

It is difficult to relate these superscriptions to the music with which they appear. With the 'langage' and the leitmotifs we can, for the sake of argument, agree with Messiaen that "Il est convenu que ceci exprimera cela" (It is agreed that one thing expresses another); we can agree that a musical phrase represents God the Father, another the Son, and so on. It is harder to explain a passage of music that carries a superscription in the score relating to an extra-musical program that cannot be comprehended by the listener.

We have analyzed the mechanics of the 'langage communicable' and discussed the texts it transliterates and how they fit into the larger picture of the *Méditations*. Let us now turn to the questions of acquisition, perception, retention, and comprehension of the 'langage' and of the other compositional techniques used in the *Méditations*.

We could arguably acquire Messiaen's 'langage' even though it is 'dead', because we have all the necessary information. The speed of acquisition, degree of retention, and ability to comprehend the 'langage' would depend both on the general and musical intelligence of the person learning. Because of the nature of the alphabet and leitmotifs, a person with absolute pitch would be at a great advantage over one with no specific pitch-recognition ability. Indeed, it is questionable whether someone without absolute pitch could ever acquire the 'langage' or fully translate it, because even if he or she were able to recognize some of the leitmotifs, recognition of letters of the alphabet would be difficult, if not impossible.

The main problems with musical perception are noted by Dowling and Harwood in their book on music cognition.[21] They write that "the simplicity by which psychoacoustic approaches succeed becomes, itself, an impediment to the exploration of complex stimuli whose perception is dependent on both content and experience."[22] These are the main problems with perception of the 'langage': we are dealing with complex stimuli, and we have problems of context and experience.

What about cognition? Dowling and Harwood write that "the immense amount of information transmitted in the sound wave is selected and organized by the cognitive systems of the listener, and it is the result of that cognitive processing that is experienced and remembered."[23] Unfortunately, Messiaen's music is difficult to comprehend because the melodic lines generated by the 'langage' do not sound like melodies we might reasonably expect someone to have heard as part of their cultural heritage. There are two problems: the often disjunct melodic contours of the 'langage' are not conducive to retention, nor is the timbre and dynamic the same for each phrase in the 'langage'. This brings us to yet another problem, that of discerning which material is part of the 'langage' and is therefore carrying extra-musical information, and which is not. The 'langage' is difficult to distinguish because other music in the *Méditations* is similar in style, timbre, and dynamic. Messiaen does not herald or announce phrases in the 'langage' in any way, but integrates them into the compositional whole.

Another obvious disadvantage of the 'langage' is the length of time required to 'say' something. Steven Pinker has observed that casual speech is perceived at ten to fifteen phonemes per second, but can be understood at an even faster rate.[24] With Messiaen most single phonemes last over a second, a rate at which the human brain finds it difficult to retain the small amount of information given over such an extended period. Aquinas's phrase "La relation réelle en Dieu est réellement identique à l'essence" in *Méditation III* takes around five seconds to say, Messiaen's paraphrase "Relation en Dieu est identique à essence de Dieu" a bit less. Spoken in the 'langage' it comprises the whole of *Méditation III,* and takes Messiaen 2'23" to play, or 143 seconds—making it nearly thirty times slower. It is difficult to understand because the individual parts of a melody are perceived in succession, not all at once, and we cannot move backwards and forwards in this temporal line to recover what has been lost or to see what is coming up. There is also the problem of memory which, as Eero Tarasti notes, is "not only repetitive but creative."[25] Tarasti proposes a paradigm of expectation which, like Eugene Narmour's expectation-realization theory, suggests that identification of patterns in musical material sets up expectations for continuation of the music in the mind of the listener. The continuation of a piece can be analyzed by showing how a composer disrupts or fulfills this expectation. Because of the nature of its construction, Messiaen's music generated by the 'langage' does not conform at either the macro- or the micro-levels to an identifiable pattern, and consequently defies analysis following a paradigm of expectation. This may explain why Messiaen used so many shorter note values for his alphabet. It is possible that he was aware of the problem of comprehending a phrase prolonged to this extent and deliberately chose shorter note values in order to reduce the time it takes to enunciate each phrase.

Perception and retention of the information conveyed in the 'langage' is one problem, comprehension is another. Part of the problem is that for any language to be understood some effort on the part of the listener is required. Messiaen's 'langage' requires a great deal of effort from his listeners because the language is a foreign one. By virtue of its extended semiotic system, and the problems of perception and retention noted above, Messiaen's language is more complicated and difficult to understand than that of a speaker talking to us in a spoken verbal language we do not know. There is also the question of semantics. Jean-Jacques Nattiez suggests that "semantic analysis of a musical work must be able to verify whether the meaning that a composer invests in the work is perceived and understood by the performers and listener—and if so, how."[26] Supposing that through extensive study we have perceived all the information in the *Méditations* and comprehend that it includes Aquinas, bird song, and plainsong among other things, how do we interpret this information? Saussure says that "to explain a word is to relate it to other words,"[27] but surely to explain Messiaen's music in verbal terms is to limit it. Interpretation depends on the background, training, experience, and general intelligence of the listener. We can never be absolutely sure that a sign has been correctly interpreted with the import it was given by the person using it, and, as John Blacking warns, "as soon as we analyze music with speech, we run the risk of distorting the true nature of non-verbal communication with both the structural conventions of verbal discourse itself and the analytical categories of grammar that all educated speakers have assimilated."[28] Pinker suggests that "when we listen to speech the actual sounds go in one ear and out the other; what we perceive is *language*."[29] When we listen to the *Méditations* what we hear may well go in one ear and out the other, but what we perceive is *music*.

In the Preface to the score of the *Méditations* Messiaen talks about two other influences that give us some clues for understanding the piece. The first is the Rosetta Stone. This stone, a small slab of black basalt found in 1799 near Rosetta in the Nile Delta, served as a key to the interpretation of Egyptian hieroglyphs. Its inscription, dating from the second century before our era, is repeated in Greek, hieroglyphics, and demotic script (a cursive form of hieroglyphics).[30] The Englishman Thomas Young deciphered the name of Ptolemy from six identical cartouches and, by examining the way bird and animal characters faced, discovered the direction the other hieroglyphics should be read. The Frenchman Jean-François Champollion then went on to decode the whole script after realizing that the hieroglyphics did not constitute a writing system but a phonetic system. The language system of the Rosetta Stone uses a variety of signs: some are alphabetic, some syllabic, and some determinative (standing for the whole idea or object previously expressed). Messiaen thus adapted several concepts from the Rosetta Stone in his *Méditations*; the most notable is the use of the cartouche. In the Preface Messiaen wrote of his fascination with the use of this sign to enclose royal names on the Stone.[31] To enclose a musical theme in a cartouche that can be recognized by a listener is impossible; nevertheless, Messiaen chose to highlight the words *Père, Fils,* and *Saint Esprit* by placing them in cartouches above their music each time they appear (see pages 10 to 12, and 61 to 66 of the score). The *Thème de Dieu* is treated in the same way on pages 26 and 28.

Three interesting questions arise concerning the parallels between the Stone and Messiaen's system. First, is the 'langage communicable' an equivalent to the hieroglyphics, and, if so, in what ways? In fact, the 'langage' is not the same as hieroglyphics because, rather than being an essentially different language, it is a merely a reduction and adaptation of French. Second, supposing all the other information were lost, is it possible to work out what the rest of the piece says from Messiaen's cartouches? The answer is simply no. The words enclosed in cartouches do not provide enough information about the alphabet or the grammatical structure of the 'langage' for the system to be deduced from the cartouches alone. This would only be possible if the names in the cartouches used the alphabet of the 'langage' and were not leitmotifs unrelated to this alphabet. Third, is the text in the 'langage communicable' saying the same thing as the other passages of music that have text superscriptions? This is also not the case. All the text in the 'langage' is taken from Aquinas and expresses complex Trinitarian theology, whereas the texts used in the *Méditations* also include the eleven additional superscriptions.

The second clue that helps us understand the *Méditations* is Messiaen's discussion of communication by angels. Messiaen has treated the subject of angels many times.[32] The *Méditations* differ from the other pieces because they do not invoke angels in any pictorial way.

The reference to angels in the Preface is based on Aquinas's writings on "The language of the angels" (*Summa theologiæ*, Question 107), and on Messiaen's highly developed personal theology. The angels described by Aquinas are formidable. Messiaen considers their means of communication "almost frightening", and quotes from the *Duino Elegies* by Rainer Maria Rilke, who describes all angels as 'terrifying'.[33] Messiaen agrees with the Aquinian belief that angels communicate "sans langage, sans convention, et plus merveilleusement encore, sans avoir à tenir compte du temps et du lieu" (without language, without convention, and most marvelously of all, without consideration of time and place).[34] This view of communication by "mental concept" is interesting because it points to the limitations of communication via human language of any sort (musical or verbal). It also gives what may be a key point to understanding the *Méditations*.

My theory about how angelic communication helps us understand the *Méditations* has two parts. First, Messiaen could be attempting to communicate with the angels, writing a piece that can be comprehended in all its aspects by them, because if angels can communicate with a sophisticated system that has no heed of time or space, they can surely interpret the various semiotic systems in the *Méditations*. From this perspective Messiaen can be seen to be trying, albeit in a mundane way, to join the ceaseless praise of the angels as written for example in the

Liturgy of Saint James.[35] Angelic themes are expressed throughout the *Duino Elegies*, and, as we know that Messiaen was familiar with the *Elegies*, this quote from *The Ninth Elegy* may expresses more of Messiaen's view of angels:

> *Preise dem Engel die Welt, nicht die unsägliche, ihm /*
> *kannst du nicht großtun mit herrlich Erfühltem; im Weltall,*
> */ wo er fühlender fühlt, bist du ein Neuling. Drum zeig /*
> *ihm das Einfache, das, von Geschlecht zu Geschlechtern*
> *gestaltet, / als ein Unsriges lebt, neben der Hand und im*
> *Blick.*
>
> (*Die neunte Elegie, 53–57*)

[Praise this world to the angel, not the unsayable one, you can't impress him with glorious emotion; in the universe where he feels more powerfully, you are a novice. So show him something simple which, formed over generations, lives as our own, near our hand and within our gaze.]

(*The Ninth Elegy, 53–57*)

Messiaen may subscribe to Rilke's notion that although praising God is essentially pointless because of His omnipotence and omnipresence, one can still praise God to the angels. It is also possible that Messiaen developed his 'langage communicable' to express his thoughts on the Trinity fulfilling the prophecy of Rilke: "daß ich dereinst, an dem Ausgang der grimmigen Einsicht, / Jubel und Ruhm aufsinge zustimmenden Engeln." (Someday, emerging at last from violent insight, let me sing out jubilation and praise to assenting angels).[36]

Second, taking this a step further and applying the medieval concept of anagogy, it may be that, as mere humans, we do not need to understand what is being played in the *Méditations*. Instead, rather like gaining grace by standing in the light from a stained glass window high up in a cathedral without being able to distinguish the detail of the picture, simply hearing the music of the *Méditations* may be spiritually efficacious to us.

It is clear from the preceding discussion that language is an expression of thought, and that signs are used to express thoughts. The American anthropological linguist, Benjamin Lee Whorf, suggested that language determines perception and thought. The Whorfian Hypothesis posits that because we think in a language, our thoughts are restricted by the nature and content of the language, and the expression of these thoughts is similarly confined by the limitations of the language.[37] An extension of this hypothesis, known as linguistic relativity, suggests that "differences in languages cause differences in the thoughts of their speakers."[38] In Messiaen's case his 'langage' is extremely restrictive which, as we have already seen, produces problems of translation and interpretation. His semiotic system, however, is very complex, and constitutes an almost complete language system.[39]

In the light of Whorf's hypothesis, I suggest that Messiaen's complete semiotic system in the *Méditations* uses an additional dimension to present his thoughts about the Holy Trinity. This dimension escapes the confines of verbal language and moves to a realm where thoughts are encoded and decoded on several levels, one of which is purely musical. The combination of levels of encryption produce what is, in human terms, the ultimate and most complete means of communication. In his chapter entitled "Mentalese" (a word used for the language of thought), Pinker argues that "there is no scientific evidence that languages dramatically shape their speaker's ways of thinking."[40] Following a thorough and convincing argument he concludes that "knowing a language, then, is knowing how to translate mentalese into strings of words and vice versa."[41] It seems clear that Messiaen has translated his mentalese into a sophisticated semiotic system, which in some areas bypasses verbal constructions at the encoding and decoding stages. The purely musical coding produces a connection between the composer and listener that operates at a different level from verbal language. The concept is not a new one. In 1842 Mendelssohn wrote a letter to Marc André Souchay in which he revealed:

> People usually complain that music is so ambiguous; that it is doubtful what they ought to think when they hear it; whereas everyone understands words. With me it is entirely the converse. And not only with regard to an entire speech, but also with individual words; these, too, seem to me to be so ambiguous, so vague, and so easily misunderstood in comparison with genuine music, which fills the soul with a thousand things better than words. The thoughts which are expressed to me by a piece of music which I love are not too indefinite to be put into words, but on the contrary too definite. And so I find, in every attempt to express such thoughts, that something is right, but at the same time something is unsatisfying in all of them... [42]

We cannot put everything we perceive or understand about the *Méditations* into words, nor should we. Messiaen is speaking with the tongues of men and angels, not to us but to God, and at times we may not fully understand him because he utters mysteries with his spirit.

NOTES

[1]*The Holy Bible, New International Version* (London: Hodder & Stoughton, 1987).

[2]The seven modes of limited transposition are scale systems devised by Messiaen which form the basis of his melodic and harmonic style. *Deçi-tâlas* are rhythmic patterns which Messiaen derived and modified from the 120 *deçi-tâlas* of Sharngadeva. Both are described in his *Technique de mon langage musical* (Paris: Leduc, 1944).

[3]Saint Thomas Aquinas, *Summa theologiæ* (Cambridge: Blackfriars; New York: McGraw-Hill, 1964-).

[4]Several ideas mentioned here are developed at length in my doctoral dissertation: *The Unspoken Word: Olivier Messiaen's 'Langage Communicable'*, (Ph.D. Dissertation, Harvard University, 1998). I am grateful to Paul Lekas for his comments on this essay.

[5]Almut Rößler, *Contributions to the Spiritual World of Olivier Messiaen* (Duisburg: Gilles und Francke, 1986), p. 51.

[6]For a comparison of the techniques described in each Preface see Thomas Daniel Schlee's dissertation *Olivier Messiaen:'Méditations sur le mystère de la Sainte Trinité'* (Ph.D. Dissertation, University of Vienna, 1984).

[7]To avoid confusion the alphabet is always denoted with lower case letters, pitches are denoted with capitals.

[8]The sound attributes of the various aspects of the 'langage' are not indicated in the Preface, they have to be abstracted from the score itself. The following are the registration indications for each occurrence of the 'langage':
>   1) [I, 10/1 - 12/15]
>   Positif: Clarinette, Quintaton 16, Cornet 5 rangs— Positif en 16, 8, 4
>   2) [III, 26/1 - 28/11]
>   Récit: Bombarde 16, Trompette 8, Clarion 4, et tous les Fonds 16, 8, 4
>   3) [VII, 61/7 - 66/6]
>   Récit: Trompette 8 et Bourdon 16

From this it is clear that the specific timbre is different each time the 'langage' is used. There are two commonalities to each registration: each uses an eight foot reed stop (Clarinette or Trompette), and a sixteen foot foundation stop (Fond 16 or Bourdon 16). Otherwise the sound is very different.

[9]All translations from French in this essay are my own.

[10]Claude Samuel, *Olivier Messiaen: Musique et couleur* (Paris: Belfond, 1986). Translated by Thomas E. Glasow as *Music and Color: Conversations with Claude Samuel and Olivier Messiaen* (Oregon: Portland Press, 1994), p. 143.

[11]Places in the score (Paris: Leduc, 1973) are indicated thus: [movement, page/measure].

[12]The cases are: nominative, vocative, accusative, genitive, dative, ablative, and locative. Messiaen does not give a 'formule musicale' for the nominative or vocative but does give one for the privative, a grammatical term indicating negation, absence, or loss.

[13]Ferdinand de Saussure, *Course in General Linguistics* (New York: Philosophical Library, 1959), p. 67; see also p. 119.

[14]Saussure, *op. cit.*, p. 131.

[15]I refer readers again to my dissertation, which provides a more complete discussion of this and many other ideas mentioned in this essay.

[16]See Rößler, *op. cit.*, pp. 89 and 138.

[17]For reference to the score see *vers* in [XI, 76/5] [XI, 77/4], *Fils* in [XI, 76/4] [XI, 77/3], *Père* in [XI, 76/6], and *Dieu* in [XI, 78/1].

[18]The passages from Aquinas are: (1) The Trinity, book 1, question 33, "The Person of the Father," article 4, conclusion; (2) The Trinity, book 1, question 28, "The Divine Relations," article 2, conclusion; (3) The Trinity, book 2, question 37, "Name of the Holy Spirit," article 2, conclusion.

[19]The original Latin reads: *Unde remoto a Patre quod non sit genitus, cum tamen sit principium generationis, sequitur consequentur quod non sit procedens processione Spiritus Sancti, quia Spiritus Sanctus non est generationis principium, sed a genito procedens.* (Hence, once being begotten is denied of the Father, while he yet remains the principle of generation, it follows logically that he is not one proceeding by the procession of the Holy Spirit; the Holy Spirit is not a principle of the begetting, but is the one proceeding from the one begotten.) *Summa theologiæ*—The Trinity, book 1, question 33, "The Person of the Father," article 4, conclusion. Volume VII edited and translated by T. C. O'Brien (Cambridge: Blackfriars, 1976), pp. 22-23.

[20]Steven Pinker, *The Language Instinct: How the Mind Creates Language* (New York: HarperPerennial, 1995), p. 232.

[21]W. Jay Dowling and Dane L. Harwood, *Music Cognition* (Orlando: Academic Press, Inc., 1986).

[22]Dowling and Harwood, *op. cit.*, p. 85.

[23]*Ibid.*, p. 176.

[24]Pinker, *op. cit.*, p. 161.

[25]Eero Tarasti, *A Theory of Musical Semiotics* (Bloomington: Indiana University Press, 1994), p. 64.

[26]Jean-Jacques Nattiez, *Music and Discourse: Toward a Semiology of Music.* Translated by Carolyn Abbate (Princeton: Princeton University Press, 1990), p. 126.

[27]Saussure, *op. cit.*, p. 189.

[28]John Blacking, "What Languages do Musical Grammars Describe?," in *Musical Grammars and Computer Analysis*, M. Baroni and L. Callegari, eds. (Florence: Olschki Editore, 1984), pp. 363-370; p. 364.

[29]Pinker, *op. cit.*, p. 159.

[30]Information on the Rosetta Stone is condensed from articles in the fifteenth edition of the *Encyclopedia Britannica*.

[31]Preface, p. 5, line 16.

[32]The following movements refer specifically to angels: *La Nativité du Seigneur:* VI—"Les Anges"; *Les Corps glorieux:* III—"L'Ange aux parfums"; *Quatuor pour la fin du temps:* II—"Vocalise pour l'Ange qui annonce la fin du temps," VII—"Fouillis

d'arc-en-ciel, pour l'Ange qui annonce la fin du temps"; *Visions de l'amen:* V—"Amen des Anges, des Saints, du chant des oiseaux"; *Vingt regards sur l'enfant Jésus:* XIV—"Regard des Anges"; *Saint François d'Assise:* Act II scene 4—"L'ange voyageur," Act II scene 5—"L'ange musicien"; *Éclairs sur l'au-delà:* VI—"Les sept Anges aux sept trompettes."

[33]Rainer Maria Rilke, *The Selected Poetry of Rainer Maria Rilke.* Edited and translated by Stephen Mitchell (New York: Vintage International, 1989), pp. 149-211. The quote "All Angels are terrifying" occurs in two of the ten elegies: "Ein jeder Engel ist schrecklich" (*The First Elegy,* line 7), and "Jeder Engel ist schrecklich" (*The Second Elegy,* line 1).

[34]Preface, p. 3, line 18.

[35]At his feet the six-winged Seraph; Cherubim with sleepless eye,
  Veil their faces to the Presence, as with ceaseless voice they cry,
  Alleluia, Alleluia, Alleluia, Lord most high.

[36]*The Tenth Elegy,* line 1.

[37]Pinker acknowledges the influence of Whorf's teacher Edward Sapir, and calls it the Sapir-Whorf hypothesis (*op. cit.,* p. 57). It is actually an old idea, supported for example by many of the early Romantics.

[38]Pinker, *op. cit.,* p. 57

[39]The only element missing from this total language system is a visual stimulus for the 'listener', who, given the nature of the language, might perhaps be better described as the 'receptor'. There is a way of performing the *Méditations* which adds the visual element and removes many of the problems of reception and comprehension noted above. Images projected onto a screen in the performance venue could indicate which leitmotifs and bird songs were being played, could indicate passages in the 'langage', and could display the superscriptions written in the score at the appropriate time.

[40]Pinker, *op. cit.,* p. 58.

[41]*Ibid.,* p. 82.

[42]Quoted in Deryck Cooke, *The Language of Music* (Oxford: Oxford University Press, 1959), p. 12.

The Spiritual Layout in Messiaen's Contemplations of the Manger

Siglind Bruhn

Between 23 March and 8 September 1944, not long after returning from war imprisonment and shortly after completing his String Quartet *For the End of Time*, Olivier Messiaen wrote one of his great piano cycles: *Vingt regards sur l'Enfant-Jésus*. The word *regard* is commonly translated as "look" or "gaze," and the title is thus often translated as "Twenty Looks Upon the Infant Jesus." However, interviewers and students claim that the composer used the word *regard* in a wider sense, one that also encompasses the notion of different "perspectives" or "views" of the Jesus-Child. The French word *regard* thus seems to pose problems of translations comparable to those of Schoenberg's favorite "Anschauung." Messiaen himself, in his Author's Note that prefaces the score, speaks about the "contemplation of the Infant-God of the manger," upon whom many eyes are laid. Given the ambiguity of the English word "look," I have decided to adopt Messiaen's explanatory term for the translation and thus speak of *Twenty Contemplations of the Infant Jesus.*[1]

Among those who are contemplating the Child in the manger are not only human beings and anthropomorphized heavenly persons, but also what the composer calls "immaterial or symbolic creatures": Time, the Heights, Silence, the Star, the Cross, and even the Awesome Unction. Messiaen's list of all that influenced his conception of the cycle includes an astonishing array of sources: "bird song, carillons, spirales, stalactites, galaxies, photons" as well as "the texts of [the Belgian Benedictine abbot] Dom Columba Marmion, the writings of Saint Thomas Aquinas, Saint John of the Cross, and Sainte Thérèse de Lisieux, as well as the Gospels and the Missal." As Messiaen emphasized, two other writers, Dom Columba Marmion in *Le Christ dans ses Mystères*, and after him Maurice Toesca in *Les Douze Regards*, have made allusion to the eyes of the shepherds, the angels, the Virgin, and the Heavenly Father laid upon the infant Jesus, a concept which he then expanded to twenty scenes or contemplations.

Here is an overview of the titles, together with my English translation:

I   *Regard du Père*
     The Father's Contemplation

II   *Regard de l'étoile*
     The Star's Contemplation

III   *L'échange*
     The Exchange

IV   *Regard de la Vierge*
     The Virgin's Contemplation

V   *Regard du Fils sur le Fils*
     The Son Contemplating the Son

VI   *Par lui tout a été fait*
     Through Him All Was Made

VII   *Regard de la Croix*
     The Cross Contemplating [the Infant Jesus]

VIII   *Regard des hauteurs*
     The Heights' Contemplation

IX   *Regard du temps*
     Time's Contemplation

X   *Regard de l'Esprit de joie*
     The Spirit of Joy Contemplating [the Infant Jesus]

XI   *Première communion de la Vierge*
     First Communion of the Virgin

XII   *La parole toute-puissante*
     The Almighty Word

XIII   *Noël*
     Christmas

XIV   *Regard des Anges*
     The Angels' Contemplation

XV   *Le baiser de l'Enfant-Jésus*
     The Kiss of the Infant Jesus

XVI   *Regard des prophètes, des bergers et des Mages*
     The Prophets, the Shepherds, and the Magi
     Contemplating [the Infant Jesus]

XVII   *Regard du silence*
     Silence's Contemplation

XVIII   *Regard de l'Onction terrible*
     The Awesome Unction Contemplating [the Infant Jesus]

XIX   *Je dors, mais mon coeur veille*
     I Sleep But My Heart Wakes

XX   *Regard de l'Eglise d'amour*
     The Church of Love Contemplating [the Infant Jesus]

In what follows I will argue that a close examination of the musical symbols used throughout the cycle, and the spiritual messages for which they stand, reveals a striking structural design that is not easily evident from the outside and has not, to my knowledge, previously been ascertained. What one discovers is a somewhat unusually determined layout, encompassing an initial "exposition" followed by an intricate but extraordinarily symmetrical interplay of pieces constituting what can be termed "development," "contrast," and "synthesis."[2]

THE EXPOSITION OF THE CENTRAL SYMBOLS

As will be shown in some detail below, the five initial pieces of the twenty-part work can usefully be considered as an "exposition" in kind. They jointly present the full array of musical components that recur cyclically throughout the *Vingt regards*. These components are here introduced in their basic form and matched with their respective spiritual message, which will remain consistent throughout the cycle. The spiritual contents thus conveyed encompasses Messiaen's principal thoughts regarding his faith in general and the Incarnation in particular: God's fatherly, divine love and Mary's motherly love, the mystery of the Incarnation and the exchange of natures, as well as the symbolic implications of the Star of Bethlehem and the Cross of Golgotha.[3] The basic musical symbols representing these spiritual events span phenomena of pitch and rhythm, horizontal and vertical tonal organization, structural design, texture, developmental transmutation, as well as three themes. Here is a list of the symbols:

(1) four of Messiaen's "modes of limited transposition": modes 2, 4, 6, and 7;
(2) the key, and particularly the key signature, of F♯ major
(3) the basic forms of four symbolically used chords
    - the F♯-major triad with added sixth
    - the bell chords of the "shock of grace"
    - a 3-chord progression in contrary motion, based on the tritone
    - a chromatic cluster over the lowest piano key
(4) two symbolically employed pitches E and A♯
(5) asymmetric processes of vertical growth and warping
(6) rhythmic palindromes of highly complex forms
(7) the superimposition of several dimensions in stretto canons
(8) the basic forms of the three most significant cyclical themes (the *Theme of God*, the *Theme of Love*, and the *Theme of the Star and the Cross*)
(9) bird song

In the context of this volume of essays, where most of the building blocks of Messiaen's music have been dealt with in great detail, very few remarks regarding the nature of this material will suffice. Despite the fact that Messiaen does use modes 3 and 5 occasionally in the *Vingt regards*, the four modes of limited transposition he introduces in the "exposition" of this cycle prove the most important ones in the composition. A comparison of these four scales reveals that they are subtly interrelated in a way that Messiaen exploits: modes 2 and 6 complement one another, sharing four pitches and adding another four each; modes 4 and 7 are almost identical, in that mode 7 is but an extension of mode 4, adding one pitch in each hexachord. Here are the basic forms of these modes:[4]

mode 2:	C	C♯		D♯	E		F♯	G		A	B♭
mode 6:	C		D		E	F	F♯		G♯		B♭	B

mode 4:	C	C♯	D			F	F♯	G	G♯		B
mode 7:	C	C♯	D	D♯		F	F♯	G	G♯	A	B

As I will show later, these relationships are not merely material in terms of scale degrees, but carry symbolic meaning of their own.

The key of F♯ major appears not as a diatonic scale but as a tonal area supported by I–IV–V progressions. The fact that it is notated, more often than not throughout the cycle, with explicit six-sharps key signature, is significant in a composer who otherwise prefers local accidentals. So consistent is Messiaen in this distinction that the visual emblem of "a key signature" as such comes to be perceived as reminiscent of F♯ major even in the one piece, no. X ("The Spirit of Joy...") where the tonality does not literally appear but is only symbolically evoked. Finally, it is on account of the singular importance of this key in Messiaen's work that one feels justified in interpreting the chord A♯-C♯-D♯-F♯ as an "F♯-major chord with added sixth, in inversion"—a reading otherwise not self-evident in a twentieth-century tonal environment.

The way in which the nine musical symbols listed above are introduced in the five pieces of the exposition, shows a web of intricate symmetries. Most striking is the many-faceted relationship between nos. I, III, and V on the one hand, and nos. II and IV on the other. While some links would become apparent only after an analysis more detailed than this chapter allows, most shall be pointed out here.[5]

1   2   3   4   5

GOD'S LOVE in its comprehensive form determines beginning and end of the five pieces I perceive as exposition. No. V ("The Son Contemplating the Son") is designed as a variation of no. I ("The Father's

Contemplation") in that the lowest of the three strands in the piece that closes the exposition restates the entire harmonic, melodic, and rhythmic argument of the opening piece. GOD'S LOVE is thus musically presented as constituting both the source and the goal of the Incarnation.

In the opening piece, GOD'S LOVE appears as the only presence, the single truth, epitomized by a combination of three determinants: the thematic phrase that Messiaen labels *Thème de Dieu (Theme of God)*, the Biblical quotation in the subheading (Matthew 3:17: "And God says: 'This is my beloved Son in whom I am well pleased'..."), and the performance indication, which specifies the desired mood of the piece with the words "mysterious, with love." This exclusive presence of GOD'S LOVE in the opening piece prepares the ground for the interpretation of many other aspects of the Christian doctrine within the cycle. Messiaen's faith does not allow for a strictly transcendental God who remains aloof from humankind. Nor is the Divine Presence—whose praise, as he repeatedly claimed, was the foremost purpose of all his compositional activity—a wrathful God whose anger must be appeased and whose kindness must be won. Messiaen's "Father" is God-Father, whose love predates everything.

Musically, GOD'S LOVE is embodied in what constitutes the largest group of musical symbols to appear in this cycle: the six-sharps key signature, the tonal environment of F♯ major, the pitch arrangement of mode 2 in its three transpositions, the melodically dominating pitch A♯, the *Theme of God*, and the inverted F♯-major triad with added sixth.

Theme of God

EXAMPLE 1:
Theme of God

All except the chord appear integrated into the brief thematic cell from which the entire opening piece, laid out in two structurally corresponding stanzas followed by a coda, is developed.

Also in this very opening piece, Messiaen introduces his second most important cyclical theme, the *Thème d'amour (Theme of Love)*.

EXAMPLE 2:
Theme of Love

The four-chord sequence that constitutes this theme, clearly identified and labeled in the score only after the exposition, appears very much concealed here.[6] In "The Father's Contemplation," the *Theme of Love* is enveloped within the conclusion of the second stanza —furnishing, as it were, the final message before the coda. Messiaen seems to express musically his conviction that GOD'S LOVE offers the basis for humankind's LOVE OF GOD as well as, intimately related to it, for human love in general. In Messiaen's spiritual cosmos, "love" must be understood always in its idealized form. It is experienced by humans, but whether directed at God or at other humans, it remains in its true nature an emulation of God's love for His creatures.

The fifth piece concludes the exposition by reiterating this message from a different angle. The fact that "The Son Contemplating the Son" quotes "The Father's Contemplation" in its entirety is to be read as Messiaen's musical ascertation of the Christian conviction that GOD'S LOVE, in its encompassing and original form, supports the incomprehensible relationship of the Divine Son and the Child of the manger. The duality of aspects is depicted in a surprising yet most logical way. The uppermost of the three layers that make up the main texture of this piece presents a sequence of seventeen three-note chords, in a rhythmic phrase that consists of four tripartite palindromes followed by a tail of increasing rhythmic values. The middle strand, whose seventeen chords are of four notes each, presents the same rhythm in an augmentation by $1\frac{1}{2}$.[7]

EXAMPLE 3:

the rhythm in strand 1:
(3-note chords, mode 6^3)

the rhythm in strand 2:
(4-note chords, mode 4^4.)

The phrase in the upper strand is repeated twice, that in the middle strand once. As a result, the two aspects of Jesus, presented rhythmically as two dimensions of the same idea, diverge after a joint origin and merge again at the end (3×1 equals $2 \times 1\frac{1}{2}$), a symbolic depiction of the mystical identity of the dual aspects of Jesus' nature. Furthermore, the consistent number of voices in each textural layer (three in the upper, four in the middle) as well as the microstructural arrangement of chord types within the rhythmic palindromes (very regular in the upper, developmental in the middle strand)[8] provide clues for understanding which aspect of the Son each of the two upper layers in "The Son Contemplating the Son" represents. In the uppermost strand, the Trinitarian numeral 3, paired with a great regularity in chordal sequence, suggests the divine aspect. This aspect is portrayed as "looking down upon" a sequence of 4-note chords. Often contrasted with the Trinitarian 3, the numeral 4 is, since Presocratic cosmological speculations about the four elements as building blocks of the world, semantically connected with the idea of the earthly, the worldly, the material. Together with the somewhat more amorphous structure of the chord progression, which overrides the small-scale palindromes, this "earthly" numeral seems to symbolize the human aspect of the Son.

This interpretation of the two textural layers is corroborated in two ways through the composer's choice of modes. The chord sequence in the upper strand is taken from mode 6. This is the mode that, as the pairing in the first overview has attempted to show, is related to mode 2, the mode of GOD'S LOVE, with which it creates an interplay of complementing and sharing. The mode-6 aspect of Jesus' dual nature, then, is musically defined as that which is complementarily related to God's nature. The chord sequence in the middle strand, by contrast, is taken from mode 4. This is the pitch collection of which mode 7 is a mere extension. Mode 7 will be presented in the cycle's second piece in its one and only symbolic connection: as the mode of the Star of Bethlehem and the Cross of Golgotha, the two hinges of Jesus' human life span. The mode-4 aspect of Jesus' nature is thus matched to the mortal aspect of His nature. (Actually, Messiaen's numerical symbolism extends its play to the modes and their transpositions: for the divine aspect, the *3-note* chords in the upper strand are taken from the *3rd* transposition of *mode 6,* while the "worldly" aspect is represented by *4-note* chords in the *4th* transposition of *mode 4!*)

Finally, the concluding piece of the five-part exposition introduces a further component that is central to Messiaen's musical language: bird song. The juxtaposition of "The Father's Contemplation" with the musical representation of Jesus' dual nature that was discussed above covers only the initial segments of both stanzas and of the coda, while each of these sections ends with GOD'S LOVE accompanied by what Messiaen understood as nature's rejoicing over God's creation: the virtuoso treble cadenzas of bird-song imitation.

1   2   **<u>3</u>**   4   5

If the opening of the exposition was devoted to the Father and the concluding piece to the Father supporting the divine-and-human nature of the Son, the central piece of the exposition is explicitly dedicated to the precarious identity of the divine and human aspects of the Son. In the prefacing remarks for this piece, Messiaen speaks of the "awesome human-divine commerce." Musically, Messiaen expresses his reading of this awesome commerce by pitting an immutable, descending opening component against a succession of figures that, in twelve sequential transformations, undergo various symbolic processes. The composer makes it clear that he identifies the inalterable initial component with God when he writes, in his Author's Note, *"Dieu, c'est... ce qui ne bouge pas"* (God is that which does not change). Messiaen seems to reiterate in this piece one of the key messages of the exposition and of his faith in general: God precedes all development and anchors everything; yet, although the source of all unfolding, He does not interfere with or modify an event once it is initiated (the twelve transformations to which the group of components is subjected follows abstract laws). The Incarnation of Christ, the exchange of natures, becomes musically evident as God's reaching out to humankind (*descente en gerbe* writes Messiaen for this figure, "descent in a shower of sparks"), a gesture in which God approaches his creatures while nevertheless remaining unchangingly the same.

Besides showing God's relationship to humankind, no. III also speaks of Jesus' relationship to the world. From God's downward-directed gesture emerges a three-note figure that will grow from chromatic smallness to the imposing power of a two-octave leap; the remaining components develop in ascending direction but with intricate warping.[9] Jesus' growth, God's outstretched hand in the "awesome commerce," is musically represented as a vertical expansion in both height and depth, occuring throughout twelve transformations. It is mirrored, or inversely imitated, in the concluding three-note segment of the asymmetrically spreading figure at the beginning of the second bar, a fact that invites interpretations regarding the human participation in this "commerce."[10]

Messiaen reiterates here also the number play that characterizes no. V, the other expositional piece dealing with Jesus' duality. Once again he posits the numerical symbol for the Trinity against that of the material, human realm. Within the two-bar unit on which "The Exchange" is based, a first bar with *three beats* and *three musical segments* (two for what Messiaen calls "God's shower of sparks," one for Jesus' growth) is complemented by a bar with *four beats* and *four musical segments* (the human element in the exchange).

Another musical symbol Messiaen introduced within the twelve transformations of the two-bar unit is that of an emblematic pitch. The first symbolically used pitch in this cycle, the melodically predominant A♯ in the *Theme of God* and the *Theme of Love*, is here matched with its tritone. The composer inaugurates the pitch E as the symbol for God's immutable presence in the two-part homorhythmic figure that concludes the two-bar unit in "The Exchange." E is the only note here that does not participate in the twelve-fold warping transmutation but remains steadfast and changeless. Once alerted to the significance of the pitch E, one notices that in the first bar of the unit, E fulfills a similar, albeit more indirectly realized function: it constitutes both the point of departure for the vertically growing gesture in the "exchange" and the goal towards which it aims.[11]

Through such musical depiction of God's repeated and unchangeable support in spite of human fallibility (depicted in the warping of the "human" components), "The Exchange" thus prepares symbolically for "The Son Contemplating the Son." In V, God's love supports the Son against the hardships and misunderstandings in the world; in III, God's consistent presence anchors humankind in its difficult attempt at a dignified imitation of Christ.

1   **2**   3   **4**   5

The two intermediate pieces within the exposition, "The Star's Contemplation" and "The Virgin's Contemplation," present different yet complementary aspects of affection and recognition on the one hand, of premonition on the other. The flash-like ascent of the star in the opening bar of no. II has its counterpart in the plunging figure that interrupts Mary's motherly gaze upon her son in no. IV, bars 18/19. The gentle, utterly unpretentious tune of Mary's lullaby in IV, set in a multi-voiced texture, counterbalances the threefold, vertically expanding bell strokes that herald the birth of the Savior in II. Furthermore, both the star over the stable and the lullaby next to the manger conceal a second meaning, a deeper knowledge. The Star of Bethlehem functions not only as a guide for the people who trust in God and come to worship His Incarnate Son, but also (in Messiaen's understanding, where it appears linked to the Cross) as an indication that the life just begun is fated to end in a dreadful death. Similarly, Mary's pure joy over the child just born to her is overshadowed by the premonition that a sword will pierce her heart as her son meets his destiny.

Musically, the Virgin's love itself appears composed of two contrasting aspects. The gently rocking rhythm and the naivité of the tune come across as an expression of her intimate motherly response. On the other hand, with a tonal material whose coloring is audibly related to that of "The Father's Contemplation" (see, in both IV and I, the melodically predominant A♯ and the conspicuous use of the F♯ major triad with added sixth), Messiaen reminds us that Mary's motherhood is very much an expression of GOD'S LOVE for humankind.

Another feature linking the two intermediate pieces is the fact that both II and IV can be read as conceived in contrast-stanza form (II: A-B, A-B, etc.). Significantly, the piece explicitly dedicated to Jesus' life on earth between Bethlehem and Golgotha, no. II, remains structurally incomplete: the third stanza-pair omits precisely that which constitutes the principal element of the piece, the *Theme of the Star and the Cross*—as though there was more to be said about this later, and not all of it stood under the benign sign of the Star that gives this piece its title. The prophetic aspect is thus presented here both in the label given the theme and in the build-up of anticipation for a conclusion under another heading. By contrast, the layout of alternating stanzas that underlies "The Virgin's Contemplation" appears complete. What is more, the element in segment B (which circles around C♯ and, as I have shown elsewhere, can be interpreted as symbolic for Mary's foreboding) enriches the second occurrence even of section A, thus taking over more and more of Mary's lullaby tune and overlaying her previously innocent joy with a small voice of apprehension.

THE DEVELOPMENT OF THE
SYMBOLS OF THE DIVINE

Within the five expositional pieces that I interpret as the exposition of the cycle, Messiaen has introduced the central musical symbols and determined the direction of their spiritual interpretation. Pursuing this line of thought further, the remaining fifteen pieces seem to be grouped in a striking manner, falling into three groups. Nos. VI and XX, the framing pieces of the cycle's body after the exposition, are in a group of their own. Although these two pieces draw significantly on the symbols outlined above, they are, as will be shown later, complex syntheses of large numbers of symbols rather than delving into particular aspects; for this reason, they deserve special attention and will be discussed later under a separate heading. Of the thirteen pieces surrounded by these syntheses, the composer devotes seven to further exploring single aspects or groups of symbols, on which he sheds additional light by developing the corresponding musical material.

It is intriguing to notice which numbers Messiaen has chosen for this "development section" within the cycle, or rather, how he has distributed the developmental pieces throughout the work. Having chosen to place them exclusively at odd numbers, he has created a perfectly symmetrical distribution.

6   **7** 8 **9** 10 **11** 12 **13** 14 **15** 16 **17** 18 **19**   20

In their titling and religious contents, these seven developmental pieces span the entire spectrum from the concrete to the abstract. Four of the numbers relate to the Infant Jesus. Among these, three address aspects that were often depicted in folk-art vignettes: the first stirring of the infant in his mother's womb and the first contact of the smiling new-born with the people he was sent to redeem. While these three pieces thus musically celebrate the "sweet child of Mary" in aspects that are somewhat remote from the narratives of the Gospels and only found in legendary, non-canonical traditions, the fourth piece in this group, no. XIII, deals with the Holy Night from a perspective that highlights the timeless significance of the event. Not the shepherds and magi who populate the scene around the manger are evoked here, but instead the annual celebration of the birth of the Son of God and the initial moment of the "good tidings" about human salvation. It is worth noting that this piece, which among the vignettes relating the concrete scene in the stable at Bethlehem is the only timeless one, is placed exactly at the center of the fifteen pieces following the exposition:

6   7 8 9 10 **11** 12 **13** 14 **15** 16 **17** 18 **19**   20

A fifth piece of this developmental group, no. VII, occupies a place on the dividing line between the concrete-pictorial and the abstract-conceptual. It deals with the opposite aspect of the birth at Bethlehem, the Cross of Golgotha whose dark shadows loomed already over the star-lit manger in the exposition (no. II).

The remaining two numbers (IX and XVII) complement the exploration of the central symbols by probing into the mystery of the Incarnation. Messiaen addresses here two aspects that challenge our common understanding of what it means to live in this world. We are asked to imagine a world in which communication and time, two central conditions of earthly experience, have more than one dimension. He suggests as desirable a love so spiritual as to be *sans bruit de paroles* —devoid of the noise of speech, one of the central ways of human self-expression—and projects a world in which the nature of time as we know it will be questioned. The two pieces devoted to these explorations are again positioned at symmetrically corresponding places:

6   7 8 **9** 10 **11** 12 **13** 14 **15** 16 **17** 18 **19**   20

While, significantly, the three pieces portraying the "sweet Jesus-Child" as well as the central piece "Christmas" are not entitled *regards*, the composer chose to mark the three pieces whose spiritual message stretches our human comprehension with headings that, deceptively simple as they appear, similarly stretch our logic. We are asked to imagine the Cross, Silence, and Time as spiritual actors, or, in Messiaen's explanatory circumscription, "The Cross's Contemplation," "Silence's Contemplation," and "Time's Contemplation" [of the Infant Jesus].

Musically, the three pieces devoted to the new-born child are conceived as extensive enlargements of individual symbols introduced

in connection with "The Father's Contemplation" and its first variation
in "The Son Contemplating the Son." The three pieces are placed as
nos. XI, XV, and XIX in the cycle; separate enough to avoid the impression of too compact a suffusion of sweetness, yet so regularly
spaced that they convey the importance Messiaen attributed to the fact
that all manifestations of God's presence among us are imbued with
love.

6   7 8 9 10 **11** 12 **13** 14 **15** 16 17 18 **19**   20

Several highly intriguing developments of the primary symbols of
GOD'S LOVE can be observed in these three pieces.

- In "First Communion of the Virgin" (XI), the *Theme of God* is
the dominant element. The basic phrasal group is structured as
a free imitation of the large-scale phrase structure in nos. I and
V. Here, however, the initial transposition of mode 2 is never
once abandoned. Similarly, the *Theme of God* dominates the
principal section in "The Kiss of the Jesus-Child" (XV), albeit
in a tonally redefined version and thus, as it were, in humanly
embodied form. In "I Sleep, But My Heart Wakes" (XIX),
however, the *Theme of God* itself is no longer discernible; its
message has been transferred entirely onto other symbols
related to GOD'S LOVE.
- The mode of GOD'S LOVE, mode 2, is heard in "First Communion of the Virgin" in combination with short passages in modes
4 and 7. For moments, this tonal setup diverts our attention
from the expectant mother's bliss towards the task and fate of
the child that will be born. (Mode 4 was introduced in the
exposition as a symbol for Jesus, son of Mary; mode 7 stood in
exclusive connection to the *Theme of the Star and the Cross*,
the endpoints of Jesus' earthly life.) In "The Kiss of the Jesus-
Child," mode 2 is heard in all three transpositions, thus enveloping everything. Finally, in "I Sleep, But My Heart Wakes,"
mode 2 governs only the B sections, even here interrupted by
manifestations from another, modally unidentified sphere.
- The tonality of F♯ major, the third symbol of GOD'S LOVE, is
conspicuously absent in "First Communion of the Virgin." It
is, however, substituted by B♭ major, a key that in light of
mode 2 is closely related to F♯ major. "The Kiss of the Jesus-
Child," by contrast, begins in an F♯-major context which, emphasized by the full key signature, functions clearly as its tonal
frame of reference. Finally in "I Sleep, But My Heart Wakes,"
a transformation has taken place that redefines the contextual

frame as content: for more than a full minute, we hear nothing but F♯ major. In this way the composer conveys a clear and unambiguous message about the theological significance of GOD'S LOVE, which is not merely the backdrop against which other events unfold, but ultimately, through Jesus, the only reality that counts.

- The major triad with added sixth which, particularly in the context of F♯ major, was identified as the chordal manifestation of GOD'S LOVE of humankind, but which also recurs as one of the symbols of humankind's LOVE OF GOD, does not play any role in "First Communion of the Virgin." In "The Kiss of the Jesus-Child," by contrast, the "chord of love" is heard repeatedly in each phrase. It is further emphasized by two cadences resolving into the chord and by an eight-bar passage built on nothing but this sound. In "I Sleep, But My Heart Wakes," the F♯-major chord with added sixth is absent from the A sections but very prominent in the B sections, and even more so in the final segment of section C, which is almost entirely devoted to displaying this harmony.
- The *Theme of Love* does not play any role in the first two pieces of this group. Not surprisingly then, it proves central in the third piece of the group, "I Sleep, But My Heart Wakes," in which the *Theme of God* does not explicitly appear.

In this subtle manner, the three numbers developing the musical symbols of the cycle's opening piece allow us to observe a shading of the one message. This spans all the way from the emphasis on love as God's gift of mercy, through God's love as it reaches humankind at the moment of Jesus' arrival on earth, to humankind's reciprocal love of God.

The second piece of the *Vingt regards sur l'Enfant-Jésus* is developed in no. VII. "The Cross's Contemplation" clearly relates to "The Star's Contemplation" not only in that it takes up the complete chant of the *Thème de l'étoile et de la croix* in its characteristic mode 7, but even more so in the complex, metaphorical expansion of the shift of perspective initiated in no. II.[12] Beyond these most salient components, no. VII also draws on elements of nos. I and V. First, it features in prominent position, as a kind of pedal, an A♭-minor triad with added sixth. This chord is strongly reminiscent of one of the symbols introduced in "The Father's Contemplation," the F♯-major triad with added sixth. It seems as if Messiaen wanted to stress, albeit in a somewhat subdued (minor-mode) coloring, that even Christ's death on the Cross was conceived as an act of God's Love. Second, Messiaen quotes here the superimposition of modes 6 and 4 that was distinctive of the two strands representing Jesus' dual nature in "The Son Contemplating the Son." In the context of the exposition's final piece, this modal juxtaposition represents the two aspects of Christ's coming into this world: as the Son of God and the son of Mary. In the context of the Cross of Golgotha, this duality takes on an extended meaning, superimposing the SUFFERING AT THE CROSS of God's Son, an act whose redemptive significance surpasses our comprehension, with the more immediate blessing of the INCARNATION OF THE WORD, manifested in Mary's child.

The same expositional piece, no. V, also informs no. XVII, although it is developed quite differently here. The initial section of "Silence's Contemplation" features a superimposition of two distinctive rhythmic sequences that are easily recognizable as derived from "The Son Contemplating the Son." Moreover, modally this piece extends the idea of the dual nature of Jesus by juxtaposing the interpretation of Christ as the INCARNATION OF THE WORD (mode 4) with that of the CHILD IN THE MANGER (mode 3).[13] Here, too, mode 2 as a symbol of GOD'S LOVE plays a significant role, albeit not, as in no. V, in the form of a third textural strand. Instead, it is prominently displayed in the framing passages of the middle section.

"Time's Contemplation" develops—and thus illuminates—a segment of the exposition that remains largely elusive when first heard. The coda of no. II, "The Star's Contemplation," presented the contrary motion of two strands with three three-note chords each. These chords, each built as a superimposition of fifth and augmented fourth, are unrelated to anything heard in the main body of the expositional piece both tonally and with regard to tempo, gesture, or any other parameter. Since Messiaen does not seem to have included any hint that might enlighten the interpretation, the impression they give in their original context is at best that of being "outside of" the regularly pacing, strophic piece. When developed in "Time's Contemplation," the same chord sequence recurs as one of the two themes representing aspects of time. As revealed in the comparison of the amorphous, emotional, centrally anchored features of the first theme with the abstract order, superhuman passionlessness, and extreme range of the second theme, theme 2 represents the divine aspect of Time in contrast to the human aspect in theme 1, or: theme 1 stands for time as we humans know it, while theme 2 epitomizes its eternal dimension. This is one case where Messiaen postpones the disclosure of an intended symbolic attribution, to reveal it later, in a developmental piece. Only with the benefit of hindsight do we recognize the dimension of "divine time" in the coda of "The Star's Contemplation" as one more aspect at play in the stable of Bethlehem.

The same symbolic representation of eternity also features prominently in the cycle's celebratory central piece, "Christmas," whose refrain in its two upper strands is based on the chord just associated with "divine time." In addition, no. XIII is notable for its development of the chromatic bass cluster. This feature was introduced at a structurally memorable moment in no. IV, "The Virgin's Contemplation," where it symbolized Mary's awe at the thought of her child's destiny. The same bass cluster recurs first, in similarly underemphasized position, in XI, "First Communion of the Virgin," before it assumes its outstanding role as a rhythmically shaped bass pedal in the refrain sections of "Christmas."

In conclusion, I think there are good reasons for the following general reading of the symbols as used by Messiaen in the expositional and the way they recur in the developmental pieces of this cycle. The five-part exposition introduces the basic mysteries of faith: God's love, the devotion of the Virgin, the dual nature of Jesus, and the Star of Bethlehem which, in view of Christ's destiny, is overshadowed by the Cross of Golgotha. In the seven pieces that develop the symbols established in the exposition, Messiaen seems to explore the human response to these truths. These responses range from a joyful, celebratory mood through experiences of mystical love to meditations of the human condition as determined by finite time and space. Consistent with this view that the developmental numbers introduce the human perspective is the fact that the only symbol that is newly added within the seven pieces is one that highlights the most human aspect of the Infant Jesus: mode 3, the symbol of the *Child in the Manger*.

CONTRAST: JOY, ADORATION, AND PROPHESY

As has been shown so far, of the fifteen pieces after the exposition Messiaen reserves those with odd numbers for the development of the musical and theological symbols. This leaves the even numbers from 6 to 20. Of these, as mentioned earlier, the two framing pieces constitute something akin to large and complex syntheses. This chapter, then, deals with the intermediate pieces:

6   7 **8** 9 **10** 11 **12** 13 **14** 15 **16** 17 **18** 19   20

While these pieces maintain occasional links to the primary material of the *Vingt regards*, a further exploration of the main symbols, whether musically or theologically, is clearly not their intention. Rather, they represent a group that, together, furnishes moments of contrast within the cycle.

The six *regards* can usefully be grouped into three pairs. Each of these pairs, one realizes with amazement, deals with one aspect of the way in which the birth of the Son of God at Bethlehem is perceived.

6   7 **8** 9 **10** 11 **12** 13 **14** 15 **16** 17 **18** 19   20

The first pair is devoted to expressions of *joy*. The jubilant music of the songbirds in "The Heights' Contemplation" represents, as always in Messiaen's œuvre, both nature's rejoicing over God's grace and a manifestation of God's presence in nature. The relationship is made here specifically through the composer's referring to the heights above the manger. The wording, reminiscent of the biblical "Glory to God in the highest" (Luke 2:14), seems to evoke God's indirect presence through the song that praises Him. The allusion to the biblical verse further suggests that the birds in the heights above the manger may act as substitutes for other beings who in popular spirituality are usually entrusted with this praise: those jubilant angels who are among the first to hail and celebrate the Savior's birth.

Similar indirect representation occurs in the partner piece of "The Height's Contemplation." No. X, "The Spirit of Joy Contemplating the Infant Jesus," speaks of the ecstatic dimension of God. This Spirit of Joy is not entirely identical with, yet somehow related to and certainly here representative of, the Holy Spirit. Moreover, the wording points once again to an indirect presence of God Himself: Messiaen in his prefacing lines remarks that he had always been profoundly convinced that God is full of happiness, bliss, and the joy of love (*la joie d'amour du Dieu bienheureux*). The Spirit of Joy is, then, a further aspect of God.

Both pieces in this pair thus entail a threefold chain of representation (birds—Bethlehemitic angels—God being praised in the highest, and Spirit of Joy—Holy Spirit—the blissful God) whose common source is Messiaen's joyful God.

6   7 8 9 **10** 11 **12** 13 **14** 15 **16** 17 **18** 19   20

The second pair of even-numbered contrast pieces explores two aspects of the way in which God enters into contact with the world. No. XII, entitled "The Almighty Word," refers to an abstract concept that is granted quasi independent existence here. "The word was with God," we read at the beginning of the gospel of Saint John, immediately qualified with "and the word was God." The Word creates the world and—this was of utmost importance for Messiaen—the Word is that which incarnates in Jesus. On a different level, a similar claim can be made about the majestic angels in XIV: they are God's messengers, but at the same time self-assured, independently judging beings. Messiaen's angels are not fashioned after those heavenly musicians of the sacred arts and crafts who, particularly since the Renaissance, had become ever more full-cheeked and Victorian. By contrast, they are exalted beings like the ones we know from Michelangelo's paintings, the opening lines of Goethe's *Faust*, or Rilke's *Duino Elegies*. Those angels are self-confident, superior beings with an opinion of their own about the Incarnation of God's Son, and this opinion includes, so Messiaen believes, the very articulate astonishment over the fact that God should have chosen the human rather than the angelic realm in which to manifest Himself.

6   7 **8** 9 **10** 11 **12** 13 **14** 15 <u>**16**</u> 17 <u>**18**</u> 19   20

The pieces coupled in the final pair of the presently discussed group are musically linked in a very conspicuous way: both feature closely related, palindromically designed framing sections. In terms of the characters who are contemplating the child in the manger here, no. XVI, "The Prophets, the Shepherds, and the Magi Contemplating the Infant Jesus" presents human beings who, while remaining nameless, are distinctly specified. The three groups of people pondering the birth of the divine Child in the stable at Bethlehem are of very dissimilar background, and nothing but an event of such momentous proportions could have united them. Historically, the life-time of the prophets does not literally allow their presence in the holy night; geographically, the Magi travel from very distant countries to the stable of Bethlehem; and socially, the shepherds represent, in contrast to the learned and anointed men, the class of the simple people with whom Jesus was preferably to interact later in his life.

In contrast to these picturesque persons whom Messiaen imagines contemplating the infant in no. XVI, "The Contemplation of the Awesome Unction" rests on a concept that is as abstract as the other one is concrete, and not immediately accessible. In which way these ostensibly unrelated pieces are nevertheless closely linked, and inform one another even theologically, can only be shown in a detailed analysis that would be beyond the scope of this essay. Components at play include the awe-epitomizing lowest pitch of the piano, the symbolic imagery related to palindromic frames, and the interpretive aspects encapsulated in the composer's choice of dynamics.[14] Perhaps more than anywhere else in this piano cycle Messiaen employs here his eloquent musical language to open our eyes and ears to an unexpected theological message.

In summary, the six pieces of "contrast" reflect the manner in which the world as a whole, in all its facets, reacts to the Incarnation of Jesus. We meet animals and humans, the abstract powers behind the Creation (the Word) and behind the anointment as Christ (the Awesome

Unction), as well as superhuman beings (angels, the spirit of joy). We witness bird song and tam-tam ostinatos, hunting horns and the playing of shawms, as well as ecstatic dance. But we also hear prophesies of exterior and interior conflict, and doubts about the adequacy of this world as the place of God's Incarnation.

Despite such emphasis in the contrast pieces on the reaction to the event, a closer look allows to discern traces of the cycle's primary symbols. Again symmetrically distributed, these almost secret links occur above all in the second piece of each pair. While "The Height's Contemplation" contains no memories of expositional material, "The Spirit of Joy Contemplating the Infant Jesus" features all of the musical symbols connected with GOD'S LOVE. (The *Theme of God* is being remembered, albeit in distortion; mode 2 dominates the hunting song of the "ecstatically blissful God," and Messiaen underscores this reference even further by using a general key signature and the F♯-major chord with added sixth.) Where "The Almighty Word" is linked to the exposition merely through the awe-symbolizing chromatic bass cluster introduced in "The Virgin's Contemplation" and further explored in the refrain of "Christmas," "The Angels' Contemplation" takes up the compound palindrome of the rhythmic sequence first heard in no. V, "The Son Contemplating the Son," as well as the asymmetric growth of no. III, "The Exchange." Finally, the framing sections of the third pair are both built on the chord that was introduced in the coda of no. II, "The Star's Contemplation," but only the second, "The Awesome Unction Contemplating the Infant Jesus," reestablishes the contrary motion and thus confirms the connection to what in X, "Time's Contemplation," was retroactively determined as the symbol of timelessness.

ALPHA AND OMEGA

The two extensive pieces that bracket the interspersing pattern of developmental and contrasting numbers explored above both represent syntheses, theologically as well as musically. No. VI, entitled "Through Him All Was Made" (after the prologue of the Gospel of Saint John), represents a look back towards the past, towards our origin, and traces "all things" to the moment of God's Creation.[15] Correspondingly no. XX, "The Church of Love Contemplating the Infant Jesus," is directed toward the future. The agent to be imagined next to the manger here is the community of Christians, the Church that, historically, will not come into being until more than thirty years from the event at Bethlehem, through the ministry of this new-born child.

Musically, these two pieces are not only by far the longest of the *Vingt regards*; they also present entities of completely independent dimensions and character, and thus summarize the cycle's compositional material and ideally complement one another.

Structurally, the pride of independence in these pieces is particularly striking. The Creation piece "Through Him All Was Made" is conceived as a complex fugue. Its ten sections encompass a palindrome of mammoth proportions (sections I/II/III recur, after section IV, which functions as a free central unit, in exact retrograde as sections V/VI/VII), followed by a canon (section VIII). The piece climaxes in the *Theme of God* (section IX) before it is wrapped up in an extensive coda (section X). Similarly, "The Church of Love Contemplating the Infant Jesus" begins as an imposing edifice built, in a largely mirrored structure, on the alternation of palindromically growing units. It, too, climaxes in a recollection of the *Theme of God*, which Messiaen presents here one last time in the form of a complete variation of the cycle's opening piece, "The Father's Contemplation." As this brief comparison reveals, the two pieces correspond to one another with regard to their large-scale features, without therefore creating any specific likeness.

Remarkably, both pieces introduce conspicuous musical material not heard anywhere else in the cycle. Suffice it here to mention the most conspicuous: in the Creation piece the fugal subject and counter-subject as well as the five-chord sequence that appears repeatedly interspersed with those components, and in the Church-of-Love piece the rondo-like rotation of material and the "theme of growth" (or "theme of missionary power"—not so named by Messiaen who only writes *"thème 1"*). Both pieces also recall the cycle's main symbols, in such a way that, together, they simultaneously reintroduce and embrace every one of them. Bird song is the only exception. Somewhat surprisingly, this feature does not play a role in either synthesis, apart from very brief figures that could be heard as reminiscences of what we otherwise know as lavishly extensive glorification.[16]

This very absence of Messiaen's beloved bird song in the pieces devoted to the exploration of the past and the future, the origin whence all life came and the goal whither the Child is to lead humankind, encapsulates a symbolic message in its own right. Could it be that Messiaen's particular fascination with the feathered singers of God's glory rests not least on their living fully in the present, on the fact that they represent for him a reality not touched by concerns of past and future: the glorious, joyful, timeless Now?

NOTES

[1] In order to avoid further possibilities for misunderstandings in these titles, I have chosen to use the direct genitive wherever possible ("The Father's Contemplation"), and rephrase in all other cases. "The Contemplation of the Father," but even more so "The Contemplation of the Cross" would not make it clear whether somebody is contemplating the Father or the Cross, or rather, as is Messiaen's intention, the Father and the Cross are contemplating the Child in the Manger.

[2] While observations of the structure under this angle have not been made with regard to this particularly multifaceted cycle, the idea that Messiaen's may be laid out following intricate patterns whose strands interweave is in itself not entirely new. Harry Halbreich, in his exhaustive overview of the composer's work up to the late 70s, has shown convincingly that the ten movements of the *Turangalîla-Symphonie* follow a scheme that groups nos. 2, 4, 6, and 8 ("the movements that are most developed, richest in memorable tunes and lyricism ... associated with the development of love"), nos. 3, 7, and 9 ("of violently opposite character, shorter ... also the most high-strung, the most difficult, of tragic and even sinister character. ... They represent the pole of death, but are perhaps the most fascinating for the analysis and the most novel, richest in terms of the future."), the first, introductory movement, and finally the two pieces that conclude the two halves of the cycle, nos. 5 and 10 ("two immense Dionysian scherzi ... the latter has in addition the role of a reminiscence, a synthesis."). See Harry Halbreich, *Olivier Messiaen* (Paris: Fayard / Fondation SACEM, 1980), pp. 374-375.

[3] In what follows, I will render in CAPITALIZED words those spiritual messages that appear enshrined in a musical symbol or group of symbols and recur as such.

[4] Note that Messiaen referred to the basic form of each mode as "first transposition," a labeling that may appear a bit confusing given our common understanding of the term transposition. He abbreviated the various transpositions with superscripted numbers; thus "mode 2^1" stands for the first transposition (or, the basic form) of his second mode.

[5] For an in-depth discussion of each of these pieces see the relevant chapters in Siglind Bruhn, *Images and Ideas in Modern French Piano Music: The Extra-musical Subtext in Piano Works by Debussy, Ravel and Messiaen* (Stuyvesant, NY: Pendragon Press, 1997). A somewhat more detailed account of the structural play at work in the cycle can be found in Siglind Bruhn, *Musikalische Symbolik in Oliver Messiaens Weihnachts-vignetten: Hermeneutisch-analytische Untersuchungen zu den Vingt regards sur l'Enfant-Jésus* (Bern/Frankfurt: Peter Lang, 1997).

[6] Compare I: bar 15 with, e.g., VI: bar 170.

[7] For an in-depth discussion of this rhythm and its persistent significance in Messiaen's work, see Robert Sherlaw Johnson, *Messiaen* (London: J.M. Dent and Berkeley, CA: University of California Press, 1974 and 1989; now Oxford: Oxford University Press).

[8] Were one to represent the chord types with letter names, the result would be:

strand 1 = a b a',   c c d,   a b a',   c c d,   e d c' f f,
strand 2 = g g h,   h i i',   g g h,   h i i',   k g g l m

Of these two patterns, the first is configured in agreement with the rhythmic palindromes that characterize both versions of the phrase, while the second overruns the boundaries of each pair of palindromes with a developmental structure of its own.

[9] Cf. III, bars 1 and all odd-numbered bars through 23.

[10]Cf. III: bars 2 and all even-numbered bars through 24.

[11]See the E that, in bar 1, forms the angle-point of the bifurcating development throughout the twelve transformations of the unit, and E as the target notes in bar 24.

[12]As mentioned earlier, the third stanza of "The Star's Contemplation" breaks off where the listener expects the recurrence of the theme, which constitutes roughly the second half of each stanza. "The Cross's Contemplation" in its entirety is nothing but a very slow, very much thickened version of this missing half stanza. Furthermore, as only a more detailed analysis could show satisfactorily, the change of medium that happens on the larger scale between the initial 2 1/2 stanzas (= "The Star's Contemplation") and the final 1/2 stanza (= "The Cross's Contemplation") exists in microcosm already in the *Theme of the Star and the Cross* itself. This theme consists of three verses, as it were, of which the first 2 1/2 are set in unison, while the final 1/2 is suddenly scored in thick chords. For an in-depth analysis, please see Siglind Bruhn, *Images and Ideas in Modern French Piano Music: The Extra-musical Subtext in Piano Works by Debussy, Ravel, and Messiaen* (Stuyvesant, NY: Pendragon Press, 1997), part III, chapter 3.

[13]For more details on the symbolic interpretation of Messiaen's use of the modes in his *Vingt regards*, as well as on the interpretation of this juxtaposition, see S. Bruhn, *Images and Ideas...*, part III, chapter 5.

[14]See Siglind Bruhn, "More Prophets Than Expected: Religious Symbolism in Olivier Messiaen's Christmas Vignettes," and "Frames that Expand our View: Religious Symbols in Two of Messiaen's *Vingt regards sur l'Enfant-Jésus*"; papers presented, respectively, at the annual meeting of the Semiotic Society of America (Santa Barbara, CA, Oct. 1996) and the Society for Music Theory (Baton Rouge, LA, Oct. 1996). See also the chapter "Incarnation and Suffering" in the above-quoted *Images and Ideas*.

[15]Not surprisingly, the sixth piece was the last Messiaen composed for the cycle. See Harry Halbreich, *Olivier Messiaen* (Paris: Fayard / Fondation SACEM, 1980), p. 220.

[16]Cf. XX, bars 18 and 30.

The Contributors

Jean Boivin teaches music history at the Université de Sherbrooke (Québec, Canada). He received his Ph.D. in musicology from the University of Montreal in 1992. His book *La classe de Messiaen* (Paris: Christian Bourgeois, 1995), based on extensive interviews with the composer's former students, was acclaimed by the French music critics and awarded the Bernier Prize from the Académie des Beaux-Arts de France. He has since given many lectures on Olivier Messiaen's music, thought, and heritage, both in Europe and North America, and published a number of articles on various aspects of Messiaen's career as a pedagogue and composer.

Siglind Bruhn (Ph.D. Vienna 1985) is a musicologist, concert pianist, and interdisciplinary scholar who, having taught at the Pianisten-Akademie in Ansbach, Germany and at The University of Hong Kong, is now affiliated with The University of Michigan as a Research Associate in Music and Humanities. She has published eight monographs, two of which deal prominently with Messiaen; a ninth study, which explores Hindemith's opera *Mathis der Maler* and its reading of Grünewald's *Isenheim Altarpiece*, is currently in press with Pendragon Press. Her current research, under the working title *Musical Meditations on Poetry and Painting: The Sonic Sisters of Ekphrasis*, focuses more broadly on the way early twentieth-century European composers create meaning in their musical language.

Camille Crunelle Hill received her B.M. and M.M. degrees from Northwestern University and her Ph.D. in musicology from the University of Kentucky, jointly with the University of Louisville. At the University of Louisville, she received the John Hankins Writing Award in Music History, a Graduate School Dean's Citation, and a grant from the Modern Language Department for study in Paris and Salzburg. She is presently Associate Professor of Music at Elizabethtown Community College, Elizabethtown, Kentucky and a 1997 national winner of the NISOD award for excellence in teaching.

Ian Darbyshire is currently preparing a Ph.D. thesis at Lancaster University, U.K., on the manuscript sources for the early Tudor festal mass. His forthcoming publications include an edition, with Roger Bray, of Fayrfax's mass *O Quam Glorifica* for the Early English Church Music series. The edition incorporates his conclusions about postulated notational reworkings represented in the surviving manuscript sources.

Roberto Fabbi was born in Reggio Emilia, a small Italian town between Milan and Bologna, in 1960. After the haphazard musical adventures of his youth, in 1988 he graduated in "Discipline delle Arti, della Musica e dello Spettacolo" from Bologna University, with a thesis on Messiaen's *La fauvette des jardins*. His field of interest is twentieth-century music. He contributes to specialist reviews and publications, as well as writing for theaters and musical institutions. He is currently the music librarian at the Teatro Municipale Valli of Reggio Emilia.

Theo Hirsbrunner studied the violin as well as composition and musicology in Bern and Paris, and taught music theory and history at the Conservatoire in Bern, Switzerland, until 1987. The author of books on Debussy, Boulez, Messiaen, Ravel, and Stravinsky, he is also an expert on Wagner, and follows developments in avant-garde music. He has lectured on European music of the nineteenth and twentieth centuries in Europe, the United States, Australia, and Japan.

Nils Holger Petersen studied music theory and composition before he turned to getting degrees in mathematics (M.Sc.) and theology (Ph.D). He is presently a Research Lecturer at the Center for Christianity and the Arts, Institute of Church History, the University of Copenhagen, Denmark, and an external professor of Gregorian Studies at the Centre for Medieval Studies at the University of Trondheim, Norway. He has published work on the Latin music drama in the Middle Ages and on medievalist aspects in modern music drama of Western Europe. He is also a composer of instrumental music as well as of operas, including the medievalist opera *A Vigil for Thomas Becket*.

Larry W. Peterson, Professor of Music at the University of Delaware, holds degrees from Texas Christian University and The University of North Carolina, Chapel Hill, where he was a Woodrow Wilson Fellow. He has received awards from the National Endowment for the Humanities, the John F. Kennedy Center for the Performing Arts, and the Delaware Heritage Commission among others. He develops multimedia materials for the teaching of opera, which achieved second place in the

1991 Masters of Innovation Competition as well as recognition from EDUCOM and Technology Tools for Today's Campuses (a CD ROM produced by On the Horizon).

Andrew Shenton studied at The Royal College of Music and London University. His master's thesis (Yale) concerns the renaissance of sacred art in post-war Britain; his doctoral dissertation (Harvard) is on Olivier Messiaen. Shenton has received many major prizes and awards, including Harvard's Slim, Paine, and Merit Fellowships. As a conductor and keyboard player he has toured extensively in Europe and the United States.

Robert Sherlaw-Johnson was born in Sunderland, Great Britain. After graduating from the University of Durham, he studied piano and composition at the Royal Academy of Music, London, and subsequently in Paris with Messiaen, Nadia Boulanger, and Jacques Février. He is currently Fellow of Worcester College and University lecturer at the University of Oxford where he was awarded the degree of Doctor of Music in 1990. He became a Fellow of the Royal Academy of Music in 1984. He has published a book on the music of Olivier Messiaen (Oxford University Press) and has composed works for many different genres, including a number of piano works, which have recently been released on compact disc with himself as pianist. He has also made recordings of Messiaen's piano music, including the complete *Catalogue d'oiseaux.*

Jean Marie Wu earned her B.M. and M.M. in piano performance at the Peabody Institute of The Johns Hopkins University. She won the 1997 College Music Society Mid-Atlantic Chapter Award for "Sound and Color: Olivier Messiaen's Expression of Faith" and is currently writing her Peabody doctoral thesis "Rhythm, Color, and Birdsong: Olivier Messiaen's Musical Language of Faith." She is the founder/director of the Baltimore Center for the Creative Arts and serves on the faculty at Essex Community College and Dundalk Community College in Maryland.